letters to a best friend

AN IMPRINT OF STATE UNIVERSITY OF NEW YORK PRESS

letters to a best friend

Richard Selzer
edited and with a preface by Peter Josyph

All illustrations by Peter Josyph,
except anonymous photograph of Troy, NY, on page 12

Published by
STATE UNIVERSITY OF NEW YORK PRESS, ALBANY

© Richard Selzer / Peter Josyph 2009

All rights reserved

Printed in the United States of America

No part of this book may be used or reproduced in any manner whatsoever without written permission. No part of this book may be stored in a retrieval system or transmitted in any form or by any means including electronic, electrostatic, magnetic tape, mechanical, photocopying, recording, or otherwise without the prior permission in writing of the publisher.

For information, contact State University of New York Press, Albany, NY
www.sunypress.edu

Production and book design, Laurie Searl
Marketing, Fran Keneston

Library of Congress Cataloging-in-Publication Data

Selzer, Richard, 1928–
Letters to a best friend / Richard Selzer ;
edited and with a preface by Peter Josyph.
p. cm.
Includes bibliographical references.
ISBN 978-1-4384-2721-8 (alk. paper)
1. Selzer, Richard, 1928—Correspondence.
2. Authors, American—20th century—Correspondence.
3. Josyph, Peter—Correspondence.
I. Josyph, Peter. II. Title.

PS3569.E585Z46 2009
818'.5409—dc22
2008054152

10 9 8 7 6 5 4 3 2 1

Sir, more than kisses, letters mingle Soules;

For, thus friends absent speake.

—John Donne

Contents

Preface by Peter Josyph ix
COME ON UP AND WE'LL HAVE A FINE DAY

LETTERS
1988–1992

You Will Believe in Civilization, 1988	3
Sleepwalking and Daydreaming, 1989	9
Into the Cave of Aeolus, 1990	97
Lazarus Rising, 1991	137
Driving the Quill, 1992	169
Notes	217
Bibliography	235
Editor's Acknowledgments	237

Preface by Peter Josyph

Come On Up and We'll Have a Fine Day

When this correspondence was just under way and we were working on the book *What One Man Said to Another*, I had a conversation with Richard Selzer about the art of the letter. We were sitting in the solarium of the three-storied house that has been his residence for over forty years. This narrow white room, which extends the width of the house, relaxes you with a sense of easeful habitation—more so, even, than his spacious livingroom. There is a rattan couch, rattan chairs, a glass-top table littered with letters, tapes, manuscripts, and books. Foliated nicely with a row of hanging plants, the room looks out on a lovely lawn and garden that Richard's wife, Janet, enjoys tending. For a second backyard, the large old house atop St. Ronan Terrace has the outskirts of Yale University where, before he became a full-time writer in 1985, Richard Selzer was both professor and practitioner of surgery.

"It's very odd who becomes your correspondent," he said. "You don't choose your correspondent: your correspondent chooses you."

"It's not necessarily the people one cares most for, is it?"

"Absolutely not," he said. "It's like a target, and you aim your arrows at it. *Our* letters are different, and I have two or three other correspondents, people I'm trying to *reach*—reach their feelings and their minds. But for the most part my correspondence is with people who, if I met them, I would not be particularly thrilled. They are just addresses. There are hundreds and hundreds of these letters. I usually write six to ten letters a day, at the end of the day. The letters I write to you, you can tell that I write them straight out."

The solarium at St. Ronan Terrace, with typed pages of Richard Selzer's diary.

"Do you ever think: 'Wait—this is a good way of saying that,' and copy it into a journal for later use?"

"I don't do that," he said, "but sometimes in the morning, when I'm at the library and I'm having my hot cocoa and my first cigarette, I have my notebook open. It's before I start my day's work. I will, say, think about you, and I'll jot down things that I want to say to you. Then, at the end of the day when I go to write to you, I'll open the page of that notebook and I'll put that in." More recently he indicated that now and then the letters do influence the diary. "Sometimes I write something in a letter to you, and then, when I'm writing in my diary that day, I'll think: 'Hey, that's not bad—I'll put that down here too.' But that's rare."

I asked him to name some of the best letter writers.

"Well, *you* are," he said.

"Be serious now."

"You *are*," he said. "You are the best letter writer I have ever known, without exception. People don't write *letters*—people *aren't* letter writers. *I* am a letter writer: I write *letters*. *You* write letters. I *love* the idea of talking to people in letters. I never take out a sheet of foolscap, say: 'Dear Peter,' and think: 'I'm just going to get this off my chest.' No! I sit down to make this letter worth it to you when you open it up. They're all the same length because I only write on two sides of one sheet, but everything in it is exactly designed to entertain you or stimulate you or confirm our friendship. A little bit of it has to do with our work, but what I really want to do is *reach* you. And when I get one of your letters I'm thrilled. At the end of a day of isolation and solitude, it's my chance to have a conversation. It's a funny thing, but I think in my letters there is a third persona. The letters are lighthearted, ironic. I'm trying to charm you, make you smile."

"There *is* a distinct Selzer that doesn't exist anywhere else but in the letters," I said.

"That's because when I sit down with that piece of paper and my Mont Blanc pen," he said, "I shuck the cares of the world. I am not trying to write for posterity, I am not dancing on a stage, I am indulging myself in a carefree act of speaking to a friend. The letters flow out. I write them late in the afternoon after a vodka, and so vodka uncorks the wit—up to a point. I never correct them. As you see, nothing is crossed out. These letters are an effusion from a mind sitting there in its pajamas, its bathrobe, and its slippers."

Yes, but Richard Selzer is every inch a wordsmith. Both his letters and his conversations flow naturally, but he is adept at tempering and structuring them spontaneously. He never forgets himself with words. With a good correspondence, as with the blowing between horn players improvising off of each other's riffs, it isn't easy to say whether it's art or society because it is both of them at once. Richard Selzer is one of the best, most dedicated practitioners of the epistolary art, and in this sampling you will see how committed he is to entertaining his friend long distance, no matter the circumstances or the storms raging around us. Whatever else it is, this is a book about two men who value a friendship balanced upon words; men for whose friendship the phone is a thief; men who are comfortable with the U.S. mail. If Richard wants to tell me something, he can rest assured that I will know it within a day or two. That's soon enough, unless you savor the delusion that all communication is an emergency. Waiting for a response provides just the right interval between us, and between the present self and the past, enabling us to read a little piece of our own history as told by someone else.

And told in English sentences. This is important for a pair of dedicated writers—one accomplished, the other striving to be—who appreciate a guaranteed readership of one. If a reason to send a letter is to receive one, a reason to read a letter is to write one. If correspondence is a form of literature, its practitioners needn't choose between the prose poem, the memoir, the short story, the satire, the eulogy, the rhapsode, or outright lying. A letter can be all of these, and all at once. It is also a solitude, an interior monologue that, once it is given a stamp, converts into a civil conversation. If *What One Man Said to Another: Talks with Richard Selzer* is a record of conversations between friends over the course of one year, this correspondence can be viewed as the friendship itself. The title *Letters to a Best Friend* is Richard's idea, and it might be accurate, but it can be misleading.

"It's hard for people to understand," I said to him recently, "that the person to whom you've written all these letters isn't a factor, isn't important, in your life here."

"It is the correspondence which is the life," Richard said. "If we lived in the same city and saw each other frequently, we might not even be friends. That we live apart sets the only condition in which a correspondence is maintained: distance. When the friends are together, there aren't any letters. Madame de Sévigné, whom I admire so much, wrote wonderful letters to her daughter, but when she *visits* her daughter there are no letters and the reader is left out in the cold."

"When Flaubert and Turgenev get together in Paris—"

"There are no letters! And the reader feels insulted that he is being excluded. In our case there is no hiatus because we correspond all the time. Your letters are in my hand, being read, the minute I come home. Sometimes, when you write a particularly good letter, I will reread it a number of times. The letter that you wrote about the two metalsmiths in Virginia, making a cross out of the Trade Center steel, I thought was a wonderful work and I read that a few times. I read it as much for its power as for the information. Now and then you do that, you turn out a little beauty."

Kind of him to say so, but it is solely his doing that I advance in the discipline, learning, by example, its rules, its liabilities, its parameters of caprice and indulgence. Learning, too, that a letter can go forth without brilliance, without drama, even without episode, but it must have a sense of humor, it must have grace, and it must have buoyancy. If there is no *lift* in your letter, don't send it.

If cellphones have shown that apparently polite people were really just awaiting the right instrument of rudeness, email has shown how educated people have been longing for an excuse to be illiterate. Had he lived to see email, Churchill, who wanted schoolboys whipped only for not knowing English, would have had to whip us all. But Richard Selzer *adores* English. An unbroken chain of fine letters full of English, written off the cuff, without revision, is a creditable achievement, and he produces them with such a smooth sense of ease that you feel empowered by it—until you try it for yourself. As email mitigates against such a performance, on the very few occasions I have emailed Richard I have done it with trepidation, lest I truncate one of the most energetic examples of the correspondential art.

It must have been around 1994, when Richard was sorting through a shipment to an archive in Texas—the Institute for Medical Humanities—that he gestured toward the drifting mounds and boxes of notebooks, pamphlets, mailers, tapes, postcards, and letters on the floor of his small study, saying: "Feel free to rummage around. If there's anything there that interests you. . . . Of course, all your old letters to me are there too. Would you ever have thought they'd make their way to a library in Galveston?" Kneeling on the carpet of this cluttered room on the second floor—"my scriptorium," Richard has called it, although most of his writing is done in the Yale Sterling Library, to which he walks every morning and where he spends the bulk of his day—I separated out all of my letters and took them back. When we met again in the kitchen, I said: "Two pages, three—my letters are too much. Henceforth no letter longer than a page."

"Thank you," he said.

This was a hard lesson: the correspondential quality—and the courtesy— of withholding. It is not that there are any inherent restrictions as to subject. In the way that comedians can tackle any issue they can manage to make amusing, correspondents can do the same if they can make it interesting, *and*—and this is the point—brief, for a ramble is something more and something less than a good letter. As you will see, there are few topics on which Richard Selzer cannot be interesting, and as for brevity, the short form has always been his expertise. Like Henry David Thoreau, Richard Selzer is a born diarist—I have never seen him without a notebook in his case—and most of his published work is composed by the selection, expansion, arrangement, and refinement of journal entries. However soon they outgrow it and need to be transplanted, even his short stories start as seedlings in his diary. He has never tried to conceal this dependency on his diaries. "In writing my diary I find myself at the top of my form," he has told me. "And it's worth talking to yourself. It's a kind of *folie à deux*, a schizophrenia, in which the writer and the reader are the same person."

These letters, too, constitute a kind of diary, and those that are completed over the course of several days are diaristically dated by him accordingly. Letters that chart the course of a single day accrue the geography, the architecture, the dramatis personae of Richard's rounds. But when I mentioned that his letters float *above* the days on which they report, he said: "That's because I *don't* want to tell you the story of my life every day: I want to make art. These are what I *do*. It's a form of my work. Letters are definitely a genre—and I think it's one of the best."

A letter, however personal, is full of information, gazetting a world of one for a sole subscriber. It is also a forum in which queries will be answered, suggestions considered, preferences affirmed or rejected—even chastised or ridiculed. But good correspondents have too much to offer to let your last letter shape the course of their pen. The surest sign of a dull correspondent is the dutiful ticking off of everything you wrote to them, as if your letter were an assignment. The notion of response, in its literal sense, is almost incidental to these letters, most of which carry the unspoken imprecation stated openly in one of Charles Lamb's letters to Coleridge: "Write, when convenient—not as a task, for here is nothing in this letter to *answer*."

Also critical to the health of a correspondence is the degree to which its practitioners take each other seriously, an x-factor as indefinable as it is indispensable. Too fine a regard can be as disruptive as too little, or none at all. Even Richard's most overt solicitudes should not be abstracted from that dimension between the literal and the rhetorical that can only exist in the correspondential moment. You will learn to take with a grain of salt the protestations and promises with which this book abounds, not because they are likely to prove false, but because they are meant to be true the way music is meant to be true.

That experience of seeing my own letters in Richard's scriptorium also made me wonder why a man of such a wide range of cultural connections had continued to write to me, for writing to me meant, of course, reading me—and I never, for a moment, believed that my letters were the best of his experience. There had to be something else at play, but I refrained from asking about it until a recent conversation, also in the sunroom at St. Ronan Terrace (which hasn't aged or altered at all), also devoted exclusively to letters, only the correspondence was now a dozen years older. The talk told me as much about what had remained the same as it did about the little that had changed, and it confirmed my suspicion that, excluding emails, and with the exception of one woman, Pirkko, with whom Richard has corresponded for over twenty years, I had effectively become his only regular correspondent.

"It's completely a mystery," Richard said, "who becomes the correspondent of one's life. It's a person who is, somehow, *the perfect receptacle*. You see this when you read the marvelous letters of Byron and Lamb. It's inexplicable why their letters poured out in those directions, but it's the whole secret of the epistolary art. As Emily Dickinson would have said: 'It's just a happen.' And it has become very important to me, this correspondence. Sometimes, when I've spent a fruitless day at the desk, I'll write to you and I'll feel: 'Well, I did something.'"

"It's *never* a chore?"

"Heavens no, it's no effort at all."

"That's not an illusion you create from hard work, as you would with a piece of fiction?"

"I could sit there and write six a day, it would be fine. To set about writing a short story—to have the architecture, the layers of meaning, the characters, the setting, all come together—*that's* work. Writing a letter—to you—is a pleasure because I know you're going to read every word and you'll enjoy whatever I say, no matter if it's stupid or not, and I have the absolute freedom to say whatever I want. I don't think about it ahead of time: I just go. When the page is full, I stop."

"But do you still write to me in the afternoon?"

"Yes," he said. "In the morning I still have hopes of writing something more formal. After I've come back from lunch, in the library, I'll write a letter to you, or perhaps, when I've gotten home and had a vodka, I'll write another. The other letters that I write are nothing like the ones to you. I calibrate myself at a certain level, for a certain state, and when I'm in that condition that I wasn't in before and won't be in after, I don't talk like that to anyone else. I have your face in front of me—I have you in my thrall—and I aim my letters *at* you. I've no idea what's in them. Do I tell stories? Certainly they've nothing to do with current events. You could read these letters and think that we lived in the seventeenth century, because I have turned my back on the world, in a sense."

Richard has made the same point about his diaries.

"When one reads the diaries of Samuel Pepys," he has told me, "one has a view of the era in which he lives. Anyone reading my own diaries a hundred years from now would hardly be treated to a vision of our time. It is all an attempt to play with the language and my own personal thoughts. It has none of the greatness of diaries that are major historical documents." When I protested that for me it was often the most intimate of diaries—Kafka's, for instance, or Delacroix's—that bodied forth the time and place in which they were set, he said: "That is not the case with me. I wish it were."

"But Selzer's times," I said, "are no less the times than the *New York Times*'s times."

"Then why don't I write about the war in Afghanistan?" he said. "Or the Rushdie business? I don't. It may be true that if someone, years from now, read all of my work, including the memoirs, the diaries, the letters, the book of talks, they would have a certain narrow vision of the time. They would see how a boy grew up in Depression Troy and went to Yale, became a surgeon, served in Korea, came back and made a life in New Haven, and then started, eventually, to write—they would see that small story, with all that involves. But they wouldn't have a grand view of society."

Rummaging one day through boxes in Richard's solarium that were bound for the archive, I happened upon a sheet of what appeared to be discarded notations from his diary that had been typed, for some reason, all in capital letters. One of these is worth recording, partly because a version of it appears in his letter to me of December 10, 1989; partly because it's an interesting—if debatable—description of his life. "For fifty-eight years," he wrote, "I lived with the intensity of a puppet, every movement exaggerated, jerky, predictable, and dictated from above. At fifty-eight I reached up to snip the strings, and ever since have sprawled, floppy and contented, in an overstuffed chair."

Well, not exactly. As these letters will show, the insularity of Richard's world—"my little ancient life," he has called it, or "the lovely quietude that attracts no attention"—is not as narrow as he suggests, and his resignation to it is far from complete. Richard's response to disappointment, for instance, is often a display of acceptance or indifference that is grounded as much in psychic self-protection as it is in true contentment. Even if that contentment is real, it is never more than a step away from protest and outrage (when Richard writes to me "So, fiercely, to go on is all," the *fiercely* is important), as if the shadow of a Selzer-who-might-have-been always hovers over the man who'd rather walk every day to his library than anywhere else in the hemisphere. This is stated with delightful clarity in his essay "Going No Place," and it comes across in a recent letter about that very thing—walking to the library—in this case through a blizzard while the Bush administration was gearing up to invade Iraq.

> This morning I trudged to the library. The unsullied snow muffles the drums of war, so I didn't mind the trek; I relished it. When I think of all the appointments broken, the meetings postponed, the flights cancelled, my heart leaps up. A blizzard serves to humble the arrogant. You and I never did matter to the government, the economy, the culture, so we aren't in the least discommoded. We hadn't made any appointments; nor were we to attend a meeting; and certainly we weren't planning to go anywhere. So let us dance a jig and sing tra-la-la.

Another undated fragment, also recounting a walk to the library, typifies how it is often the smallest moments, the whispered thoughts, that inspire the most interesting passages in his work.

> Just today, at the corner of Sachem and Prospect on the walk to the library, I felt a kiss come right out of the air and press itself to my lips. A moment later a pretty young woman came jogging by. Had it belonged to her? Did she want it back? I was about to run after her and ask, but just then she turned up Grove Street and into the cemetery, which I took as a message from the dead to act my age.

Thus it does not much matter to the vitality of the letters, or the diaries, whether Richard is in his garden or at the end of the world. But the reader will easily see that he is hardly a recluse. When you walk the streets of New Haven with him, it seems as if everybody knows him from some incarnation of his life. And the breadwinning he does at the lectern—as "a strange migratory bird that roosts on podia"—has taken him all over the world, a world of which he has long since seen quite enough—at least in the life of a public speaker. Here is another fragment:

> I used to like to travel. "The stranger is a guest sent by the gods." So spoke Homer. If the usage I have received on my travels is any measure, I have been under divine protection, for I have been made so welcome at the Abbey of San

Giorgio Maggiore in Venice; at Annecy; on the island of Kauai; in Halifax; in Galveston; and in a hundred other oases. Time was, when I found it easy and even intoxicating to fling myself in any direction. Light of heart and light of hand, I went abroad with no more luggage than one of the Apostles. Now, if forced to go away somewhere, I prepare with all the solemnity of one preparing to depart this life.

Of course reading good letters in a book is not the same as finding them in the mail. Many's the morning I have stood in the bright sun of a parkinglot, leaning against the door of my car, reading a letter from Richard Selzer before I resume the day. Then it operates within me as a read thing, forming into an answer, which I might half-compose before reaching my destination. When I lived at the edge of a cliff on the North Shore of Long Island, I drove winding roads inland to my studio in St. James, reading Richard's letters as I went. I knew Richard's hand as well as I knew the turns in the road, so I negotiated them equally. Or I would simply stash the letter, unopened; but as an unopened letter isn't an unimagined one, I would absorb it as an unread thing until enjoying it during lunch or at the far end of the day.

I have pursued an exchange of letters with a fair range of people, but such letters have never become a way of living, only a way of communicating. It is easy to think of correspondence as once-removed from life, whereas it is really a distinctive way of *being in the world*, so that even on a day when no letter is exchanged, a day on which you haven't even bothered to go for the post, you are aware of your attachment, your interdependency. Wondering whether a letter is waiting for you, there is the flow of mindwriting as your thoughts and adventures tend toward communication: *I have to tell Richard*. But there are deeper dimensions to being a man of letters that are harder to describe. A married man who doesn't think of his wife all day will not forget that he is married. This subconscious sense of connectedness is more than a life-enhancer: it has been a life-saver. When all else fails—all else will often do that—there will always be a letter to be written and received.

A correspondence is a place, but it's a place of paradox: you inhabit it all the time, and yet it's a world to which you go, and it is not like other habitations. You can work all day on a novel and yet you must still write a letter. You can read until your eyes ache and yet you need to know what's enfolded in that envelope. It is not news of illness at St. Ronan Terrace that prompts me, occasionally, to want to mail out two words only: *Don't die*. It is a way of saying: *I need you in the world*. More exactly: *I need you, Sir, to talk to me*.

Given that anyone can duplicate typing, whereas only a specialist can impersonate script, it might be said that a handwritten letter, like the handwork of an

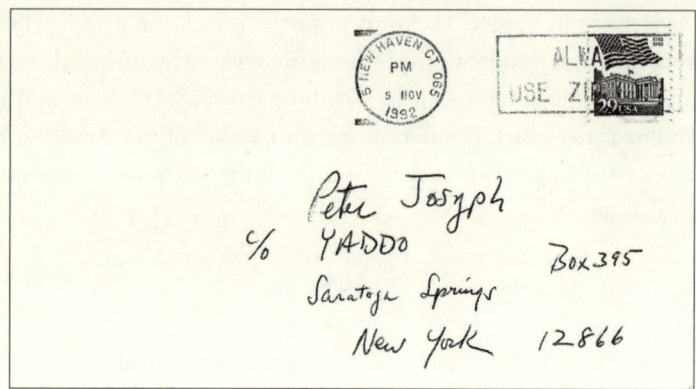

Envelope of a letter from Richard Selzer to Peter Josyph, November 1992.

artisan or artist, is the body renovating and extending itself outward. If art gets the best of us, then through the art of the letter some of the best of Richard Selzer has been folded into an envelope and shipped to my address. When I open my postal box and see the familiar handwriting, I do not think merely: "There's a letter," I think: "Richard's here," for I am, in a way, seeing him in the flesh, but it's the body transubstantiated as ink. And if you are living in a world of unsolicited ads, unpayable bills, slides and manuscripts returning in self-stamped packages that look as if they have gone through a war, what a mercy it is to see that small white envelope addressed to you in pen by a warm familiar hand that isn't your own. The unopened envelope alone is a lift, a message in the bottle reaffirming that the remotest islands of self are not wholly disconnected. A letter arrives, proving once again that your friendship is real; proving that you, too, are real. A man breathes better if he is worth writing to. A letter remembers you, therefore you exist. With two such letters in one post, you feel as if you own half the world.

Unless it were from a mistress or an officer of the day, the adventure for a writer represented by an envelope cannot occasion the boasting associated with roustabouts like Hemingway, Cendrars, Casanova, Kerouac. But I see it as an adventure, and there is a touch of pride in playing the roles of recipient and reciprocator, roles that can lead to a bragging of their own.

"Richard Selzer and I have corresponded for close to twenty years, sometimes twice a week."

"Twice a *week*?"

"Sometimes twice a day."

It is as if you were keeping a T.-rex in your den. Regular correspondence: does such a creature exist? And what manner of man would keep it? Perhaps correspondents are, in fact, remnants of a vanished world, but for all the talk of email and cellphones closing the continuum of letters, it is no less convenient for people to write to each other now than a hundred years ago. If letters aren't written because people can't be bothered, we shouldn't exaggerate the bother. Machiavelli, who wrote charming, sometimes Selzer-like letters from his farm in Sant Andrea outside of Florence, had to send them in duplicate by two different messengers to double the slender hope that they would reach their destination. In our correspondence not one letter has gone astray—unless in Richard Selzer's home. Occasionally a letter that is interrupted, lost, and then completed months later will conclude in another season, another year even, or else it is paired with a new one. "Just found this under a rug." "Fragments, these are. I have a drawer full of them." "I keep starting letters to you, then falling into a trance and they don't get mailed at all." "Here's one that I wrote but have been using as a bookmark for ten days. Since you don't get any other mail, here it is." In September 1992, a letter arrived dated July 24. At the halfway mark it reads: "Cut to September 18. A recent archeological dig in the ruins of my study turned up this fragment of the Dead Sea Scrolls. Should I toss it, or lateral it to the only human being remotely interested?"

To enjoy these letters it is not necessary to have read *Mortal Lessons*, *Taking the World in for Repairs*, or *Down from Troy*. As he has stated, Richard is not quite the same writer here as he is in the short stories, essays, and memoirs that have made his reputation as one of the finest prose stylists of his day. But readers of Richard Selzer will, I believe, find in these letters many of the qualities that inform his published works, and they offer glimpses into the process by which—and the chaos in which—those works were composed, published, adapted, and performed; or, in the case of Richard's play *The Black Swan*, almost-but-not-quite-performed for many years. The letters will also tell you much—never *too* much— about the character and the day-to-day life behind the pen that opened up a new way of writing about the body, about the act of entering into it, and about what it means for us to own a corporeal form. I say *not too much* because the writer who never forgets himself with words never forgets himself with himself either. Relaxed as he is in the letters, I doubt that Richard has ever written to me without protection. "I am a person who is on guard, secretive," he has told me. "For all my apparent openness, much remains held captive and unspoken. That is the way I have learned to survive. So even in moments when I am moved to extend myself passionately, it is never complete, and always there's an element of selectiveness. I don't believe I'm unusual in that. Nobody tells everything."

Through my friendship with Richard Selzer I have been privileged to have, at arm's reach, a living example of what it is to be a professional writer. If, as Hemingway said, being a writer means finishing things, for Richard it means never not having something to finish. It is said that after he blotted the last page of a novel, Balzac would take a clean sheet, dip his pen, and begin another. This is Richard Selzer, for in the years I have known him I have never once seen him *in between*. Despite what he says about putting his work aside in order to visit with his family, there is no time off. He is full of writing all the time.

As an editor I have tried to place these letters in context, but only to facilitate enjoyment. This is in keeping with my correspondent's one stated preference for this volume: "It should be entertaining." The number of letters necessitates a shortening of some, exclusion of others. Occasionally I have excerpted a sequence of letters and presented them unsalutated, heightening the impression of a journal writ for another and enabling the chronicle to briefly accelerate without losing its principle threads. In discussing the free hand with which he punctuates the titles of his works or works-in-progress—with underlinings, all caps, quotation marks, acronyms—Richard and I have agreed that it was a shorthand for rules with which he is perfectly conversant, and those rules will be applied to the printed letters. But when a title isn't punctuated at all, it often signifies something interesting.

Take the short story "Luis," which was published in *Imagine a Woman and Other Tales* and was adapted into a piece for dancers and voice by the Cleveland-based VERB Ballets in November 2006. Until this tale has been completed, the title is printed here the way Richard wrote it to me: Luis. With this name, Richard is referring to both a poor Brazilian boy who lives in a São Paolo dump, and the work of fiction in which the boy appears. But in his letters to me, Luis is a form of artistic possession of which Richard will not be free until, at an uncertain date of deliverance, "Luis" begins life as a story, the character Luis dwells squarely within it, and the author escapes to other concerns. Meanwhile, Luis is practically everywhere in Richard's life. When he reports: "Spoke only to Luis, did everything but blow into his ear until finally he spoke back to me," he is talking about a fragile figure in formation, its outlines shifting, its voice indistinct, its course uncharted. Every day Luis is both an order and a chaos. Half-creating a character brings the power and the existential pressure of forming a life. Luis: there he is—there he *may* be—*now* what? "This morning saw another millimeter of progress in the tale of Luis." "Poor Luis, who is lying on the dump while I race about the barnyard clucking out of my amputated head." "Ah Luis! You ask after him. There is nothing to report, as I have jilted him for the arms of West Point. No chance of a reconciliation until October 1." When Richard is uneasy about his brother's surgery in a Baltimore hospital—perhaps too distractedly to focus on Luis—it's as if he is disappointed to not be able to fly to Brazil and to Baltimore simultaneously. And when he does get to Brazil, Luis might have vanished. In a letter that arrived only yesterday, a passage concerning a new, as yet untitled story encapsulates this symbiosis, demonstrating that Richard's approach to writing—or writing's approach to him—has not essentially changed.

"The story?" he writes. "It desperately needs to be done with, as it has become detrimental to my health, peace of mind, physical and mental equilibrium, and whatever else can be disrupted by the terrible act of creativity."

When a letter includes passages from one of these works-in-progress, a punctuational challenge arises for which there is no solution. Richard is not, properly speaking, quoting from his work. For one thing, he knows his sentences well enough to render them from memory and he is, in a sense, writing, or rewriting, *in* the letters. Sending me Luis is a way of testing and proofing Luis. For another, the inclusion of these sentences is, to me, part of the chronicle of Richard's daily adventure—Luis is one of a number of things that happened to him today—and the distinction between reporting on something written and reporting on something that happened is nicely blurred. This is most evident when a story is told, by turns, in the voice of the narrator and the voice of the correspondent.

"Did I tell you about the wooden whistle he's found?" Richard asks about Luis. "After clearing out the muck that clogged the holes, he blew into it and was startled at the lovely, low sounds which seemed to come from someplace distant, yet be very near. Each time he blows into the whistle, his mind is set to dreaming. He sees pictures which fade as soon as he stops, return when he blows again. Show me the artist who wouldn't die for one of those."

As not one phrase of this paragraph appears in the published story, this is my own Luis, different from the pages called "Luis" in *Imagine a Woman*. With such a passage I am privy to a story in the works, but I am, after all, reading a letter, not a book: an intimate report from the artistic interior. My Luis lacks the certainty, the certification of print. My Luis can run for cover, change his name, or perish of creative malnutrition on the dump in which he is fated, allegedly, to die of radiation. Any day a letter could come in which Luis has been scrapped, so this story about the death of Luis is inseparable, for me, from the story of his borning.

As long ago as 1989, when I first contemplated this series of selections, I wanted it to end on an upbeat note for both Richard and the reader. My own success, I supposed, would be just the right development on which to conclude. Having been forced to fret, for so long, about the diversified life of a correspondent who had rarely, and fleetingly, achieved self-support, Richard would, in the end, receive a piece of heartening news and the Maestro (as I call him) would write to me in tones of celebration and relief. I decided I would probably have to scratch this idea until a letter from Richard arrived, dated December 5, 2002. Simple as it is, the last line of this letter made me see what it meant that I, for all my faults and failures, was still a buddy of his, and that this was success enough on which to close a volume. Or, better, on which to open it.

RICHARD SELZER TO PETER JOSYPH

Caro
Noon.

It has been snowing for hours. There are several inches on the ground, with the certainty of more to come. To be snug, warm, and dry in my library, surrounded by books, makes me happy. Outside, it is silent, with few vehicles. The city has the look, the texture of a city of a hundred years ago. Walking to the hospital for lunch quite refreshed me. Now, back in the library, I read; I sleep; I get up and walk around a bit, now and then I write a few words. O keep your Paris, your Bangkok, your Santiago de Compostela—all I want is right here.

4 p.m.

We are securely tucked under the snow, as I'm sure you are too. The noble shuttle bus driver saw to it that I got within 100 yards of home, then waited to make sure I did not slip and fall. I still retain some of the fun of snow—not the sledding or snowball fights, but the lesser joys of purity, cleanliness, the sense of deposition. It is no small pleasure to feel the flakes upon your eyelashes, wear them for a minute or two like opera glasses, then move on.

December 6.

The pneumonia has taken its toll, as the mirror declares. I have aged a year in a month. Why not? I have walked for a long, long while hand in hand with Time.

Evening.

I light the candle I keep on the desk to tempt the muse. I'm one of those who feel that electricity has come at a great cost to the senses. The electric light does not exist that can fill a room with a soft pulsatile glow and moving shadows. Electric light is raw, glassy: it gilds everything with the same savage brilliance. No crevice is safe from it. A flick of the switch and poof! out goes any mystery.

December 9.

Slowly emerging from the pneumonia. I could use a balloonful of Alpine air every once in a while, but otherwise I am on the mend. This illness has solidified my feeling (long held) that I do not (never did) need a wife. I need a valet and a rickshaw. He would do everything—cook, clean, transport (he would alternate as the runner between the shafts), draw my bath, launder, massage, encourage, buck up, and otherwise mend the carcass and its spirits. It would help if he could play the guitar.

DECEMBER 11.

Your letters make me sad. To me, you are not a failure but a fully realized human being. What can be done to stir up the sediment and allow it to settle in a new and different pattern? If *you* are a "failure," so was Edgar Allan Poe. Success, failure, anyway—it doesn't matter much. Now and then, when I have managed to write something I like, I am "happy" for a bit, but then I realize it doesn't matter all that much. Only my rapture for literature remains. I continue to read the plays of Shakespeare at the rate of one scene a day—like vitamin pills.

Come on up and we'll have a fine day.

letters

1988–1992

A view that is typical of Richard Selzer's walks around Yale University.

you will believe in civilization

1988

DECEMBER 10, 1988

Dear Peter,

    You are a true friend, traveling all that distance to see me again. It was a grand reunion indeed. Next day I spent the morning writing at the Yale Club, of which I am not a member but a sometime squatter. They have a nice clean Men's Room, so I do not have to be spied on while peeing, which is what happens at Grand Central.[1] Then I had lunch with the man from the *New York Times Magazine*. It is depressing to learn just how a magazine is run and by what unimaginative minds. For instance, no unsolicited article is even *read*. Of the many hundreds solicited each year, less than 5% are accepted. Furthermore they take pride in paying very little. One is to be grateful only for being included. I ate my ziti and listened and decided not to give them anything. At sixty, one can begin to fight back. If not now, when?[2]

    I started reading Stendhal's *Life of Henri Brulard* on the train coming home. It *is* delightful. I especially like him when he writes about his love life.

Wouldn't he have made a delightful friend? You certainly are seeing to it that I receive an education. I have devoured each one of your generous gifts. When you come to see me in New Haven, I'll force my pets on *you*. Today I must type, for my sins. It is the bat story, "Pipistrel" [in *Imagine a Woman*], that I told you about at Yaddo.

Your friend

Richard

P.S. Forgive all my stupidities with the medical students. It is what they like, and need, to hear.

December 11, 1988

Dear Peter,

When you come, I shall be your devoted cicerone about Yale. Not one of the beauties of Yale will be excluded. The galleries, the libraries, the colleges—all shall be yours—as well as the key to my house. My wife, Janet, will respond with warmth to any gallantry or blandishments you might muster. We'll walk and talk and you will once again believe in civilization.

Today I attended a performance of scenes from operas—done by the excellent Yale School of Opera. An amazing young basso and a mezzo of note. I cried. But then, I always do at the opera. It's a reflex—nothing to do with the cerebral cortex. It's an atavistic phenomenon having to do with a mother who sang opera. A poet friend of mine alternately deplores and is ravished by my shameless infatuations with art and love. I can't help it. I'm a mess.

You are right—the medical students feed off me ravenously, and I know it, and humbly accept it. I *love* them, and would give them parts of me—my wrist, my earlobe, whatever—if I could. I am so happy that you came to see me in my *other* life. As for Yaddo, I want you to apply again at once. Don't wait for me. I'm too disorganized. I'll come up and take you to my beloved Troy, and we'll see all the marvels there. You will by Troy be *elevated*.

Tell you what: when you come, bring work. That's the way it is here. I'll put you on the third floor with buckets of space and we can both go on with our tasks. It's the way it works best. *Henri Brulard* is absolutely wonderful. I love that man, I do. Thanks for making me look at him.

Love

Richard

December 19, 1988

Dear Peter,

Have I told you that your letters are the best of my entire life? I purr when I see one lying in my mailbox. No one has the epistolary art in greater part. I am delighted that you will come to New Haven. Bring work, you will have a whole floor of this house to yourself, and we shall have fun alternately interrupting and avoiding each other. The privacy rules are not nearly so strict as at Yaddo. What good news about the further sale to Agnieszka! Do bombard her with slides, and suggest a pre-paid visit. Go West, young man. (Offer her my body, if you must.)[3]

If you hear from a producer named Barbara Maltby, open the door. I will have sent her your way. She wrote, claiming to be a fan, asking for a few hours of advice on a screenplay about a doctor suffering from burnout. I declined, but gave her your name as someone who could be hired to mend whatever is wrong with it. She opened the letter with the words *Robert* and *Redford* in immediate succession, to get my attention. Seems she has worked "a great deal" with that one. One never knows.

I have tidied up the last two essays for the book and must now dictate the whole mess and have it typed decently. In order to do that I have taken out my little bag of whips so that each time I flag, thwack! It's called flagging and flagellation, or up! up! Flaggart! I'll let you know if it works. The director of the Oakwood Cemetery in Troy said it would be okay to come up and visit the Crematorium, so I'm planning to do that in January.[4] If you like, we can do that when you come? As for Verdi, I agree with your sister. He is the best. Never wrote a wrong note that I can see. For your opera, you should pick a dark romantic tale full of murder and incest. I'll think.

I've thought. What about *The Black Swan* itself?[5] I'll throw in some thoughts for you to ruminate. Tonight I must go to a dinner party, God help me. And considering the "wormy circumstance" (Keats) of my wardrobe, I shall be a scandal. Never mind, I shall steep my hair "in weird syrops" (Keats) and all will be well.

Love

Richard

P.S. No! You may *not* take us to dinner, and that's that.

December 29, 1988

Dear Peter,

Happy New Year! So I shall expect you on the 9th or the 10th. Whether we go to Troy or stroll these groves of academe will depend on the weather. It'll be a last-minute decision. I loved your conversation on the film set with the Japanese actor, and I am glad to see that you are working, however miscast as a cop. Actually, you are *my* kind of cop.

My wretched book is dictated and at the typist's. I have a bad case of ennui over it. To cheer me up, the Japanese book arrived. It is very pretty and is called: からだの宇宙誌. In case you were dying to know, that's *Mortal Lessons*. Also yesterday a lady from *Time* called and kept me on the phone too long for an article she's writing on American medicine. I said quite stupid things as well as a few lies. I will get much angry mail and a handful of death threats.

That Barbara Maltby—producer—phoned. I again urged her to contact you. Here's the thing: she *does* work for Redford. They hired a writer to write a screenplay about a doctor who suffers burnout—having to do with a malpractice suit, etc. The script is "flawed." In fact I gather it is no good. Since they hired and paid him for a rewrite, he is to do that, but they wanted to come discuss it "for two to three hours." No, I said. No time. Besides, I am working with a writer who is doing a screenplay based on my work with a related theme. Who is it, she wanted to know. Peter Josyph, I replied. I tell only as many lies as necessary. We left it

Richard Selzer's home on St. Ronan terrace in New Haven, Connecticut.
Above the porch are the windows of his study or "scriptorium."

that she'd think and get back to me. If she does, I'll sic her on you. Maybe they'll hire you to doctor the script? If they do, I'd then be more than happy to consult. We must keep plotting. It's the only way.

Thanks for [Eugen Herrigel's] *Zen in the Art of Archery*. It came today and I'll save it for bedtime. You must stop buying books for me. Buy peanut butter for yourself.

I was told today that the philtrum (she put her finger over mine)—it's the sweet little groove from nose to upper lip—is caused by the shushing finger of the angel who warns the newborn baby not to reveal the secrets of the life before birth. Should I believe her?

Love

Richard

sleepwalking and daydreaming

1989

JANUARY 14, 1989

Dear Peter,

It *was* the grandest visit. Know that you are welcome in this house *ad libidum*. Just let me know when, so I can evict whoever is sleeping in your bed—unless I think you might benefit by the company therein.

I'm sitting at my table in the sunroom having just read both of your letters. And the answer is (in the words of Molly Bloom) Yes, yes, yes, yes, yes. The Talk is a great idea—there is nothing so civilized. We'll do it for our own sakes and let the world eavesdrop if it wants to. We must think how to do it. Already, one is as skittish as a bride. I do think that some editing will be necessary to eliminate the ums, ers, and yeahs, and to place the talks in some narrative form. I'm ready to begin any time, so we must decide how to arrange a schedule that will not keep us from our other High Arts. A good bit of it will require that we sit face to face. Some might be done by your sending me questions to which I could respond into a tape recorder and forward to you. But *you* must be the one who decides on the format and editing. The Joseph Campbell/Bill Moyers book [*The Power of Myth*] might be a good model.

Thanks loads for the Richard Burton tape of Donne. I'll hear it tonight over a pitcher of vodka. And for [Malcolm de Chazal's] *Plastic Sense*, which I have peeked at and find just to my taste. Chazal reminds me much of Francis Ponge—I'll send *you* that one.

Two Presbyterian preachers came this week and interviewed me for hours for a Christian youth magazine. Very genial bearded gents who love Jesus rather a bit too much. My unabashed atheism turned them both pale. Then came a would-be author bearing the manuscript of his 500-page novel for me to read. So you see that I get nothing done. It's just as well. There's too much of me as it is. I did scratch out a few lines of Crematorium, however. Please let me help you place *your* novel when the time comes. Borchardt will read it.[1] Good news, that, about Agnieszka's check, and that you will see them this month. Be irresistible. Express my regrets. And for God's sake stop spending your money on *me*. That was not the idea. Be of good cheer and we shall prosper together.

Love
Richard

P.S. Thanks, Yaddo, for bringing me Peter Josyph.

January 19, 1989

Dear Peter,

"Get up," I said to my pen this morning.

"Nothing doing," it replied. "I shall *not* get up today. Or ever again."

"There, there," I soothed. "It's just an attack of malaise. In an hour you'll feel better and we'll work."

Whereupon it discharged a pale blot of ink onto the page and swooned among my fingers. No amount of stroking would tease it erect. Either it needs a blood transfusion or a visit to Dr. Kinsey. Such is my state of impotence these days. I thought you ought to know—you, who have embarked on a rendering of my stories for the movies and who has determined to Talk with me in the coming year. I am not worthy of your perspiration. Just a broken-down scribbler whose Muse has called out a cheery ta-ta! Think it over, dear boy, before you spend your treasure on such an one as I. But then, you are besotted, and I can only take comfort in the thought that the most beautiful flowers are fed with manure.

I do hope you are preparing for your reunion with Agnieszka. Be sure to use the right spoon for your soup and don't guzzle your tahini. I want her smitten and captured, you hear? Even more politic would be to smite and capture Art. The way to a woman's purse is through her husband.

I will try to type up my Crematorium notes tonight, because tomorrow must be spent on Grub Street preparing for my sermon at the First Baptist Church in Worcester. I go up on Saturday and am required to stay at the home of some parishioners. And me—incompletely housebroken! And yet another dinner party with "conversation." Their last speaker was one Scott Peck, bestselling charlatan and psychobabbler. I never thought I'd sink so low. As for the year ahead, let's plan and plot and inch forward. I just wrote a recommendation for a guy to go to Yaddo. He ain't a thousandth of you, so why don't you apply again and tell them I am your recommender? It can't hurt. A letter from Robert Brustein today asking When?[2] So I shall gather myself together soon and go—with your plays in my valise. Come to New Haven soon. I'll load the pantry with whole wheat pasta and cheese and tofu. And I'll keep the toilet plunger within arm's reach for you.

Love

R

January 20, 1989

Dear Peter,

You are a marvel! A phenomenon! A daemon! A first draft in hand and so quickly. While here I sit scribbling, then erasing, then pausing "to commerce with the skies" as Milton put it. I shall try to answer your questions with as few lies as possible.

(1) Oddly, I do not recall a single overt instance of anti-Semitism during my years in Troy. Not that Troy, of all cities in the world, was free of it. Only that I was spared. Perhaps the town, exhausted by its poverty and sickness, had no energy to sustain a racial hatred; perhaps growing up with a Catholic sensibility and clearly projecting it, I was taken for a gentile. At age ten I owned my secret rosary which I kept hidden in a shoe in the closet. I remember the day my mother found it and walked into the kitchen where I was doing my homework—dangling it between thumb and forefinger. "I believe this is yours?" she said and dropped it on my notebook. Nor ever was another mention made of it. Nor do I think my father—family doctor to the Irish poor—came in for any racism. He was as much

loved in the town for his obvious lack of materialism (we, too, were poor) as for his own catholicism (small c). While it is not unthinkable that an outraged patient might have blurted a racial epithet, it was not *their* way. A punch in the nose *was*. Father used no Yiddishisms that I can remember, altho' he spoke (we all did) Yiddish to my father's mother and my mother's father, both of whom lived with us. Only the presence of two old Jews in the house gave any evidence that a visitor was in a Jewish home.

(2) Yes, I'll play and sing the songs my mother taught me, such as "What Are the Wild Waves Saying," "The Kashmiri Love Song," "Carissimia," "The Golden Links of Love Are Broken," etc. Be prepared to weep the way all Troy wept when she lifted her delicate soprano at the music hall—like a white mouse ringing a little silver bell.

Tomorrow's the day I drive to Worcester and the Baptists. I'll be home at 5 p.m. wearing a halo and an animal hide. Yesterday I was asked to go to Barbados with Janet for five days of teaching in what is called Continuing Medical Educa-

Old photograph of the Selzer family home at 45 Second Street in Troy, New York.

Current view of 45 Second Street.

tion. Janet says we should do it, but what will become of me in Barbados? Shall I snorkel? Or *be* snorkeled? I loath the beach, nor is there an iota of the Caribbean tourist in my bones. Nor am I to be paid. It is to be of service. Of how much service need one be? Tell me, Sir. I am a poor flibbertigibbet and wish only to retire behind my quiet and unmolested door. Also, I am incapable of enjoying myself away from my notebook and pencil.

Love
Richard

P.S. Thank you for Maxwell Perkins. I'll devour it.

JANUARY 23, 1989

Dear Piotr, Kamarad

I entirely agree with you on the way we should proceed with the Talk. Of course you are right and I place myself in your capable hands. We'll start at Columbia, then. I'll be staying at the dorm overnight. If I come in early that morning we could meet and start, go to the talk, work afterwards and perhaps the following day—just to get it going.

I am terribly pleased about the Bicentennial Room.[3] I shall, by all means, ferry over to see the show, my emphysematous chest further expanded with pride. And yes, you must come back with me to St. Ronan Terrace after that. But come *before*, too. Janet is most amicably disposed, so you must have done something right. Just let me know ahead of time so I can plunge out the toilet. If you can find time to boat up the Hudson with me to Troy, we'll explore the Crematorium together.

I'm just back from Worcester, where I gave the sermon at the First Baptist Church! Glorious. And I was not struck by lightning at the pulpit. Talked about medical ethics, death, euthanasia, etc., to 600 bright, argumentative congregants. I loved them. The pastor is splendid and the music ethereal. I had to stay overnight at a parishioner's house—which I did *not* like. No smoking or drinking, so you can imagine. Today I spent eight hours at my desk and ended up with 200 words (Crematorial). It is not the way a grown-up should behave. Chatted with cronies about the Koran, Islam, etc., and had lunch with two grand Yale undergraduates. So you see that I am frivolous to the *nth* degree.

Tell me all about your Agnieszka meeting. I long to hear everything. *Everything*, do you hear?

Love

Richard

JANUARY 26, 1989

Dear Peter,

The pen just gave out—a lovely, silent little death—the kind I wish for my dearest friends, so I am writing to you in rare and priceless graphite. Actually it is my favorite. I love being able to use the rubber eraser and stopping now and then to sharpen the tip. Those little bits of business add a lovely feeling of craft to scribbling. And the smell of the pencil is enough to awaken the whole of my buried childhood. It is the most nostalgic smell of my life.[4]

Last evening at 5 p.m. I addressed an audience at the Medical School—"Instructions to the Architect" was the idea—or "How to Build a Hospital." Actually it was about Lady Jane Grey, windchimes, fountains, and centaurs. The roomful seemed mighty sleepy to me, as though they had been up all night stanching a flow of blood, which made me struggle to soldier on and carry them on my back. It was murder. In fact one guy, a math teacher, came up afterwards to tell me that I had annoyed him. He had come anticipating an architectural discussion, not a lot of bullshit about the sensual imagination. I told him to go home, think it over and write me a letter, then we'd see about it. What would you have done?

Today I inched ahead on the Crematorium piece and I am getting quite happy with it. I have almost finished the memoir part, and now it is time to describe the interior of the building, so soon I must go up to Troy—on location, as you film people put it. I need a tour of the place, a talk with the caretaker (who also does the incinerations), and a xerox of the original plans. It is very far from morbid but instead is quite lighthearted. My agent said we'll send it to the *New Yorker*, but I don't know. If they put people in Hell for indecisiveness, I'll be there.

I finished the Maxwell Perkins letters and enjoyed them. What a decent man. Which brings me to your novel. Just say when and if you want me to offer it to my agent. Your play, *Adventures of a Red Ball*, is just wonderful. You must really have two superb actors. It is subtle and complex underneath. Your letters are a joy to me, but I don't want you to take time away from your work to write me. Only if you want a change of pace.

Love

Richard

February 3, 1989

Dear Peter,

The whole Columbia gig made me feel like Moliere's *Le Médecin Malgré Lui*. I arrived home at 12:30 p.m. in a state of profound exhaustion. If it had not been for you and your sweet and solicitous care, I should have perished somewhere during the proceedings.[5] Thank you, my dear and good friend. You are the most thoughtful of human beings. I picked up your letter at the post office and, yes, I want to begin anytime you say. Whenever it suits you, come up to New Haven and we shall commence.

At a recent dinner party, an otherwise faultless woman, upon hearing that I hail from Troy, leaned close and said: "Troy is the asshole of North America." To which I cried: "Then thank God for it, or you would be even more bloated and full of shit than you already are!" I should have died at that moment. Never again will I be so ready to enter the Kingdom of Heaven as when I defended my native land from so poisonous an epithet.[6]

Today a sluggish pen due to the vicissitudes of yesterday. But *Lear's* magazine called to say they have taken my article, so I am solvent again. And I am invited to give the Commencement Address at the Mayo Clinic in May. Tomorrow night I speak to Yale on Surgery as Religion. We'll talk about shamans and the sacred work of the hands. Would you could be there to shore me up. If I live to be a thousand I'll never forget sitting in that Inferno called Grand Central Station—with you. Oh, Gods! It is to touch the dark underside of metropolitan life. Peter, however can I thank you for your many kindnesses toward me? You are a real friend. I haven't got so many of *them*.

Love
Richard

FEBRUARY 5, 1989

Dear Peter,

Today is this family's expected date of confinement and it is snowing.[7] Those two put a man in a mood of reflection. In addition to which, the Crematorium has been squatting on my head like a bird of prey with its talons embedded in my scalp. Why did I begin this obsession with such a building in the first place? Is it just one more pathetic grope for faith? On that score there is nothing to hope for or to worry about. The combination of Catholicism and Judaism with which my childhood was beset has permanently secured my atheism. Nor is it a maudlin yearning for the past, which, truth now, was no joke, and mostly bitter as the apples of Sodom. Let's just say it is a woeful exploration into the cave of my life. Then too, there is Troy which, in my case, "age cannot wither nor custom stale."

When I think of Troy I think of death—Father, Mother, and all the rest. I've seen a great many dead people since I left Troy—cadavers in the anatomy lab, the legions of patients I've watched die in the hospitals where I've worked, young men with AIDS, Korean farmers blown up by land mines. The settling, the solidification of death is engraved on my mind. I have become its *familiar*. But it all started in Troy, which has had short shrift from the twentieth century. In 1917 the Spanish flu arrived to do battle with tuberculosis for the citizenry. By the time that was over there wasn't a doorpost in town that hadn't worn Madonna lilies. The flu, having eaten its full, flew. And left us galloping into the Depression, the vanguard of which we achieved in 1926—way ahead of the rest of the country. And there we stayed until the war came along, not to rescue so much as to distract us. It wasn't til fifty years later that Troy has begun to lift its head from the wallows.

That's not quite it. In one aspect of life, we flourished—prostitution. What with the river traffic and the railroad and men coming up from Hudson and

Poughkeepsie and down from Saratoga and Vermont, we were *busy*. It's a wonder the plumbing on Sixth Avenue stood it. Sixth Avenue—that's where the houses were—three blocks of *them*, as my mother called them. Jesus Christ simply could *not* have died for the likes of *them*, she said. It was all wasted on me. Youth was not my time. Some people do not come into bloom until they are elderly. Only when I left Troy did I figure out how to charm the birds down from the trees. Now I've got that down pat, so don't fret over it.

So much for reverie. Friday night I spoke to a warmhearted crowd at the Yale Hillel organization. I didn't read, only blabbed on about such trivialities as the Resurrection of the Flesh and dreams. After everyone left—at 11:30 p.m.—the rabbi broke out the cognac and I got home at 1 a.m. having made a dozen new friends. When are you coming to New Haven? Let this letter be the spur. And tell me how the painting room is going. I'll be back on track in my next letter. I know it's going to be a good week because I won $47 in the lottery. Affluence is just around the corner.

Love
Richard

FEBRUARY 8, 1989

Dear Peter,

You cannot imagine how desolate I was to read your letter.[8] It just *couldn't* have happened. Not to *you*, whose every impulse is to create, not destroy. I can't accept it, I can't. But the marvel of it is that, like a phoenix, you have risen from the ashes and have prevailed. Now you *must* come up as soon as possible. We'll immerse ourselves in the work and rebound with vigor from this calamity. I am at your disposal entirely. Your rooms are waiting. I want to be part of your work. If I had your phone number I'd call you tonight to insist that you come now. Also, it is *not* your fault. If anyone's, it is mine for letting you stay with me at Grand Central Station when I should have made you go. I berate myself all over the place. Never mind, I intend to make it up to you by hurling myself into these projects with a full heart. You have my promise. We'll civilize the world yet.

I am laboring over my Crematorium—it is devilish hard—but I strain at it every day and all day. I think it will be a thing that has not been done before. When you come we will surely talk about it—and about death—which has been with me all my life—both friend and adversary.

The Mark Twain [William Dean Howells's "My Mark Twain"] is a beauty and I enjoy it every night in bed. Your taste is so fine. I trust it now. I shall try hard not to feel malice toward the people who stole your work. Malice eats the spirit up and leaves nothing behind. Let's just spend all that in *work*. But in the freshness of the wound, let me say that I'll never forget your kindness in staying with me at the station, regardless of the ugly consequences. I wait to hear that you are coming *pronto*!

          Love

          Richard

It's 2 a.m. and I am unable to sleep thinking about the robbery. To think that we were sitting in that antechamber of Hell drinking club soda while it was taking place! If I hated to go to New York before, this has solidified my horror of that city. I feel guilty for having suggested you come to Columbia in the first place. We'll just have to try to put it behind us and go on. I cherish the notion that good things are coming for you and that perhaps *because* of this incident, Fate will be shamed into granting you a shower of successes. I am a rather gentle man to whom this sort of thing is insupportable. I can't digest it. I imagine it's like being raped. Let me leave it alone, then, and go to sleep. Tomorrow, I am resolved to stop chewing it over and try to pay attention to my sentences and paragraphs again. Do you the same.

          Love

          R

FEBRUARY 21, 1989

Dear Peter,

    Gone not twenty-four hours and already I miss you. Which informs me that I *do* have a touch of masochism in my soul, if not my body. Your 4000 questions are still swarming about my head like bats in a cave. Since I got nothing done yesterday, I must gird up my loins, loin up my girds, and write these damn speeches for Utah—*NOW*. But first this note to express my utter satisfaction with the way you are directing this book. You have an authoritative and masterful way, and it succeeds in drawing from me what has been squatting way down in my medulla oblongata for decades. I thought I had forgotten it all, but it seems I haven't. One line of conversation, I hope, will deal with writing itself, about which I like to think. Can we plan on that?

    You will be interested to know that the minute Janet got home she threw out the rest of that shit you cooked for dinner. The gleam in her eye was marvelous to see. "It's a wonder our old plumbing could take it," she said. I don't know whether she was referring to the pipes or our intestines. Never mind, you have given new life to the old term *stuck up*.

    I shall try to get up to Troy the week after next to visit the Crematorium and its caretaker. Then I can finish the piece. I'm immensely pleased that you like it.

And I am on page 85 of your novel. It is terrific—mysterious and playful and full of the unexpected. I am savoring it. For the life of me I don't see how you get so much work done, and I so chaotic. I am glad to think that you are exactly the same age I was when I began to write. And with so much accomplished already and so much time ahead of you. We must plan another session in March.

Love

Richard

February 24, 1989

Dear Peter,

I trust that your uncharacteristic silence is due to total immersion in your painting. This show is a great chance for you and will be the launching pad to catapult you over the moon—like that jumping cow. I've spent the last three days shuffling papers—making piles. (1) Diary entries. (2) Notes for an essay on writing. (3) Notes for an introduction to the diary. Now begins the job of putting everything together. I'll take the writing notes with me to Utah tomorrow and see if I can move them along. I got a letter from my Japanese translator today with surprisingly good reports. *Mortal Lessons* is doing better than anticipated and will be reprinted this week. Three leading newspapers and a magazine praised it prominently, and the publisher is mulling over a visit to Japan to push it.

Yesterday came an invitation to deliver the annual Freedom address at West Point in September.[9] It is their biggest deal (Tom Wolfe gave it last year; before that, Bart Giamatti). There is to be a Richard Selzer afternoon with a parade and *me* as the "reviewing officer"! I must rehearse my salute. What does all this mean? Am I then to be dragged from obscurity after all? I *always* cry at parades and will doubtless break down and disgrace myself. I plan to talk about the freedom of the imagination—which is the last freedom available to mankind, the only one that cannot be taken away.

I keep thinking of you laboring to transcribe those tapes and my heart swells with pity. I wouldn't blame you for getting cold feet over this project. As you know, others have foundered on the same rock. I've floated the idea of the TALKING book (I don't know what else to call it) to colleagues and friends—all of whom say: *Do it*! That includes the great and near-great hereabouts. I've finished your beautiful novel. It is unique and exhilarating. Give me permission to show it to my agent and others. I won't until you say so. I understand fully your attitude toward fame and success, as I share that disinterest. *But*, I'd like to see this book in print.

Now I must pack a suitcase and go to Utah. What in heaven's name shall I do there? Look at the mountains, that's what. And work. I need to pay the family's plane fare home.

                Love

                Richard

FEBRUARY 27, 1989

Dear Peter,

This ski lodge is 8500 feet high, so guess who had to stop smoking—almost. From my window I look out at the most beautiful mountains—covered with snow and hairy with dark evergreen trees. Everywhere you look there are tiny figures sliding, hopping, crawling in what seems an utterly aimless pattern—rather like Brownian movement. If I didn't know better I'd think this mountain had a bad case of the crabs.

I gave my first talk this morning and as a result am the darling of the *in vitro* fertilization crowd (these are all gynecologists here). This afternoon I do it again and then home tomorrow, having had altogether too much food, drink, and praise. I am the only non-skier here, and surely the only man in history to bring a gray pinstripe suit and a red silk tie to a ski lodge. I haven't worn it, as one appears everywhere in jeans and sport shirt. Of course I have done no writing except in my diary. When I can, I read Mark Twain and rejoice.

LATER.

Now I've given the second talk and have received everything but a laurel wreath and the keys to Snowbird. I am much made over by the elderly ladies who make up a considerable percentage of the people here.

STILL LATER.

This letter is getting written by installments, like *Oliver Twist*. I am home. Yesterday, I began to shuffle through my notes on writing. There may be an essay there but it will take a detonation of TNT to excavate it. I'm beginning with a cure for writer's block. Speaking of writers, I received a fan letter from Phyllis Theroux. She bought *Repairs* in a supermarket in Ashland, Virginia! Next to the tomato soup, I suppose. Also a letter from Miyo Takano, my Japanese translator, with plans to publish *Down from Troy* there in English for students.[10] Along with it came the introduction written already—by a Jesuit professor at Sophia University. It's a sweet introduction. I hope they will let me add the hospital piece, the Crematorium, and the one about my mother.

Thanks so much for Donne's *Sermons*. They are a great sea of words to drown in, but happily. What passion! While in Utah I was phoned by one David Kranes, who runs Rob't Redford's Sundance Theatre there, asking to see my stupid play. Now I have to get it back from Chuck Schuster in Milwaukee. Practically everything is a pain in the ass. Except you.

Love
Richard

March 3, 1989

Dear Peter,

First things first. Your novel is a gem. Quirky, intelligent, and reeking with style and flair. I want to see it published. Please tell me if I can send it on to Borchardt and some of my editor people. I await your word. My God, Peter, you are working like Hercules when he cleaned the Augean stables! And here I sit with my head in my hand, lucky to get an adverbial clause down on paper. It ain't fair—to you. Today I typed four pages on writer's block that will be part of the essay on writing. It has to do with a pair of my pants, a candle, and Ambroise Paré's artificial rain.[11] So you can just imagine. Reading your letter and thinking things over, it occurs to me that for years I have been putting away bits of my life for a rainy day. And now that the time has come, I am spending them one by one onto a page, or sometimes in a wild spree such as we had together when you were here.

Just today I remembered that Father was the house doctor at the Home for Wayward Girls in Troy—called the Mary Magdalene House. Now that is really the oddest thing about Roman Catholicism, because so far as I know she was nonesuch, but a poor epileptic woman who was cured by Jesus. At least that is what Luke, the physician, diagnosed in Chapter 8, Verse 2: "Mary that was called Magdalene from whom seven demons had gone out." Given the choice—Matthew, Mark, or Luke—I'd rather believe the one Gospeler who was a doctor, wouldn't you?

I've been thinking a lot about Dick Ellmann lately, how he spotted me early on and browbeat me into continuing. Robert Brustein, too. Luck deposited me on St. Ronan Terrace twenty-four years ago. I thought at the time it was Mt. Olympus, what with all the gods living on it. But they've all gone off to other galaxies, leaving me here to fend for myself. How fickle of them.

The calendar tells me that March 23–27 would be perfect for another visit. We'll go to the Elizabethan Club to see the books, then to the Medical School.[12] I'll introduce you to Ferenc Gyorgyey—my librarian friend there, and you can talk to him while I keep out of sight. The Anatomy Lab, too. And a look at the Civil War letters at the Rare Book library.[13] Do please come if you can. My head is in a whirl. Your energy and enthusiasm carry me along. You are a marvel. But if *I* ask *you* some hard questions, what will you think?

And now I'm going to listen to that mysterious tape you sent. Whatever could it be?

Love

Richard

MARCH 4, 1989

Dear Peter,

Here I sit amidst the detritus of my diary, when a familiar feeling comes over me. What can it be? I ask myself. A moment later, I know. It is guilt. There you are, spending your talents on a subject that may very well in the end prove unworthy: ME. I am the farthest thing you can get from being a Great Writer. To be a GW you have had to perform heroic deeds. Your life must be full of plots, counterplots, rivalries, hatreds, and challenges to duel. I have swum no Hellespont, contracted no venereal disease—unless you want to count a dose of crabs forty years ago—and so far as I know I am devoid of enemies. Worse yet, I haven't any high and vaulting ambitions. My biography could be written on a single sheet of paper—triple spaced. Who would want to read a book of my meanderings? Having read your novel and seen your paintings and plays, I worry that you are not wasting good time on me. You must promise to tell me the instant you decide that it isn't worth the effort. I would understand completely and it would not fracture our friendship. I guess I had to say this when I read your last wonderful letter for the fourth time. Your letters are riveting. I read and reread them to make sure I don't miss anything. Mine, on the other hand, are to be read once and filed. All this having been said, I look forward eagerly to our next session.[14]

It's Saturday and the opera is *La Boheme*, so no writing between 1:30 and 5. What other art form can one have heard or seen dozens of times and still approach with eagerness? Surely not anything I will ever produce. It's humbling.

Love

Richard

MARCH 6, 1989

Dear Dynamo,

I like the title [*What One Man Said to Another*] very much. It is straightforward and inviting. Do keep it. And yes, the 17th–22nd will be just fine. I shall try to sweep out my brains for the occasion. The diary is giving me no end of trouble, and I sink back from it in despair a dozen times a day. If only I had a bit of your courage. But that is youth, and I must do with what I have left. I think I'll try to go to Troy for an overnight. I desire so much to finish the Crematorium. Then you and I can go there together in April if you wish. It's a lovely ride up there and we can talk all the way. I'll arrange for us to stay at the Parish House at RPI [Rensselaer Polytechnic Institute] with Father Gary. You are bound to be touched by the affection with which we will be received. I cannot wait to walk with you the streets of Troy, to stand by the river of my dreams. Oh Troy! Will you never let go of my heart?

The Mark Twain tape [Hal Holbrook's *Mark Twain Tonight*] is *beautiful*. I love it and am hearing it again now. Thank you. My *get* are arriving momentarily, so I shall close for this time. Only to say how thrilled I am over our joint venture.

Love

Richard

MARCH 11, 1989

Dear Peter,

I am just back from dawdling Rebecca on my knee and feeding her an ounce of sugar water. She is more beautiful than Milton's Eve on the day of Adam's rib resection. It is a week of no work *chez moi*, as Son #2 is here and we are playing together, but next week I go to Troy and will finish Crematorium or bust. I've also begun jotting down notes for West Point, which I see as a grand honor and an opportunity to orate upon the connections between medicine and the military, to which purpose I have reread the diary of Ambroise Paré that you kindly sent me. I need to set the tone *just right*, as it is doubtful I will ever again have such a chance to present this material before so committed an audience.

I just looked up from my table in the sunroom to see East Rock turned all red in the sunset. What a signal to the end of day. I expect you, having finished one labor, are about to embark upon another while I dwindle into evening without the least intention of furthering my writerish cause. I am expecting you the week after next, so gird up your loins and come. My only regret is that I can't think what to *feed* you. Yours is such a highly refined palate. But now I know to bring the electric heater to our interview room and shine it on your meatless bones so that you can speak without the chattering of your teeth. Til then, all my concern and affection.

Richard

MARCH 11, 1989

Dear Peter,

Janet and I are momentarily off to see Mozart's *Cosi Fan Tutte* performed by the Yale School of Music. Going out at night is an occasion for me. You know my usual bedtime. So I have napped and abstained from vodka and am prepped and primed for the event. Today I was a tiny bit useful. I played piano with my daughter-in-law and anagrams with my son. After which I wrote my column for the medical magazine to which I am indentured six times a year. Then I made some notes in my journal, read in Lord Chesterfield's *Letters to His Son*, and sent off my c.v. to those who have requested it. So you can see that I stir about. How it is accomplished I cannot say. From what I read daily in the newspapers about the evils of excess, I might as well relax. Between vodka and tobacco and lamb chops, the timbers of my wretched vessel are already too rotted to be seaworthy. Which suits me fine, as I am *in my place* and intend to stay put.

LATER.

Just home from the opera. Lovely—the whole thing. Such an endless flow of melody and stylishness. I am told he composed it in a few weeks. Come to think of it, that's your speed, too. And now your fine double-spaced letter has come. That's good news about the stipend for reading *Rue Picasso*. May you have many encores! And now you have two rooms to fill with paintings. Two rooms a Versailles will make when hung with Josyphs. As soon as you arrive we'll have a look at the Civil War letters, then you can decide. While he [John Vance Lauderdale] is definitely not dull, neither is he what some call a "writer," but they are beautifully *au naturel* and spontaneous.

Today I began an unmailable letter to a young woman whose attentions I am striving to stand off. Which is a situation so absurd in my life as to border on the lunatic.

Love
Richard

MARCH 12, 1989

Dear Peter,

If my hopes are realized, I'll go to Troy on Wednesday, stay overnight at the Newman Club at RPI, and take up (by capillary action) the nourishment of that ancestral land. In the matter of the *Iliad*, I have always been on the side of the Trojans. The Greeks—Achilles, Ajax, Agamemnon, Ulysses, and the others of that kidney—seem to me a spoiled, sulky, sly lot. An army of brats. I much prefer Hector, Cassandra, and pious Aeneas who survived the sack and escaped carrying his old daddy Anchises on his back. When Apollo caused Troy to be rebuilt 10,000 miles away on the banks of the Hudson (that business about the Dutch having done it is a snare and a delusion), he couldn't resist rubbing our noses in the fact that we had lost the war. Throughout the city are signs that the Greeks were here. There is a Mt. Olympus, an Albia, and an inordinate number of Greek Revival buildings. Even the "Approach" to RPI, until it tumbled down the hillside, was a replica of a ruined temple with marble steps and columns and antique statuary. Personally, I would have preferred a more Asiatic flavor in which downtown Troy would be the corner of Frankincense and Myrrh, and the suburb up on the hill would be Ararat instead of Sycaway—so named for the great number of sycophants who lived there in the nineteenth century.

In any event, *there* and there alone dwells my imagination. As you know, it has been broadly and erroneously put abroad that the nine Muses—who were the daughters of Zeus and Mnemosyne (Goddess of Memory)—dwell on Parnassus, Helicon, and a third mountain I can't remember. One day Pegasus kicked the earth on Helicon, and from that spot a fountain gushed forth. It is called the Fountain of Hippocrene, to bathe in which any artist would sell his teeth, as it is the source of all inspiration. Anyway, it's not in Greece, it's in Troy. I'll take you there to see it if you're nice.

Word from France that the play is being done. It is tremendously moving to me that my stories are to be enacted at the Hôtel Dieu in Paris—the very hospital where Ambroise Paré learned his craft. I believe in these fated tangential crossings. They happen often and I am sure to everyone, but most go unnoticed. The only one who notices is the artist, who has the knack of seeing everything in the world in relation to himself. And just so does his life take on universality.

                                                Love

                                          The Bard of Troy

THE IDES OF MARCH

Dear Peter,

I am writing this at the Parish House at RPI where I am staying for the night. The drive up was through dense fog, beneath a livid sky—just right for a journey to a Crematorium. But once inside the city limits the sun broke through and my day at the Crematorium was lovely.

I parked the car and rang up the caretaker, who arrived with two of his helpers. Tom Gibson is the most unlikely Charon you could imagine. At thirty-one he's a short barrel with a *grand* belly, blonde beard, and the map of Ireland on his face. I was given a tour, allowed to feast on all the extraordinaries, taken up into the tower and, at last, permitted to witness a cremation. You are right to be leery. Half an hour into the incineration, Tom opened the oven door and I saw the body engulfed in flames. In deference to your fragile sensibilities, I won't be descriptive here, but will, you can count on it, in the article. Enough to say that I have seen and heard what I needed to, and will go home tomorrow to finish the piece. Somehow or other (it always happens) the local newspaper got wind of my visit and there was a reporter and a photographer waiting at the cemetery. I was interviewed in the Urn Garden!

It is very strange—uncanny, even—how familiar the interior of the building is to me, tho' I have not seen it before. I had imagined it almost as it is. An untrodden chamber of my mind—like the grotto Keats built for Psyche in the ode. I shall talk it all out to you if you promise not to cringe. Being in Troy again is like having been let back into Eden. World! I am no more of ye.

All the way here, I listened to *Lucia di Lammermoor*. It is such a sublime mess. Hysteria of the larynx. Somehow it works, though. In the last act Edgardo takes forever to die. One might snicker, only that is precisely what we *all* do: stagger around bellowing for a long time before we die.

And now I am home. Last night, pasta and wine with the Catholics til the wee hours, so that I am moribund, but that ain't half-bad after all. I've read your wonderful letter. The paintings sound to me striking and unique. I shall of course come to see them when the show opens. About the dates of my letters, let me shed a pale ray of light: I *never* know what date it is. I take a wild stab at it and hope for the best. It's the sort of character defect that drives scholars loony. Don't pay a bit of attention to it.

In today's mail, the official invitation from West Point, writ by Lt. Gen. Dave Palmer, Superintendent of the United States Military Academy. Oh God! I've got to do this right. And no fooling. It is the greatest chance of my life to say something about war and peace.

The best part of this letter is that I shan't mail it, but give it to you when you arrive. Do I need to say how much I look forward to that? Writing, then, and Death, and wherever else you choose to lead me. The book will be as long as the Encyclopedia Britannica.

Love
Richard

March 22, 1989

Dear Peter,

Well, I am back in harness and it has been a *day*. I mailed off Batch #2 of the book manuscript to Georges Borchardt via UPS, which I would never have thought to do, until he *ordered* me in that direction. Batch #3 will be sent in two months, I promised. So there may yet be another Selzer book pre-humously published.

A call came from Sundance insisting that I send *The Black Swan*. No amount of demurral on my part worked, so I sent it along with Ken Cavander's version. If they still want to work on it, what should I do? I'd hate to go there for two weeks in my present frame of mind. That's the trouble with getting a literary reputation. People act blindly. I enclosed a long letter saying exactly what you had said, so perhaps I have convinced him not to proceed. I don't want to go there with this play. I would once again be an impostor.

Crematorium proceeds and I am ready to start typing. It is one step—painful—at a time. But the piece is good and I want to see it through. I'm tempted to just go and play the piano instead.

Tower of the Gardner Earl Crematorium in Troy, New York.

I can't tell you how pleased I am that you think the Lauderdale letters are worth doing. No question that there is a book out of it. I'm glad it is on your list. Wasn't I disgraceful in *almost* missing the Archie Hanna connection? It is always best to dial Heaven directly and speak with the dead.[15] I told one of my library cronies about our Talk Book and he was mightily jealous and impressed. Why didn't *he* do it? he wonders. But, I have to tell you that I am still exhausted from the last session and go to bed at 7 p.m. instead of 8. You are a cruel, heartless taskmaster. I so look forward to our Trojan War in May. And to my trip to Long Island to see your art. I'll rest up in the meantime.

Love

Richard

MARCH 23, 1989

Dear Peter,

To follow one letter upon another with such unseemly haste is undignified. But you know my habits. I've just read *Zen in the Art of Archery*. It is a gem. I'm going to read it again tonight. It is in fact about writing or painting or any other art. It is universal. I thank you for it. Today, I rewrote and revised the Crematorium. I am in the throes, I tell you, not knowing whether it makes any sense. The vision of the cremation is as strong as I can make it. I now must consider how architectural I want to be. Perhaps that is the wrong emphasis. Since the library is closed for three days, I'll spend the time typing a draft. Also, the Italian entries in the diary are ready for typing. So I have plenty to do. I did (did I tell you?) send *The Black Swan* to Sundance, but with every bit of commentary you make, and I was as negative as anyone could be. I pray that will be the end of it. I want to be free to think about West Point, and about a story that has been churning away.

Georges Borchardt knows about you, and I await word from Nan Talese.[16] In today's mail, the manuscript of a book of poems by Andrew Hudgins, another Yaddish, and it is very good indeed. I am to go line by line and express hesitations. Andrew is a fine fellow with whom I've had lots of fun. I think him the best Southern poet of our time. Visited today at the library with Claude Lopez—author of *Mon Cher Papa*, an account of Ben Franklin's stay in Paris. Also Cyrus Hamlin, Professor of German Literature who is curious about my *Black Swan*—its relation to Thomas Mann. Read also today in the *Book of Martyrs* by Foxe—about the fellows—Cranmer and Lattimer—who were burned at the stake by order of Bloody Mary. There *is* so much to learn and read. And so little time to do it.

I look forward to seeing your paintings. They sound, in the telling, ingenious and unique. So many talents, you have. And I, only this one, and that shot through with defects. More and more I feel myself to be a fluke, something born out of the confusion of the twentieth century and not destined to last. But then, I am equally struck by the fact that all the "stars" have no future either.

Love

R

March 25, 1989

Dear Peter,

Happy Easter! I've forgotten, if ever I knew, what happened to Christ in the interval between the Resurrection and the Ascension. If you know, tell me. I got a letter from a friend to whom I had described the Talk Book. He suggests you call it: *Thus Saith The Lord of Hosts*. It will grab attention, he says. But, then, he is a wicked fellow.

I spent yesterday and this morning typing the latest draft of Crematorium. There is a problem. The first and last thirds are fine—literary, memoiristic, and well-narrated. The middle third, dealing with the architecture of the building, is tedious. That is odd, because the whole initial reason for the piece was to study its architecture. Now I must decide whether to cut that severely or let it stand. The account of the cremation makes me hesitant to show it to you—considering your squeamishness. This afternoon I'll type the excerpts from my Italian sojourn. Both together came to a mere thirty-five pages, but each speck brings the manuscript closer to book size. I'm trying to get as much done as possible, because there will be no writing during the visit of the German children. I won't give up a minute of their company—not for the chance to write a second Gettysburg Address. I'm almost through that volume of the Durrell–Miller letters. They *are* interesting, without being great examples of the genre. I want to reread *Justine* now.

Today I celebrated the arrival of spring by getting a truly reckless haircut. My hair had become too heavy for my head and I was getting stooped—stupid—whatever. Also, I cut some branches from a forsythia bush and brought them inside to force them to early bloom. Since they would bloom anyway in two weeks if left attached to the mother plant, I now see it as an act of wanton cruelty. Gardeners must be ruthless—all that pruning, lopping, mowing, and thinning out. It's only a step this side of genocide. I'd go for a walk in the park but without all that hair I am too buoyant and subject to being carried aloft by any errant gust.

I have decided to hold on to your novel until after you've made yourself known to an editor via the Talk Book. It will stand a better chance then, and I don't want to use up my options. Anyway, it's all written and requires no more work on your part. Which is good, as you are as busy as a cockroach in a bakeshop. Yesterday, a friend who enjoys analyzing me said that I was neither a cynic nor a skeptic, only because I go through life with nothing to lose. Either I have lost it all already or I am stupid. He insists that everybody else is grinding an axe. I refuse to believe that.

Love
Richard

March 26, 1989

Dear Peter,

"Crematorium" is done! Only needing to be dictated, then typed. Ditto for the Italian journal entries. I need now to contact a guy whose name and whereabouts I have forgotten, to get a copy of my essay "Instructions to the Architect." Otherwise I am sunk. Sound familiar? Perhaps I should dial Heaven again. It worked for the Lauderdale letters. Imagine bothering Archie Hanna in the Hereafter with my stupid problems—all due to my senility, and having him still *care*.

It was a miracle. *Now*, you just *have* to make that book. It tickles me pink that you too have read some of those letters. I have been the only one in the world to do so til that day. And they *are* good.

Today, in an effort not to smoke (I've had only two and it is 4:30 p.m.), I walked seven miles, four this morning and three this afternoon. I am allowing myself only one more after dinner. The reason? Cough, chest pains, etc. And I've been eating everything in sight. *Maniacal* is what I am today. And must be for the next week til it all cools down. In half an hour we go for Easter dinner to a neighbor who keeps no vodka under her roof. Do you begin to see the full horror of my existence?

I've finished the Miller/Durrell correspondence and it is fine, very fine. I tried to reread *Justine*, but for God's sake it is no longer readable! Too stagey, flamboyant, phony—but with an underlying bedrock of linguistic genius. I loved it at age fifteen. At age sixty—no. I now prefer his brother Gerald Durrell's zoology essays. And how they—D & M—fancied themselves and each other as the geniuses of their time! Today they go unread, largely, and, I think, justifiably. It is Shelley's "Ozymandias" all over again. Doubtless I'll follow them into oblivion, only more quickly and glad to be there. It occurs to me that Durrell was twenty years younger than Henry Miller. So are *you* that much my junior. Take care. It is well known that old men first attract young men, then seduce and molest them. On the other hand, don't worry about it. I am otherwise preoccupied. I must spend three days this week writing a twenty-minute talk for RPI—to be given just prior to a rock concert (!) at what is billed as a Peace Festival. I'm doing it as a favor for my Newman Club buddies—no pay. But *what*, in God's name, can one say about peace just prior to a rock concert? At least I'll be in *Troy*—my Angkor Wat, my Jerusalem. That will take a bit of the sting out of it. If they sell T-shirts that say EAT TAHINI, I'll get you one.

Love
R

March 27, 1989

Dear Peter,

Borchardt has spoken. He wants to exclude the four pieces of fiction from the book and have it consist of the diary and essayistic pieces. I am a bit dashed, but will have to go along with it. Perhaps later I can arrange for a New and Selected Fiction. I swear that if I didn't need the money I'd put it *all* in the drawer for good.

I'll be back in Troy Friday and Saturday to patrol the ancient streets with my brother. We'll share a sweet mournful pipe or two. I spent the morning on the whores of Troy—figuratively—and read in Keyserling's *Travels*—marvelous. I learned of him in the Miller/Durrell letters. I am sitting in the sunroom drinking a cold beer—a joy which you persistently deny yourself for whatever dark, self-punitive reasons. As for me, I do not burn to be a monk. Than live on in Heaven with a bunch of bland sedative Cherubim, I'd sooner be in Hell. If Dante ever returns to pay another visit to the Inferno, he will find its one contented resident—me.

Love

Richard

APRIL 2, 1989

Dear Peter,

Yes, I'll stay alive, if you insist. If pleasure extends life, then this past two—really 1.4—days in Troy ought to get me to sixty-five. Not even the fact that the bottom fell out of the car in Naugatuck (en route) put a crimp in my style. Thanks to a squadron of young mechanics, it was sutured together in an hour and I was on my way again. My brother and I prowled the town and the Oakwood Cemetery—surely one of the most beautiful in the world. Dozens of mausoleums of Baroque, Romanesque, and Greek Revival genres. Lots of Dutch and Irish names. The evening was grand. Gary, the priest, made a fine dinner at the Parish House and we twelve feasted and drank. At 8:15 I rose to the podium to immense éclat. I read a small essay about my desk—do you know that one?[17] I was followed by a brilliant two-hour concert. As tall and handsome as was the piano, just so short and homely was the cello. After that, a party til 2 a.m. with good talk and wine. Met the professor of architecture at RPI—Pat Quinn—a real find. Witty, learned and affectionate. He uses my books in his classrooms, could quote chapter and verse.[18] This morning I arose at 6 and was home at noon, the mountain forests covered with ice and glittering in the sunshine.

Now I am awaiting the arrival of Miyo Takano—translator of *Mortal Lessons*—who will be here for a few days. Meanwhile, I await word from Nan Talese on *Said*. You have so many books to write. Too many? How will you do it, this side of madness? Or perhaps madness is what is required. The big news around here is that the apricot tree that Jon planted years ago will bloom while he is here, a benevolence greater by far than any handed man to man, including West Point, "Crematorium," you name it. I shall report to you the exact look in his eye at the moment.

As one man says to another

Love

Richard

April 3, 1989

Dear Peter,

Miyo Takano turns out to be a darn sweet woman who is terribly afflicted with polio. I now have a new appreciation for the meaning of handicapped. It is a matter of carrying her from place to place, then parking the car and going to get it. If I am utterly spent, what is she? She'll be here till the 7th, so watch the obituary columns for my name. She is a nun who spent twenty years in a convent before having to leave because she could no longer maneuver the corridors and staircases. Her great loves are Mozart, Keats, and Gerard Manley Hopkins. I am presently reading her book, *Gerard Manley Hopkins: The Sensuous and the Austere*. It is mighty good. Now she is translating his letters. She has many good things to say about RS. And, since *Mortal Lessons* is now in its fourth printing in as many months (5000 copies), the publisher wants to translate a second book—possibly *Repairs*. Who would have thought it?

April 4.

Sweet Mother of God! Another day of lugging Japan about New Haven. I could weep from fatigue. Three days to go. Surely this wipes out all my sins and I am eligible for the Kingdom of Heaven? Nonetheless, my Japanese has improved a good deal and I shall soon be able to sayonara with the best of them. You can imagine how thrilled Janet is to eat dinner with two people who are speaking in tongues. And how happy she is with *me* at this time. Vodka is my best and only friend. Unless it's *you*.

A moment ago came a call from *Lear's* magazine. The stupidest woman in the world and the most arrogant, she rejected my corrections to her version of what I wrote. So it is decreed that I shall appear in that *superlative* publication in a state of slovenly undress. Never forget, Peter, that you, the artist, are at the whim, caprice, and ignorance of the fakers. They have the money; you need it. Simple as that. If ever you meet a woman named Linda Gutstein (*Lear's*), give her the finger for me.

Love

Richard

April 5, 1989

Dear Peter,

Your magnificent pacquet arrived today. Best is your own marvelous letter and the play. It is a triumphant, brilliant play. I am blown away by it—the insights and the subtleties. And the smoking! You wretch, to aim at my heart so. Bandito!

yourself. But the poetry you write for the stage is electrifying. How ashamed I am that I dared to show you my pitiful *Swan*. It is no good and I know it. Don't give it a second thought. I thank you for confirming my own critique of it.

Today I spent wheeling Miyo about Yale, fetching and carrying. I have lost ten pounds. We visited the two art galleries, the Beinecke Rare Book library, translated together a dozen lines of the Gutenberg Bible, looked at the Audubon folios of birds, had lunch at the Commons and tea at the Lizzie. I am dead. She, on the other hand, is bursting with vitality. And eager for *more*. What shall I do?

Today, a welcoming letter from Colonel Hoyt at West Point. Janet says she won't go. So if you decide to come you can stay with me at West Point. It *is* exciting. But I haven't yet begun to write the address.

April 6.

And here is a note from Nan Talese. "By all means have Peter Josyph send me the TALK book." I wouldn't *send* it, if I were you. I'd call. Her longtime assistant's name is Gail—give her my regards. Ask if you might not have an audience with the Editress (don't say *that*), as it is important to do that if possible. Remember she is at Doubleday now. If she is interested, I'll get you to Georges Borchardt right away.

Miyo and I visited with Richard Sewall today for lunch at his house.[19] He is a great man. He gave her a signed copy of *A Vision of Tragedy*. Tomorrow she leaves for Tokyo. One more day and I'd be three-quarters dead. I'm only one-half now. This morning we went to the Medical Library and read the 1573 edition of Ambroise Paré's lectures. It is quite probable that he himself held that very book in his hands. I want to take you there too.

Love
Richard

April 8, 1989

Dear Peter,

Well, Miyo has left and I am in the bosom of my family. Jon and Regine will be here til April 26. Of course that means no writing, but I assure you it is very Heaven to have him here. I have, however, been secretly dwelling in my Crematorium and trying to polish a few skulls and bones in my mind. I also read a long story by a medical student in Georgia who "burns to be a writer." I had to tell him no, not now, but maybe in fifteen–twenty years. He is a great guy—open-hearted and beautiful in character. All of which is a handicap to the artist, who is more likely to be a devious and deviated prick.

Then came a strange letter from Lyon, France, requesting two articles on AIDS. No explanation, just please do it, and in French! I replied with a list of questions to be answered, so I doubt I'll hear again. The mail is full of such mysteries lately. One was a long article in favor of the autopsy as a valuable medical procedure. It was written by a professor of pathology at Bowman Gray Medical School in North Carolina. In it, he takes me to task for writing somewhere that, in the matter of being autopsied, I (like Bartleby) *prefer not to*. Wonder where I wrote *that*. I sent back a gentle riposte. Can you see why I get nothing done? And, oh yes, a letter on pink stationery from a beautiful witty woman I know. "Dearest Lovely Boykin . . ." etc. And me a grandfather!

Buona Sera

Richard

April 14, 1989

Dear Peter,

You have a fine, admirable resilience. It will be your closest ally. Those stupid rejections cannot keep you from the arcane pleasures of the Smithsonian, or from the thrilled response to Cézanne. One day you must teach me about him. About painting, I am the emptiest pitcher. I had to smile at your touching that skull with your finger. Can you imagine Hamlet being so tentative about Yorick?

Of course I write nothing, and shan't til April 24 when Jon leaves. But, I read on: Pater's *Imaginary Portraits*, the poems of Geoffrey Hill, and the Gospel of Barnabas. He was one of the Apostles, as you know. He went to Cyprus to preach, taking some scrolls that Matthew had written. From these, and from his own personal encounters with Christ, he wrote his Gospel. It is quite marvelous. In it he recounts Jesus's adamant insistence that he was *not* a god, or the son of God. He believed himself to be a prophet, purely and simply. He even scolded Peter roundly, almost fired him, for implying that he, Christ, was divine. He was visited by the angel Gabriel on more than one occasion and was given the gift of healing, which he carried out both at Nain and at Capernaum, and so became famous. Also, when he chose Judas Iscariot to be one of the twelve, he had no idea that Judas would betray him. Later he discovered that Judas, whom he had placed in charge of giving out and receiving alms, was embezzling a good percentage of it. Barnabas makes the story come boldly to life in a way that the others (except for John) don't.

I do so love reading the historical Jesus. Why, I can't really say. Surely not out of piety, for I have none of that. Curiosity? Envy? Old men who look back over their years and count what has been denied them—love *and* faith—are rather pitiable. I refuse to do that. It is craven and unattractive. You see how my flirtatious nature copes with the one, and my curiosity probes the other. So, fiercely, to go on is all. To last. But I am lucky, as I am strangely devoid of ambition in any direction. I want none of the lesser achievements. Only the lovely quietude that attracts no attention. I *do* want friendship and conviviality and good conversation. But, up to the point when I can no longer take part, and then not one inch further.

Today I baked a bread with just yeast, salt, and flour. Not one of *your* nourishing breads, but a light, feathery, crusty French loaf that I painted with milk. The smell is grand. And Janet is making lo mein with shrimp and snow peas and mushrooms. So we will have a feast. Would you eat it? Doubtless not. I received a letter from Alastair Reid, did I tell you? He has stopped writing for two years and has a small farm in the Dominican Republic. Oregano, ginger, fruit, and vegetables. After thirty-five years at the *New Yorker*, he has given it all up. I would so much like you to meet him. He is the one who spent months interviewing me some years back. It came to naught, but I don't care. He is a good, good man.

I am waiting *with* you for Nan Talese's response, but whatever it is, don't fret, we can always move elsewhere. As for my poor fiction, I think perhaps a *New and Selected Stories* would work as a book with a proper introduction. Tell me.

Love

Richard

APRIL 22, 1989

Dear Peter,

I don't mind telling you I'm on the *qui vive* about Nan's response to the book. Which is precisely the wrong way to face the publishing juggernaut. One ought always to presage rejection by the money-and-power people. It goes without saying that they know naught whereof they speak. So why do we miserable wretches continue to follow moonbeams on the dungeon wall?

Today your exhibit opens. My profoundest wishes for success. I wish I could be there to rejoice. You surely have been the busiest man in North America this spring, while I have flopped and wallowed in idleness. Well, news came from Memphis, Tennessee, that I am a genius! A professor of theatre and communications named David Lavery is about to write a book called *Genius at Work*. His idea is to write about six people who, while fully engaged in the work of the world, managed to change society through unrelated efforts. The others are: Wallace

Stevens, Charles Ives, linguist Benjamin Whorf, philologist Owen Barfield, and science-fiction writer Alice Sheldon, a.k.a. James Tiptree, Jr. Apparently Stevens, Ives, and Whorf worked in insurance; Barfield, the only other living "genius," is a lawyer in England; and Sheldon was a psychologist. I wrote immediately, angrily denouncing his use of the G-word in my instance. It seems a gimmicky idea, but since he swore not to write biography or critical essays, I have agreed to let him come here. But I shall not duplicate anything you and I have talked about, or will talk about. He's on his own.

Tonight we are having another seder here. Jon is addicted to them. The rest of us don't care. So I helped out by baking a bread, which, if memory serves, is not what is indicated at all.

Love
Richard

April 30, 1989

Dear Peter,

Returned from three days in Portland, Maine, to find your marvelous monograph on [the painter] Kevin Larkin. It is a superb piece and I congratulate you. Your affection for the man and his work is apparent.

I see that I need only to touch up "Crematorium" and then go on to the essay on writing. With regard to which I've been thinking of words that affect one physically when they are heard. *Numb* is one such. It impinges upon the bony skeleton, its vibrations being conducted from bone to bone setting off all sorts of echoes until *numb* becomes the exact opposite of its meaning—instead it is intense sensation. It's not the *umb* wherein lies the strange power of the word. *Thumb, crumb,* and *dumb* do not possess it. Nor is it the *n*—for by *number* we remain untouched. What, then? Best not to ask. It is the mystery of language. *Crackle* and *splash* are others, but they are onomatopoetic in origin and so are less mysterious, if not less magical. They seem to me to be more *skin* than *bone* words. But I can't explain. I'm sure all this sounds silly. But it is important to *me*. It has something to do with the way I write.

Both in Maine and in Edison, New Jersey, this week I met doctors who had at one time been my interns and residents. It is strange to remember that I taught them how to make incisions, tie knots. Now they are the professors and I come around not to teach, but to *remind*.

Love
Richard

May 1, 1989

Dear Peter,

What I can't, for the life of me, understand is why so gifted an artist as yourself has to have so uphill a climb when so many with less talent—myself included—squeak through. If it depresses me, I can only surmise your own feelings. In any case, I've just written to [the publisher] Ingram-Merrill and will ask [author] Bill Ober to do so at once. I could ask Annie Dillard, but I know she'd want to see the manuscript first. What do you think? In fact, if she likes it, Annie would be a good reference anywhere.

I've started making notes for my piece on writing. I am placing instinct and intuition above experience and intellect as the avenue to art. It is instinct that makes the selection of the words, and instinct that dictates the order in which they are placed on the page. Instinct, too, dictates the selection of a subject congenial to the writer's instrument. It is the same instinct that the butterfly has. The butterfly does not itself eat cabbage. But it lays its eggs on a cabbage to provide food for the larvae when they hatch. The *larvae* do eat cabbage. The butterfly did not learn this from its parents; it never knew its parents—they are dead before the eggs are hatched. It is an act beyond sagacity or wisdom. It is inexplicable by any hypothesis other than *instinct*. Somehow there's a connection here to the making of art.

I just called Nan. I couldn't resist. She only now got home from her trip and hasn't read the manuscript, but will do so right away. She said you were "perfectly charming." But we both already knew that. I gently, O so gently, prodded her toward a *YES*. We shall see. Courage!

Love

Richard

May 2, 1989

Dear Peter:

I'm thinking about writing these days. How much sleepwalking and daydreaming have to do with it. Anyway, some less-than-conscious condition from which one emerges with a jolt and begins. I have so many notes now that I dread trying to organize them into a formal essay. Perhaps I shan't. Just let them pile up and be as a reproach unto my hand.

This morning I got to the library ready to work, but couldn't. Instead I read in Eckermann's *Conversations with Goethe*. I hope our book will not be quite so windy. The most effective parts are those wherein Eckermann asks Goethe about specific works, e.g., *Werther*, *Faust*, etc. I was surprised to learn that Goethe's great love was for botany and for color, about which he developed a theory. At the end, Eckermann tells of asking Goethe's valet to let him see Goethe's body after he had died. The valet removes the shroud so that Eckermann can gaze at his master—naked. He feasts his eyes on the deep chest and strong thighs, the delicate feet; places his hand over the heart, then turns aside to let his tears flow. Very touching.

Thinking too about West Point and the conflict between the necessity to break down all national barriers, including geographical boundaries to form one world, and the deep desire of each ethnic culture to preserve its uniqueness. I favor both, but they seem irreconcilable. And the need to admit the propensity for cruelty and evil in man—e.g., the holocaust, the rape in Central Park—so that we can cap the gusher whenever it spouts.

Love

R

MAY 5, 1989

Dear Peter,

Your letters are a joy to read. Don't stop! as it is said under altogether different circumstances. I am glad to hear that the later talks were of good quality. I am ready for another session whenever you are.

I just received the news that the Random House editor to whom my essays etc. were submitted has not liked them, so that is two down and two to go. In the end, I hope to have a book composed of both fiction and nonfiction as is my wont. These agents and editors are ridiculous. Yesterday was depressing, as it marked the end of a long friendship with a writer here in New Haven. He had turned unaccountably aggressive toward me. After putting up with the abuse for a few months, I had to sever the tie. I am both relieved and sorry to lose a brilliant young friend. I hate to think it was jealousy and bitterness, but I can't think why else. Somehow I believe it was all my fault.

Alastair Reid phoned. He's in New York and is coming up for lunch on Saturday. You recall him as the one who interviewed me for months in preparation of a *New Yorker* profile which he later abandoned. I think he no longer writes at all. I look forward to his visit.[20] There was a time when he was so devoted you would have thought I had written the Gospels instead of *Rituals of Surgery*. *Non sum qualis eram*—I am not what once I was. In fact, I feel that grass is growing inside my head. To a twelfth-century Carthusian monk such as I, it all seems inconsequential. I do own up to a tendency to chuck overboard all the articles in the lifeboat, one by one, to do away with the temptation to use them—fishing hook, compass, an oar or two—and just go on drifting on the lukewarm Sea of

Do-Nothing. My ex-friend told me it is part of my "evasive and disguised personality." But what I am evading and what disguising, I can't guess. This afternoon I'm going to take a book up to East Rock Park and have a good old time. Also my field glasses. When one grows too heavy to hold, I'll switch to the other.

Please feel free to use anything in my letters to you as you see fit. They *are* a kind of *talking* and some things might fit in nicely.[21] That's good news about your show at the county attorney's building. It's the best way to hang in a place like that.

Love

Richard

May 10, 1989

Dear Peter,

Well, the man from Memphis has come and gone. He is bright and learned, but I think less of his planned book. I gather he will write one chapter on Loren Eiseley and me together, as examples of "dual career" writers. Frankly, I think it is not an issue at all. Most writers have had to work in other areas: Kafka, Melville, Chaucer, Rabelais, etc., so what's the point? On the other hand, he has given all of my work a close reading and had interesting comments. His favorite of my pieces is "Chatterbox" [in *Letters to a Young Doctor*], an unusual choice but one that pleases me. I told him about the letters of Sr. Catherine of Siena to her confessor. He hopes to finish the book in 1991. Meanwhile, I agreed to a correspondence to answer his questions.

The good news has to do with birdwatching. A few days ago I saw a prothonotary warbler, my very first. It is almost never sighted in Connecticut. It has a yellow head, blue wings, and white underparts. And goes tweet-tweet. You can imagine my excitement. Since then the rainy weather has kept me from birdwatching, which makes me as cross as—well, I won't say who. The Random House lady has said no to my nonfiction. If all goes as expected, no one will take it and I shall most happily put it in the drawer where I keep my Apocrypha. I think I can manage without it—financially—for another year. But I pray that your book will see the light of day.

David Lavery told me that Eiseley's literary persona was entirely invented. He was a recluse who lived in a hotel room and never went on most of those anthropology treks he wrote about. I am shocked. At his suggestion, I read part of Edwin Muir's autobiography, *The Story and the Fable*. I didn't like it much, tho' Muir was a sweet, good man.

It's pretty here now what with the lilac in bloom and the hibernum, and the apple tree wearing a lady's tea hat. My snow peas are three inches tall and will have to be staked one of these days. Tonight I'm planning to get in bed and read by candlelight, which, by itself, can improve anybody's prose. I should put it in my contract that my book must only be read by candle. And here comes Becky, so Grandpa must go and play. Til tomorrow, then

> I am
> The bastard son of
> Medicine & Literature
> that signs himself
> Richard

MAY 12 (OR SO), 1989

Dear Peter,

Spent the entire day in the park with wet feet, a sore back and twenty-seven other pains of extraordinary diversity. It was all fine until half an hour ago when, "alone and palely loit'ring," I was accosted by two teenagers, one of whom responded to my command to FUCK OFF! by shoving me. I fell, but wasn't hurt a bit. I hollered for help, whereupon they fled. No harm done, but I'm not allowed to go to the park alone anymore. So you can see that I am no longer a writer. I garden, birdwatch, and think of nothing. I rather like it. And may never write again. I am a bit puzzled by the fact that I haven't heard a word from Nan or Borchardt. I must say that it doesn't bode well. You're right—had I submitted my stories as well, I'd have been taken, but it was not permitted. But, most important—the Talk book—why the silence? Surely she's read it by now. I shan't call her.

BREAK.

It is the next morning and I want to thank you so much for Mozart's letters. I'll be reading them in the garden.

Gazing at my granddaughter Rebecca—age three months—I am amazed that, as a surgeon, I was often called upon to operate on such miniatures—intestinal resections, congenital malformations, an absence or excess of this or that. So far behind have I left the deeds and misdeeds of surgery that I cannot believe it was I who performed them. I am as baffled by it as a reincarnate spirit by evidence of his former existence. Now, I wouldn't trust me to trim my own moustache. Lucky for New Haven that I am no longer let loose upon the populace, but am safely confined to deciding such weighty matters as the gender of fruits and vegetables.

Lettuce, I have decided, is female; potatoes, male. Mushrooms, with those Chinese hats, are harem eunuchs guarding the chastity of the endive until such time as the Emperor is ready to stuff it with cream cheese. About cherries, can there be any doubt? Or apricots, which are the botanical equivalents of baboon testicles. But lest you think it is all sex in the garden, there is also philosophy: the truly significant in a garden pretends to be unimportant—hoping to go unnoticed among the general splendor. I witnessed this when a dry leaf that had lain all winter under the porch suddenly flew out and landed on the upstairs sundeck. Now that is epic, is it not? It is the privilege of the artist to exaggerate.

Life magazine phoned to say that "Malpractice," which they've owned for two years, will appear in August.[22] I'm a bit nervous about it, as I must ensure that any of the people involved will not be able to sue me. What with the prevailing mentality, that is all too likely, and I shouldn't survive it a second time. Pessimism? Well yes. I am not an optimist; still, I do not agree with Sophocles that it were better never to have been born. Let's see what the next week will bring.

Love
Richard

May 12, 1989

Dear Peter,

What a day of birds, flowers, tomato plants and penlessness. Were all the archangels in the hierarchy of heaven to assemble on St. Ronan Terrace for the express purpose of inviting me up to sit on a golden throne, I'd wave them away. I am blessed by this day. *Me*—a short, skinny, youngish old man with a homesickness for the idea of faith. It is more than I deserve. But tomorrow, I swear it, I'll tether myself to a desk and try to shuffle words around on a page.

In between horticulture and ornithology, the phone rang. It is one Diane Ackerman, poet, essayist, journalist whom I met once after she had reviewed *Repairs* for the *New York Times*. She is now a staff writer for the *New Yorker* and says she wants to do a piece on INTERPLAST, wants me to go along, and will by God write a profile. I quick up and told her about Alistair and said I couldn't do that again. But I would indeed like to go with INTERPLAST once more and may do just that next year. It is a thrilling idea—to do surgery again. To function. To be useful. Can you imagine it?[23]

The thought occurs to me that I am becoming too much of a *personage*, talking too much about myself. It is disgusting. It is more decorous to be dead. The dead lose their reticence and speak more freely than the living. That is the purpose, I suppose, of biography. I begin to think that I am an impostor—bent on showing off. In fact, it is farthest from my intentions. It is precisely why I have isolated myself from the New York literary establishment. And now look at me. Scandalous!

Such weird dreams I have—that wake me up at two o'clock every morning. Always I am lost, appealing to strangers who are indifferent to my plight. I cannot find my way home. Everything takes place in France or Japan, my strength ebbing. I wake up, turn on the light and read til 4 a.m., then sleep another two hours and arise refreshed. So strange. I feel quite *innocent*—having no guile, venality, or sexual ambitions in all of this. Just—*a man*. Beset. What do you make of it? Everybody thinks I am still a writer, but you know better.

Love
Richard

MAY 15, 1989

Dear Peter,

Today I wrote five pages *about* writing. I'll xerox them and send them to you. I even went so far as to type. Now *that* is *important*. It starts out with the Etruscans and ends with an Arabic poet whose *nom de plume* is Adonis, but really it is all about the way that *I* write. I also read *Hamlet*, and in Act V, Scene I, I came across the phrase "wonder-wounded hearers." It occurs at the part of the play where Hamlet sees a funeral procession including Gertrude, Laertes, and the King. Hamlet conceals himself and discovers it is Ophelia who has died. He watches Laertes leap into the grave to clasp his sister once more, listens as Laertes expresses his grief in rather high-blown terms. Then Hamlet reveals himself and addresses Laertes:

> *What is he whose grief*
> *Bears such an emphasis, whose phrase of sorrow*
> *Conjures the wand'ring stars and makes them stand*
> *Like wonder-wounded hearers?*

The notion of the stars struck with amazement by Laertes' grief is what I have always tried for in my own writing. Never once succeeded, mind you, but striving on. Today, a small but most gratifying review of the French *Mortal Lessons* in *le Figaro*, a slick magazine. I am described as "an expert, passionate land-surveyor of the fields of the human body."

A call from Borchardt: the consensus among the editors is that the essays are "weak," "inferior" to my former work. Not a word about the TALK book other than that Nan mentioned it to Borchardt "in passing." All right, then, into the drawer with my "book." At sixty-one it is easier to accept rejection than at forty when fervor is high. I feel no pain and some relief. Now I can sink supine into my bed of sloth and go birdwatching, garden, read, walk, gab—none of which require the ownership of a blasted pen. Shall I have done with scribbling, I shall consider that I am in yet another state of convalescence such as brought me recovered from the malady of surgery. Besides, I think there is some justice in it. Looking back, I see that I *have* lacked consistency and intellectual clarity. Aside from the rare flash of illumination, I've been enveloped in a dense fog of muddleheadedness. With me, writing has always been a kind of ábracadabrántic, a magic act dependent upon a deft wave of the wand and a cry of Presto! But as for our TALK, we must press on, even if it turns out that we are talking only to our selves.

Love

Richard

JUNE 12, 1989

Dear Peter,

Home! After *what* a Polynesian saga. It requires that I tell you of it in person. Only here to say that I was on Hawiian horseback for two days—for the first time in my life. Descending 3500 feet—all but vertically—into a canyon—at the mercy of a horse, with naught but sheer space all around and terrified for five hours one day, four the next. Against all advice from my colleagues, I was *that* reckless and survived. To nurse huge subcutaneous hemorrhages of my legs and thighs, and pain in every one of my joints. On another occasion I rock-climbed a cliff overlooking the sea—all way beyond the pitiful strength of a sexagenarian. What was I trying to prove? Looking back, I see it as an impulse toward self-destruction—all but fulfilled. Forgive the writing—I am in the throes of jet lag and still hurting. Duke Wellington, my guide, turned out to be a great character. Machismo with a capital M. We went wild boar hunting. I refused to shoot—to his disgust. And all the while he quoted chapter and verse from *Mortal Lessons*!

Your wonderful letters awaited me and were unto me as Balm in Gilead, I assure you. Ted Solataroff [at Harper & Row] turned down your book [*Said*] and mine as well.[24] He didn't like any of it. I doubt that he'll call me to explain. They never do. In any case, I've decided *not* to publish my book at all, and into the apocryphal drawer it has gone. I told Borchardt's this morning that I am pulling out of the publishing game and will just sit here in New Haven writing away. Really, it's just as well, as I despise the whole enterprise. Now, relieved, I can go on with my new story and forget about the rest of the "offers" which it would be a mistake to accept. I'll write as soon as I'm back from Atlanta and fill in the gaps. How exhausted I am, wanting only to lie down and rest, but tonight I must prepare for a speech, then pack my suitcase yet again and fly away. With all of Balzac's tribulations, he did *not* have to do *this*.

Love
R

June 16, 1989

Dear Peter,

I've been writing letters to you in my mind for weeks. Getting them down on paper has proven more difficult. Here at last one is. Thanks for [Hermann Broch's] *The Death of Virgil*. It is indeed extraordinary when it is not being impossible. I did love the dialogues between Augustus and Virgil. Reading them gave me the way into the story I have at last begun writing, or had, until I left for Hawaii. I am in your debt.

I'm fairly worn out after that Hawaiian adventure followed by an overnight to Atlanta from which I returned late last night. Kauai is a beautiful island floating in a sea of flowers, perfume, music. It is altogether too much for this New Englander. Marooned there, I should soon sicken and die of what some call pleasures. I rode horseback (my debut) for two days. Once, down a virtually sheer defile. I remain terrified. That I survived is entirely due to the compassion and merciful nature of my horse. Then there was the rock-climbing to which I dared and never shall again. All this, despite my fear of heights! Surely my recklessness knows no restraint. The conference itself I gave a wide margin, having delivered the opening "oration."

I hope that by now you have rallied from your melancholy. If not, remember that sadness is the artist's best friend and put it to use. A good part of it is loneliness, my old adversary. This letter is such a hodgepodge! Chalk it up to fatigue. When next we meet, I promise to be more graphic about everything. Now, I must type "Crematorium," as Borchardt demands to see it pronto. Once, I was Richard Selzer. Perhaps I can be again?

Take care of yourself.

Love
Richard

June 16, 1989

Dear Peter,

The news you send me of the progress of *Said* is too wonderful. It is nothing short of miraculous that you have managed to make sense of the senseless—my inane meanderings. But you are a special personality—equipped to carry out the impossible. Just today, after months of silence, came a call from the man at Sundance. Verdict: the play is not ready to perform. I already knew that. He nevertheless invites me to go to Utah to work for a week or so with a dramaturge. I am mulling it over. Is it worth it, I wonder, to spend any more time on this project? I have already thrown in six months. Perhaps another week, just to see? I must let him know by next Tuesday. To be or not to be—all over again.

The new story ["Luis"] will be cast as a dark fairy tale of our time. I plan to read fairy tales for the next few weeks to locate the mood. It seems to me that in every fairy tale there is the element of *desire*—either noble or impure—with either the achievement (after many vicissitudes) of the goal—be it a beautiful princess, a pile of gold, or a magic amulet—or, on the other hand, the frustration of failure. Luis, scavenging for food or salable objects in the dump, finds the star which he had watched fall from the sky. At the same moment he had looked up to see the Virgin Mary appear in the smoke of the fire that burns there perpetually. Filled with hope for the first time, he worships, and conceals the star until it is discovered and fragmented by others. He is punished for his carelessness by the loss of his fingers and hands. He will die rejecting the "facts"—that the star was nonesuch, but a vial of radioactive powder inadvertently discarded with the waste from the hospital—but retaining the "truth" of his vision. The underlying irony will speak for itself. I hope I can write it.[25]

Love

Richard

June 23, 1989

Dear Peter,

New Haven fries. A dozen fans pretend to circulate the air at 6 St. Ronan Terrace, but what we really need is a punkah wallah—half naked—to wave a long fan such as was customary in the courtrooms of India during the Raj. I spent the morning at the Medical Library looking at photos of radiation injuries so that I can be precise in my description of the lesions sustained by Luis—my beloved character in the story. I saw no one I knew and had the feeling I had already died. Came home and tried yet again to read the poems of William Carlos Williams. I really do not like them. Perhaps I don't have the right-shaped head. Everyone is always comparing me unfavorably to WCW, so I daren't express my distaste out loud, as it is sure to be called sour grapes.

Coming home from Fairfield the other day, the train stopped for a few minutes just west of the New Haven station. I looked out to see that we were on a part of the track that is set down between thirty-foot-high stone walls—the large flat rocks having been cemented together. What was astonishing was that a luxurious growth of vines—ivy and wildflowers of all kinds—had sprouted from between the stones to form a graceful hanging garden for over a distance of several hundred feet. Quite like, I imagine, the hanging gardens of Babylon. I might have been Nebuchadnezzar himself instead of your lowly servant whose ignoble blood has coursed only through peasant veins. I die to go there on foot and photograph this phenomenon, as I think it most extraordinary. Not just beautiful but a powerful expression of the natural urge to *live*.

Of course a surgeon ought not to have a red beard. It is well known that ladybugs love to nest in them, and it would never do to have one fall into the incision and lay its eggs on the pancreas. Of course, if the beard were held in a fine-mesh snood—a sort of chin strap—I guess it would be okay.

Glad to be such a fount of information.

Love
Richard

June 30, 1989

Dear Peter,

So you're finished editing and transcribing. It is marvelous to me. Now we must resume our thrust and parry as soon as possible. You will doubtless be astonished to learn that I've given up vodka, whisky, brandy, etc., and take only a glass of wine with dinner. It has been done with disappointing ease. I had been hoping for a squiggle of delirium tremens to jog my imagination. I had no reason to abstain, only the vague sense that I should change something in my life, and vodka turned out to be what it was. No, I do not feel righteous, cleansed, or more energetic. But neither do I have any craving. What next! Tobacco? Then bury me out on the lone prairie.

The story inches forward. Luis has had to fight with knives. He wasn't hurt, nor does he hate his antagonist. If he has no friends, neither does he have any enemies. A stargazer's only enemies are the clouds. By the way, the municipal dump had once been the municipal park, but with the bloating of the city and the ocean of garbage produced each day, it had been decided that a dump was more beneficial than a park. Naturally. I really must begin to type what I have written so that I can get some picture of the narrative line.

You must tell me how the play reading went. Who heard you? I wish we might have had our Troy in early July so that you could have worked on it in Princeton, but I reassure myself that you will have much else to do—the short stories, the screenplay, the painting and God knows what else. The mail this week has been largely from readers, all of whom enjoy dissecting my work, picking their favorites, and either tossing pebbles or kissing the hem of my garment. I do enjoy them much and answer each one. Some of them are from first-rate intelligences and I am getting the inkling that my readership grows—mostly by word of mouth. That is the best way, don't you think? No word from any of the editors. Neither Nan nor Ted either called or wrote. No word from Random House either, although the lady has read "Crematorium" by now. "Desk" will be published next year in *MD* magazine.

I have my tickets for Utah and leave on Wednesday. I must give a reading there one afternoon. Perhaps I am not really one of the working writers, but an ornament. If so, I shall smite their leaders as my ancestors once smote the Amalekites.

Love
Richard

P.S. Bless Barbara for me.[26]

July 2, 1989

Dear Peter,

I imagine you at Princeton by now, altho' these will come to Long Island until further notice. Doubtless you will observe many academics on the street, the way they approach, sniff each other's crotch, then move on, having solved yet another problem. My mind is about as sprightly as a hippopotamus emerging from his wallow, and with a good deal of mud clinging. It all has to do with my lovely, innocent, blue-eyed brother Bill who has to have a colostomy next Thursday for cancer of the colon. And I am to be in Utah and not *there* to be seen when he comes out of anesthesia. It isn't fair. While I am an old man of sixty-one, he is a mere stripling of sixty-two. I have half a mind to cancel Utah and go to be with my brother.

Well, I just talked to him on the phone and I am to wait and go to Frederick, Maryland on the 14th. So I will go to Sundance, but with my mind elsewhere. I am so far gone that last night I referred to that former British prime minister as William *Gall*stone! So, I've discontinued work on the story of Luis until I can convince myself that it matters at all whether it gets written. I am very far from belief that the five fables will bear the weight of print anyway.

I am still reeling from having gone to see a movie called *Seven Beauties*. It is a shocking, vicious thing to see, made with energy and, I suppose, brilliance, but full of gratuitous sadism. Nevertheless I admit to its power. I wonder if you have seen it and what you thought. It is horror in slapstick. But then I am hardly of these times and more likely to shrink than most. Which ought to come as a surprise to the readers of "The Corpse" [in *Mortal Lessons*] and "A Worm from My Notebook" [in *Repairs*]. In that regard, I wonder what Achilles would have thought if he could have read the *Iliad* himself.

I hope your house in Princeton will be spacious and quiet—with a garden and perhaps a balcony and a lawn chair to recline in. Move it under the oak tree in the heat of the day and read the love poems of Thomas Hardy.

Love

R

July 3, 1989

Dear Peter,

Since your letters are so much longer and so much more filled with the life of art than mine, I am firing salvo after salvo of my inconsequentia at you these past days in a pathetic effort to even the score. Yesterday was spent doing orthopedic surgery on shrubbery around the house, after which I developed a four-star backache—my first—that lasted til I fell asleep at midnight. It was exactly as though I had an abscessed tooth at the base of my spine. These wandering teeth *are* a menace. Today I have only a vague ache to remind me of the martyrdom. Janet and I distracted ourselves by watching a movie called *House of Games* by David Mamet. We both liked it much, altho' the one play of his that I read left me wondering. What do you know about him?

Right now I'm reading Volume 1 of the correspondence between Rupert Hart-Davis and G. W. Lyttelton. It's a bit annoying to watch them jacking each other off, but now and then there is something perfectly lovely about D. H. Lawrence or G. B. Shaw. Both letter-writers lived bookish lives in genteel poverty and had all sorts of private opinions about everything. I'm not sure you'd like it as much as Oliver Wendell Holmes or Mark Twain. I don't. Speaking of poverty, I do hope you have received your share of the New York State grant money so you can buy the summer supply of tahini and bulgur or whatever it is you slather your mucous membranes with. My new diet of NO BOOZE is unbroken, and unbreakable, save for wine with dinner. The only result is a loss of four pounds, with, I suppose, more to shed. I think that I had been composed of four parts vodka and one part tissue. Like a martini! I doubt it will prolong my life for more than one minute.

The story notes (typed) have reached twenty-five pages, with another twenty waiting in the notebook. Then comes the puttery. I don't by any means have a half-Nelson on this tale, but am still at the feint-and-dodge stage. Oh for the facile pen of Joyce or Carol or Oates. They would have knocked it off in twenty minutes. I am aiming for January 1 and counting on the fable of the tortoise and the hare at the finish line. It is a strange experience to be *existing* on St. Ronan Terrace but to be *living* on a dump in São Paolo, Brazil.

                     Love

                      R

JULY 5, 1989

Dear Peter,

 Halfway to Denver where I am to change for Salt Lake City, the connections already having been missed. (I love putting that in the ablative absolute—a pleasure non-Latin scholars are denied.) Now I must seek out another plane headin' out thar. All of which will discommode those assigned to meet me. Oh well, I did not design the weather. I have the same blend of foreboding and anticipation as I had at age seven when, for the one and only time, I was packed off to YMCA camp for two weeks. Of *that* martyrdom I shall not speak, only to say that two weeks in a cabin with fifteen other prepubarts is in no small part responsible for a number of my eccentricities. But now I am again on the way to camp, this time with the twin armor of easy indifference (feigned) and a small but sufficient wit to stifle savagery at the early stages.

THURSDAY.

Sundance is a place of incalculable beauty. The pen swoons among my fingers and cannot go on. We are among the mountains, laced with rushing streams and observed by the stars. There are a half dozen playwrights plus one impostor, a like number of directors and dramaturges and a company of actors. It is all hugely convivial and campy (in the older sense). As is my custom, I haven't the least idea why I am here, whilst everyone else is full of specification. I cringe each time I am asked: are you a playwright or an actor? I cannot say the word *playwright*—my mouth refuses to accommodate it. *Inspector*, I reply, and leave it at that.

 There are eight plays in various stages of completion. The end result in each case will be a staged reading. As I see it, everything is done by committee. They all swear by it. This morning I met with an improvisationalist who advised me to narrate the lives of Ken and Anna after Rosalie's death in order to find out what happens to them. A set designer told me to avoid being literal in my sets—suggest, rather; be symbolic, he said. This afternoon I meet with the first of three dramaturges to get their reactions. Very little is sinking in, as I am thinking constantly about my brother. Everyone has or seems to have exquisite manners. I may have to leave early—a hard thing to do, as any definitive action would be a "statement." Of the sixty-five present, I am the oldest by far. What happens to other people when they reach sixty-one? Have they all been disposed of? Why aren't they ever where I am? It's quite sinister. Listen to me! Whining, puking, and all of that when I should be congratulating myself on having been smiled upon by Fate.

Anyway, just outside my window is a mountain with the vague shape of a supine Indian Princess. The mountain is always referred to as her or she. Which is cute enough, but these poor Utahans don't know that every Tom, Dick, and Harry of a range has a Sleeping Indian Maid—they are a surfeit in the marketplace. I won't tell them. Speaking of princesses, here is one story I *choose* to believe. Young Princess Elizabeth, while visiting her manor at Bisley, quite suddenly died. Maybe the Catholics killed her. For political reasons a young village boy who bore her a striking resemblance was dressed up in ruff and farthingale and sent off to impersonate the princess. It was this boy who grew up to be Queen Elizabeth I. Which explains all her swearing at the bishops and her teasing and taunting suitors without once ever coming across.[27]

There is a beautiful woman here who used to be married to a man I used to know. She is teaching *imagery* to the playwrights and actors. I've signed up for a private session, as I don't want any of my images to get around. She is, maybe, a witch and could use them to cast spells. It being 90°, I have retreated to my room where I pace in my BVDs. And write letters like this one instead of concentrating on Luis.

Oh, there he is! Sitting on his heels at the dump. Looking up, he caught sight of the white wing of a gull slicing the gloom. Did I tell you about the wooden whistle he's found? After clearing out the muck that clogged the holes, he blew into it and was startled at the lovely, low sounds which seemed to come from someplace distant, yet be very near. Each time he blows into the whistle, his mind is set to dreaming. He sees pictures which fade as soon as he stops, return when he blows again. Show me the artist who wouldn't die for one of those.

This letter has gone on at disgraceful length about matters somewhat less than riveting. Still, it is a painfully clear portrait of my present situation.

JULY 7.

The theatre folk are, each one, friendly, attractive, and industrious. If there is a lack of profundity (thank God), there is an absence of pretension. The ethnic mixture is equally black, Latino, and us cauks. In these surroundings I might have stumbled into Eden. I live alone in a cedar-wood cabin on the forested flank of a mountain. From far below comes the sound of falling water. Ah, that is to sleep by. Remember Ambroise Paré.

This canyon is ringed by mountains, some still with snow on the higher crags and declinations. How they carve up the sky, not apologetically like the Catskills, but boldly—with tomahawks. Spruces, pine, and cedar flow up the pleats to the tree line. Thereabove, the waving layered sandstone. The whole achieves *fluidity*. In a moment the landscape will simply undulate itself out and away. Along the path, red and orange poppies, moth mullein, reddish thistle, Solomon's sash, wild geranium, and others beyond my ken. Never is one out of earshot of a fast-moving stream, visible only as a silver shot far below, and only now and then. Here do I read, write, walk, and daydream. Thus, like every immigrant before me, have I brought to the new land the customs of my tribe.

R

JULY 13, 1989

Dear Peter,

    I arrived last night to find that a tornado had passed right up the terrace. We are a mess—and no phone or lights. All day I've been standing around the ruins listening to men tell me how much it will cost to disencumber ourselves of the fallen trees. A lot. Basta! Tonight I'm giving a reading at Yale—I'll read "Pipistrel" for the first time. (a) I'm not in the mood. (b) Maybe it won't *read aloud* well. Tomorrow morning I'm taking the train to Maryland to see my brother.

    All in all, Sundance was a good experience. Your plays are in the hands of the authorities there and I should hear by September. The readings I attended were a strange mixed lot. Many of the actors I thought superb—especially the blacks in the cast of a play based on the Tuskegee experiment. Since this was my first ever encounter with theatre people, I must say I was charmed. Sweet, vulnerable, and friendly they were. Rather like *you*, but never so intelligent or learned. How lucky I am to have been invited there. Starting Monday I'll hurl my old bones on the dump for Luis to pick over. I *need* to finish this story. Since I have no phone, I am incommunicado with Borchardt and Random House. That, at least, is lovely—I don't care what the world is doing behind my back. Must quit here for now, as I have to go to the auditorium.

Love
R

JULY 19, 1989

Dear Peter,

    Such a racket outside as the workmen and machinery remake the backyard to the equally obnoxious tune of $10,000, which I don't have but which Janet says will come from the sale of my next book. About all of which I have bitten my lip, swallowed my

Lion outside the entrance to Richard Selzer's home on St. Ronan Terrace.

tongue and gnashed my teeth—in a magnificent performance of restrained orality. Doubtless she needed to do it to exorcise herself of the tornado horrors. The apricots are ripe and need picking and cooking tomorrow. Was Henry James so beset? Tonight I'm off to Hartford for a benefit reading for hospice. A joyous chore—but a chore. As for Luis? Can those dry bones live? In Holy Writ, perhaps, but from where I sit only by a miracle.

Sundance. Four dramaturges gave much advice and conflicting recommendations on *The Black Swan*. The upshot is that I will rewrite in the fall—after West Point. I'm to return to Utah next July if I satisfy the powers that be meantimes. I beheld the process out there—plays being written by committee, much talent, but not a drop of genius. Still, I enjoyed so much the company of actors, directors, and dramaturges. Lively, affectionate people. We all ended best friends. Best was birdwatching—I saw a lazuli bunting! Turquoise head and white wing bars—but do you care? No, philistine.

Borchardt presses. I am to go either with William Morrow for two books or with Random House for the fiction and Weidenfeld & Nicolson for the nonfiction. My impulse is to throw the fiction to RH and the nonfiction to WN. Honestly, I don't *care*, only that I must stay alive to finish Luis, rewrite *The Black Swan*, and prepare for West Point. I hope your painting gets itself done and hung and that you become rich and famous. The time in Princeton should do you the world of good.

Love
R

July 25, 1989

Dear Peter,

The Chinese Grotesques?! My God, do you really think so? But why not, after all? I'll help with Frank when the time comes.[28] The Indian panels done, are they? And installed? I didn't know you had to paint more for *The Legacy*. That seems to go on and on. Your project with Kevin is a fine idea. It is grand that you have cemented your relationship with the Arts Council.

Today is my first opportunity to return to Luis and I've turned hamfisted at it. The morning yielded up nothing of worth. I long to have done with this bleakest of stories and bound off to recapture the gaiety and childishness of Chaucer.[29] Meanwhile there are the publishers. Random House is itching to do the fiction. I spoke to [editor] Becky Saletan today. Her enthusiasm is contagious. Now Harvey Ginsberg [at William Morrow] offers a *three-book* contract—(1) fiction; (2) essays; (3) journal. OR, alternatively, a two-book contract—essays and journal. With the latter I will not have a book to publish next year or even the year after that. What would you do? Well you don't have to say, as I've just decided: the fiction goes to Random House, the other two to Morrow. What a relief not to think of it again, only to write it all, which will take the rest of my thinking life. Considering that there are some trillion other planets in the universe, it is impossible to exaggerate the unimportance of everything. If I were a gambler, I'd be like Bassanio in *The Merchant of Venice* who chose neither the gold nor the silver but the leaden casket "Which rather threaten'st than dost promise aught," being of the firm opinion that beauty is more likely to be found in unlikely places. By the way, you know I haven't really ever seen your paintings, a lapse I hope one day soon to repair. Why should so many others have had that pleasure and not I?[30]

Love

R

July 27, 1989

Dear Peter,

No, No, No. Don't be depressed. Not in this heat. It's just not supportable. Wait til October. I always do, and somehow with the grand natural elegy going on all around, a sweet gloom is almost pleasurable. So quit it. Yesterday I drove out to Richard Sewall's pond for a swim and plan to go again today. All things considered, it's not a bad place to drown in privacy—i.e., to submerge and fail to come up. If ever I vanish, you'll know where to look for the bloated carcass.

Now I'm just back from another swim at Richard's where I found the place occupied by a couple of painters, interesting pleasant guys whose work I hope to see. One turns out to be the roommate of an editor at *Art & Antiques* for whom I once wrote a piece on the anatomical drawings of Casserius. I no longer have a copy of that essay and will have to try to get one from him. Next time you come, let's have Frank take us down to the bowels again to see them [in the Yale Medical

Historical Library].[31] Your title for the Lauderdale book [*The Wounded River*] is great. Do use it.

Here's Luis:

The next night she was there standing in the path. She had brought a piece of calico with a printed pattern. He watched her fold the square of cloth neatly into a narrow band, pressing it with her hands. Standing close, she reached up and tied it about his brow. All the while Luis stared down at her like an animal that does not know whether it is to be beaten or caressed.

—Where did you find that? he asked, for want of something to say.

—I have always had it, she replied. It was the first thing anyone had given him in ten years.

—Now you look . . . she began, but could not finish for the sudden hard pressure of his mouth on hers. Later he showed her the seven stars in the neck of the Bull.

—The same God who made the stars made this too.

She gestured about her.

—God! he said, and snorted.

Where this story is going is anyone's guess. I surely don't know myself.

Love

R

P.S. Now cheer up, you.

CIRCA JULY 28, 1989

Dear Peter,

I don't know whether I wrote to you yesterday or not. Such is the disarray of my brain, all of whose gyni have inverted themselves to become sulci, and vice versa, so that the few thoughts that stagger around in it have no idea where they are. This morning saw yet another false start on the fable of Luis. This is murderous. But there *must* be a way in and I'll find it or bust. Here he is:

"It was the time of the shooting stars. From where he hunkered, Luis gazed at a sky that seemed to be within arm's reach. Even with the dump sucking slowly, sensuously at his bare feet, Luis felt himself to have been drawn upward, that he too, like the great jaguar and the one-legged man, dwelt among the stars. In the strange pale light of a quarter moon, his skin took on a blue-violet color. He remembered the death-face of his father, still warm on his mat in the corner of the hut; remembered the last gurgling breath after which the mouth fell open to show the edge of his teeth, which seemed to Luis the ivory-colored edge of human existence that only the death of his father had revealed to him."

Well, does that set the tone, or not? Probably not. I gave him a sister, then erased her. Gave him a friend—Esmeralda—with whom he falls in love and whom he teaches the stories of the stars. Then I erased her too.

He had been a street thief, then a beggar, had even, when dizzy with hunger, sold himself on two occasions to gringo tourists on the beach. But now he was a scavenger. Far from hating the dump, he had grown to love it for its vitality, for the richness that he mined each night and from which he drew sustenance. He was like a fisherman who sees all around him not the surface of the water but something deeper—the shapes and patterns of rocks, the sea grasses and the fish beneath. For Luis, this municipal dump had the marvelous potential of discovery. But it was to the sky that he dispatched his dreaming mind, the night sky whose hieroglyphs he had learned to read—he who could not read.

Now you can see why I am lost. By the way, shooting stars are meteors, rocks that fall into the atmosphere and burn up in flight. They are commonly seen at certain times of the year. To the ancients they were tied up with fertility and crops. The Brazilian Indians of course did not see Orion or Cassiopeia, but the jaguar or the one-legged man chasing his wife who had been seduced by a tapir. Anyway, it is on just such a night that Luis finds the star which had fallen at his feet. What else could it be with its strange radiance—the light of angels. For one blinding instant, Luis had a vision of the universe, of worlds upon worlds stretching out forever to God. And *there*, in his hand, a fragment of that universe, a bit of evidence that had been given to *him*, to Luis, the Scavenger.

Love
R

July 28, 1989

Dear Peter,

I am utterly shocked by the horror of the rape-threat.[32] It is true that just outside the calm round of life lurks disaster. I wish I could offer a suggestion, but whatever you do or do not do will be wrong. Privately, I want to see you stay in Princeton and do your work. On the other hand there is the girl and her mother. But the fact is that *you* cannot prevent the rape from taking place. The only way to do that would be for Barbara to send her away for the rest of the summer—to relatives, perhaps. It is a matter for the police—you are only a pretend cop in movies. Besides, real rapists don't warn their victims. It is doubtless some maniac getting off on the writing of the letter. Jesus, what a malignant force lies in pent-up sperm that *need* to shoot. It is beyond all belief, and I do not blame you for feeling upon your neck the hot laughter of savage gods. Whatever you decide to do, remember that I am on your team, for whatever that's worth.

Meanwhile, as in Auden's poem "La Musée des Beaux Arts," life is going on while Icarus is falling into the sea. A woman is pounding a mortar with a pestle; a butcher is plucking a chicken; a boy is rolling a hoop—all oblivious to the tragedy. Just so I have been writing Luis, keeping up a correspondence, answering the phone, thinking about sex. Today I bought a copy of *Richard Selzer and the Rhetoric of Surgery* [by Charles M. Anderson]. It arrived at the Yale Co-Op bookstore. *Don't* buy it. I'll give you a copy. There is a shiteating photo of me on the cover, horribly smug. Is that how I come across? Added to the heat it is just too much to bear. The lady from Random House called to say that she'll be on vacation til August 20 "in case I might be trying to reach her." For what? I wonder.

About booze: I lost ten pounds in the month that I quit and have come to the realization that I shall waste away without it. So today I had a vodka and am back on the road to obesity. It's better than potatoes.

Love
R

July 31, 1989

Dear Peter,

Never mind about Princeton, prithee. Only immerse (dunk) in work and you won't notice. The immediate problem here is the underarm deodorant of the German medical student living til tomorrow in your room. It nauseates me so that I can't eat or think. I have found him a room elsewhere and will rejoice to transport him there in the morning. One takes such risks with human beings.

I spent the morning with Luis at the dump and now want only to wallow in my bed and reread the letter from the beauteous *imagist* of Sundance who wants us to run off together and never be heard from again! I am composing a weary reply full of ennui and sweet regret. Anyway, between her and the lazuli bunting, give me the bird any day.

I don't know why, but in spite of everything I feel cheerful. Things tickle me. Like the letter today from Sister Stefanie Weisgram, Order of St. Benedict, who asks will I write an article on the role of nuns in modern society for a magazine called *Sisters Today*. $5/page, she says. Of course I will. Who could turn *that* down? And two others I won't do: (1) a lady of Fairfield who asks me to come talk to twenty WASP ladies at their Literature Club; (2) a Jewish stand-up comedienne who wants us to go round the country giving hilarious readings together. Fat and ugly, she is, and unremittingly vulgar. This is my *life*.

Love
R

August 1, 1989

Dear Peter,

You are uncannily prescient. Luis tells Esmeralda that she should look at the sky after his death. He tells her exactly *where* and she will see a cluster of four new stars. It will be he, sitting on his heels and holding a hoe.

I met Ferenc [Gyorgyey] at the library, told him about the Chinese paintings. Yes, do phone or write him to discuss it. The *only* problem will be the protection of the paintings which "nobody has ever seen anyway." He himself is favorably disposed. What a dear man and good friend. He had come to look up the controversy over the darter snail endangered by the building of a dam. He is a oner.

"Cycle Michael"—tantalizing title. Keep at it. And the more I think of it, the more I like your Lauderdale project. I think it would not be difficult or long in the doing. Finally, yes, I think your suggestion of a version of "Hugh" by the Prioress would be good.[33] Why didn't *I* think of it? I am committed to Luis for all of August. Then three weeks in September to prepare for West Point. After that?

Love

R

August 4, 1989

Dear Peter,

Such a treasure trove in the mail today. Your marvelous letter, the Conrad and the Matthew Arnold. The latter two are on loan only. The first, to be yours at such time as you decide to collect our epistolary effluvium and foist it upon a vast public quivering with anticipation. As for the vodka, let it be said for once and for all time that he took it up again with renewed gusto having realized his near fatal mistake. About tobacco, you are on surer ground. It is no mere addiction as the psychologists would have it; it is the companionship of smoke without which I would go down to my grave in sorrow—like Abraham, or Lear—or whoever it was. I can't understand why "cigarettes" and "filthy habits" are always used in the same sentence. After forty-eight years in their presence, I can vouch for their politeness and charm. Cigarettes are perfect little gentlemen.[34]

I am writing this with a Mont Blanc fountain pen given to me by the interns when I retired and never used in these three and a half years. I am told it costs $120! I bought a bottle of blue-black ink and experienced the rapture of filling it this morning. It is not to be done without a box of Kleenex at hand, as the ink, crazy to escape the well in which it has been stoppered for years, leaps up in a great splash and blueblackens everything in reach. I love the ancient ritual of it, and can now fully understand Thoreau and his handmade pencils.

The doctor has just explained to Luis that his hands were injured by no such thing as a star but by radioactive cesium—a "hot" metal that emits rays that kill flesh. Of course Luis does not believe him. Why should he? It is no more credible to him than the star is to the doctor. Given the choice of which story to believe, I would take the star too. The girl, I think, does have a glimmer of understanding but does not let on. There is much to be done with the story still. It will not be done til New Year's Eve.

Love
R

August 7, 1989

Dear Peter,

Thanks for your fine letter. I haven't read the Kleist story ["Michael Kohlass"] yet, the reason being that I am in heavy seas with my own. There are a thousand difficulties and I am sinking in confusion. I think, if only you were here, you would riffle the pages once or twice and know exactly the right thing to do. The problems are those of viewpoint, order, and relevance. Perhaps I need to begin again and just tell the story right out minus the dishonesties of "art." But don't be surprised if one day you find it *dumped* in your lap along with an anguished cry of "Help!" It is getting harder and harder to write. Perhaps the powers are waning? I would dearly love to write the Prioress's say-so for *Little Saint Hugh*. After Luis, West Point, etc.—if I'm still a writer.

You ask about Derrida. He used to be at Yale every year for a semester. He is one of the original thinkers in the deconstruction of the text. He jogged through the Grove Street Cemetery every noon. I've not read him. He's too dense; I'm too stupid. I received a letter today from a gay friend who is in Bangkok (apt name?) fornicating the Thai boys. His description of the process of selection, the locale, and the *equipment* is riveting. I would be as at home among the cannibals. Or the Deconstructionists.

So it is *that* Shapiro [the novelist Jane Shapiro] whose house you sit [in Princeton]. What a lot of tangential intersections from your stay at Yaddo. Speaking of Yaddo, I gather there is a new policy. Such as I are no longer welcome. It is to be used by the new and almost new from now on. So another little pocket of light has gone dark. Never mind. I'll stay here.

If you didn't know, I'll tell you: your quote: "I have wounded and I heal" plus your misspelling of the Old Testament book makes a *jeu d'espirit* (leap of spirit). *Deuterotomy*, you wrote, *otomy* being the surgical suffix meaning the act of making an opening into an organ, e.g., thoracotomy, tracheotomy. So if we can find out what part of the body is the deuter, we can know the operation by which "I" (in the quote) wounded and healed.

Remember Luis in your prayers.

Love
R

4 P.M.

A phone call just now from West Point. One Lee Dewald is my host. He is *geometrically* correct. Called me *Sir*; is a member of the Mathematics Department. So you know it will all be done right, by the numbers. We are to arrive at the Hotel Thayer in West Point on the 20th. Then we are to be taken on a tour. Should Janet decide not to go, it will be just us. At 4:30 we meet with Lt. Gen. Dave Palmer, Superintendent of West Point. He is a historian—wrote *The River and the Rock*. Guess we should look at it. At 4:45 there will be a parade. *We'll* review it. Then a cocktail party with twenty to thirty West Point bigshots. Then dinner at the mess, then the talk, then another reception, then to the hotel. Since I can't drive at night, I must stay over. You, being nocturnally visual, can choose. Now West Point is *expecting* you. It promises to be an *occasion*. So you *must* come. I'm getting nervous about it.

Janet just announced that she ain't going, so that leaves you and me. You will be the sole (soul) witness of these events. Lee did (as he was told to do) ask about the Freedom of the Imagination. "What's that?" he asked. I said, "That's it." So he said, "Fine with us." Now I have to write it. Oh dear O dear O dear O.

R

AUGUST 8, 1989

Dear Peter,

Well look at me! I am undeniably on board a train bound for New York City. It is the 2:48 local and beautifully underoccupied. Six weeks ago, in a moment of folly, I accepted an invitation to a dinner party from Bernie Ackerman, occasional friend and professor of dermatopathology at NYU. Two or three years ago I did the same and can't remember whether I should have or not. Bernie is a horribly rich bachelor, famous in his admittedly obscure specialty. He leads the "very good life" in a three-story apartment on 70th Street at Fifth Avenue. Last time I stayed there overnight but won't this time, so I must catch the late train to New Haven and face a day of rest and recuperation—for my sins. But I've brought along your Conrad, also George Moore's *Memoirs of My Dead Life* and the original *New York Times* article—Monday, October 19, 1987—which was the seed of my story about Luis. Rereading the article, I see that it is as moving and horrific as ever. Rummaging, I also found the newspaper report in an old *Hartford Courant* from which sprang my story "The Hartford Girl" [in *Confessions of a Knife*]. I see that I do this from time to time. Well so did Shakespeare in *The Merchant of Venice*, which is a rewriting of *The Jew of Malta*.

AND NOW IT IS THE NEXT DAY. HERE'S WHAT HAPPENED:

Arrived Grand Central at 4:45. Pee'd at the Yale Club, tried unsuccessfully to buy a vodka there—you have to be a member. I used to be, but quit some years back after being thrown out for not wearing a jacket and tie—this on a day in August when temperature and humidity were both 95, and just having stepped from a non-air-conditioned train. But I still pee there, as the alternative is the Men's Room at Grand Central Station where the guys on either side of one are watching attentively, or jacking off, or both. I wouldn't mind except that I have difficulty—it puts me off my pee, somehow. From there I sauntered up Fifth Avenue to 70th Street, had an hour to kill and spent it at the Frick where I saw again my beloved Van Dyck portraits and a dozen other marvels—especially a young woman done by Ingres. Promptly at six o'clock I crossed the street. The doorman informed me that Dr. Ackerman was not home.
 "Impossible," I said. "He's having a dinner party."
 "No, no," barked Cerberus, "he always tells us [when there is a party]."
 "Well, might I use your phone to call his office?"
 "Sorry, Sir, we don't permit that."
 "Okay," I said. "I'm going away for one hour. When I come back, he'll have arrived and then you have to let me in."
 I strolled east, crossed Madison Avenue, and found a French restaurant with tables outside à la Montmartre, sat down and ordered a vodka. Next to me were three male hairdressers each of whose hair qualified him for the cauldron scene in *Macbeth*. All together their hair was a convulsion of histrionic woe. Their conversation was professional—all about spit curls and bangs and chignons, and about the stupidity, ugliness, and grotesquerie of their clientèles. Once, a young man in shorts walked by. Three heads turned. "What a lovely round ass," I heard, and turned myself to see. Well, maybe, I thought and lit a cigarette to show that I didn't care one way or the other. I also noted, walking by, any number of skinny young women with anorexia nervosa and one extremely pretty woman with two dogs of a breed that must have been created by genetic manipulation. At a given signal both dogs defecated less than three feet from where I sat. Whereupon their mistress gave me a knee-weakening conspiratorial smile, bent, took Kleenex from her pocket, and *picked up* every speck of dogshit and carried it away. I fell in love

with her at once.[35] Meanwhile, a very old man with a large rhinophymatous nose, gold chains, and bright green pants sat on my other side, handing in first another beautiful young woman. On his face a look of proprietary lust; on mine, a look of the plain ordinary kind; the hairdressers didn't notice.

After an hour of this I went back to the apartment and found that nothing had happened. No Ackerman. No other guests. Nothing. I had gone to New York on the *wrong* day. From a pay phone I tried to call the dermatopathologist's office, but was told by a recording that no one was there. I walked back to Grand Central heaving with self-loathing. I was further gone in my senility than I had thought. It was now 7:40 or so. I raced to the Oyster Bar, ate a bowl of clam chowder, and squeezed onto the 8:07 local to New Haven. Got home at precisely 10:48. An eight-hour activity which is unlikely to do anyone any good. This morning I called Bernie Ackerman to apologize. Before I could say a word, *he* was mea culpa-ing all over the place. The sound of his fist beating his breast was audible over the phone. I had *not* made a mistake. I was *not* senile. It was *he* who had forgotten the date. Strangely, the whole experience lifted my spirits considerably, especially as I got home three hours earlier than expected, did not have to sit through a dinner party, and am able to work today. To say nothing of the joy of having resolved never, never, never to go to New York City again.

What a boring story I've told!

In the mail today yet another heartrending letter from Pirkko, my Finnish friend. And an invitation to write a piece for *Art & Antiques* on any painting having to do with medicine in any way. I'm going to say yes. It's too good a chance to have a go at Poussin's *The Philistine Stricken with the Plague*, or Tiepolo's *The Charlatan*, or whatever—you pick one for me. Back to Luis. My poor, beloved, beautiful Luis.

Love

R

August 11, 1989

Dear Peter,

Today I set aside Luis and began to jot notes for West Point. It ain't going to be easy to refrain from a preachy, argumentative lecture, yet get across a few points. Byron's "Prisoner of Chillon" will open it. Then I think to bring in Ambroise Paré perhaps to show the irony of the fact that, while working at exact cross-purposes—the one bent on killing, the other bent on preserving life—medicine and the military live together in a symbiosis. Some of the great advances in medicine have been learned on the battlefield. The sick army loses the war. And

I want to tell about Paré's treatment of insomnia. Think I'll dilate a bit on the river that runs by Troy and West Point. And then deliver my thrusts. I am extremely nervous over this and will have to have a complete typed text in front of me all the time, although I shall have it memorized. I also feel the burden of my predecessors—Wiesel, Wolfe, and Giamatti. I'm glad you'll be there. It means much to me. You are invited to all the shenanigans. Plan to stay the night—altho' you may have to share my room. Not to worry: I haven't molested anyone in years. Next morning we can amble about and *Say*. On the 26th I'll be at the Lawrenceville School in Princeton. Shall you have already left? If not, I'll wangle you in, tho' by then you'll have got horribly sick of me.

Yesterday a former student, who teaches philosophy at Loyola in Baltimore, phoned to remind me that it is deadline for a promised essay for an anthology. I shall write it on surgery—the therapy of subtraction, and will try to use some of the West Point material. Help! I'm sinking. Then there are the essay for *Art & Antiques* and the Prioress and poor Luis who is lying on the dump while I race about the barnyard clucking out of my amputated head.

I fear you will think I am being too *careful* at West Point. Or too subtle. Let's see what happens.

Love
R

August 13, 1989

Dear Peter,

It occurs to me that my daily epistles may have become tiresome to you. If so, have the kindness to say so, as I dread nothing more than being a bore. I have fired envelopes at you only because I suspect that my scratchings may be your sole remaining link to (a) civilization, and (b) sanity. I also quite enjoy doing it, as you know.

The West Point talk is beginning to organize out of the fog. The subjects to be touched upon so far: (1) "The Prisoner of Chillon" and other forms of imprisonment; (2) Ambroise Paré—the symbiosis of medicine and warfare; (3) my own Korean experience; (4) the function of an army; (5) the causes of war; (6) the freedom of imagination. What do you think? I shall avoid hostility or cant. First thing is to win them over and then lunge. What worries me is that it is a *speech* and I have never given one before. Very different from my usual chat-cum-reading—the effusion of a brain in a state of moderate undress.

I do agree with you about the masturbatory nature of so many novels. Either the writer is jerking himself off with the reader as witness, or the writer is jerking the reader off. While I am put off by the former and will more often than not slam the book shut on his prick, I confess to lying back and enjoying the latter in the addled belief that it is just another example of Art imitating Life.

Yesterday I attended the wedding of the son of my beloved nurse—Ann Palkowski. The bride is the most beauteous carpentress in North America. She it was who repaired my rotting timbers—those that were holding up the garage. The wedding was very RC (which I like) but held in the only ugly Catholic Church I've seen. Jesus had worn his silliest diaper to the crucifixion above the altar. It was not a diaper, really, but a mini-skirt slung from the iliac crests to the knees. The deacon who delivered the homily is a guy I know—the heart/lung machine technician at Yale. At prayer time he called upon the congregation to ARISE! Which I had thought reserved for the Resurrection. Just plain RISE! would have sufficed. At the reception I met dozens of old nurses and patients from my former incarnation. Only two showed me their incisions. Lots of vodka and pasta, then we danced the polka and the tarantella. So now you know what a Polish/Italian wedding is like around here.

All right, all right, I'll go quietly.

Love

R

AUGUST 15, 1989

Dear Peter,

Thanks for the look at *Little Saint Hugh*. It is awfully good—so brilliantly woven together. It has quite convinced me that I must tell the Prioress's Tale one day soon. And I am eager to see you go ahead with the play. For radio, is it? I obeyed orders and kept my pencil away from the few errata. But "relishing gentiles" ought to be "relishing *lesser* gentiles." It's important to get the three *e*'s: *rel*, *less*, and *gent*, for the full value of the horrific. All followed or pursued by the *e* in Hell. Said aloud, it's good and strong. But the play is good, mighty good, further evidence, if any were needed, of your own talents.

I'm fighting fatigue today—my old adversary. I fully understand why some writers resort to amphetamines. There is little so depressing as to sit in a fog of exhaustion and know that you *must* write. I've had to contend with it all my life, though. It's nothing new. Partly now the fault of untrustworthy plumbing. My toilet and I have grown old together, the result being that neither one of us gets any rest at night. *Her* problem is arthritis of the lever. (As for my own lever, another time.) It has made a perfect Maria Callas of her—temperamental and with a histrionic vibrato in every register. Long, long after you flush she goes on plashing and gargling and would do so forever did I not get out of bed again to jiggle the handle or lift the top from her tank and rummage in the hope of disengaging her ball.

For one affected with creeping prostatism and the need to pee every two hours at night—it's called nocturia—that constitutes full employment on the night shift. Along with Catholicism and Judaism, Prostatism is a belief I heartily reject. Well, now you know why I am tired today.

Love
R

August ?, 1989

Dear Peter,

Another morning worrying the West Point affair. I'm changing tack (again!). For one thing, I do not share the liberal prejudice against soldiering that prevails around here. Feeling, as I do, that everything I am able to enjoy in life is directly due to the existence of the U.S. Army, I think of that line of Kipling: "Making mock of uniforms that guard you while you sleep." On the other hand, I despise the bellicose mentality of the Pentagon and would gladly rush to my anvil to beat the last two swords into a ploughshare.

Love
R

August 19, 1989

Dear Peter,

Returned from the library having taken a good nap on one of the benches. I had left the windows of my study open and found that Nature had done a thorough editing of my work-in-progress. A wind had arisen and blown Luis, the West Point talk, and my Troy diary all around the room—mingling them in accordance with Her Best Judgment. I have gathered them all up in one pile and now have the choice of abiding by Her decision and leaving the three-in-one as a kind of wordish trinity, or laboriously separating them into three sacrilegious piles. My instinct is to just bow to the force of Nature. A writer ought never to pray for Divine Guidance—it invariably leads to Chaos. Having written the word Chaos, I felt the need to fill my fountain pen and it is with a blue thumb that I continue.

You hint that you are collecting my letters to some far distant purpose. Surely this one will weaken that resolve. Yours, I must say, are all here in a drawer and can be used against you in a courthouse. I like your idea of writing a book—any book—in the Matisse room of the museum. Were I to do the same it would be in the Piranesi room—all those dismal dungeons, where I feel at home.

I've just looked at my schedule of lectures and readings and truly "the heart grows faint." In October I go to Mystic and Ohio. In September I am at West Point, Princeton, and Yale. In Nov. →Houston, Texas. Further on there will be Philadelphia and Little Rock and Chicago and Halifax. Just so does the old migratory bird flap from podium to podium to pay for the new backyard. Should I die on one of these ventures, it is to *you* will fall the task of cleaning the Augean stables, i.e., piecing together all the bits and pieces of my life that lie about my study. You are the only one mad enough to do it and still forgive me. By the way, *I* have a copy of your novel here. Shall I send it to Viking? Give me instructions. I shall fall upon my sword if you say so. Remember Brutus and Volumnius on the Plains of Philippi? How B commanded V—his friend—to hold up his sword so that B could impale himself on it. V's horror and reluctance, his ultimate acquiescence. *So romantic!* Nothing like that *ever* happens around here. I also love the way Achilles, mourning for Patrochus, slew everyone in sight—even sheep—to vent his sorrow. That Patrochus must have been adorable. And how Achilles *sulked* in his tent and wouldn't come out to fight the war; how, when he was killed by the arrow in his heel, the Greeks cremated him and stirred his ashes with those of Patrochus *in the same urn*. Now that is love.

Love

R

August 21, 1989

Dear Peter,

You continue to be a fountain of inspiration for me. Your brilliant quirky mind is a delight to this old hippopotamus of a writer. What an audacious thought to finish "The Light-house" for Poe as an act of pure homage. I desperately *want* to do it. What occurs to me at once is Interior Decoration—to paint the furniture, walls, windows, etc. of the Light House—all so solid and motionless with, outside, the ceaseless motion of the sea. And, living at the interface—the cell membrane between the two—the narrator. Now something must *happen*, or must be perceived by him to *be* happening (á la Poe)—e.g., the dissolution of the Light House—slow—terrifying—a merging. But when am I to do any of this? At sixty-one, one works under the very dart of death. Well, you'll have to do it, then.

Today I read the Gospel of John. I had forgotten how beautiful it is. Especially the part where Mary, the Sister of Martha and Lazarus, pours a bottle of precious oil—called *spikenard*—on the feet of Jesus, then wipes them with her hair. When Judas hypocritically complains that the oil could have been sold for the benefit of the poor, Jesus demurs and says that she is justified in anointing his body before his death, since "the poor will always be with you, but I am here for only a short time." Wow!

Love
R

P.S. Measured myself today to find I am one inch shorter than a year ago. If this keeps up I shall be buried in my hat.

August 22, 1989

Dear Peter,

Well, yes, doubtless you are right about "Lindow Man" [in *Imagine a Woman*]. And you are right again that my first impulse is to put it in the drawer. But your having pre-empted that impulse, I hereby say that I can't do that any more with a straight face. Tell you what: *You* write the paragraphs that will humanize the protagonist, and I swear I'll use them. I haven't the heart to think of it at this point, what with the muddle that is my mind, and every limb a blemish. Go ahead and do it and I'll kiss the hem of your garment. As for "Malpractice," I expect you're again right, and that a major essay could be built upon it, but I lose heart at the notion of expanding it from a diary excerpt. Best, I think, to move on. But you are a marvelous critic with an unerring eye for which I am deeply appreciative.

Today was spent on the memoir of Troy into which I have thrown myself to avoid the West Point debacle. It is, of course, next to my heart. The only other thing that happened was that Harold Bloom kissed me in the library. If you don't see him first, he's got you. I decided then and there to buy myself a pen wipe to use when filling my Mont Blanc hundred and twenty dollar artery. But I'm going to shop around for a wipe that will be worthy. None of your old cum-rags. I want it to be a relic one day for writers with *block*.

What are *you* writing? I need news of *your* work. I am thoroughly sick of mine.

Love
R

August 24, 1989

Dear Peter,

Very nice write-up! And handsome *you*! I'm inordinately proud. What a massive work you are erecting! Bravo! Four exclamation marks are all you get. Any more would not be good for you.

An unusual letter from Bill Ober today in that it has not *all* to do with sex.[36] I give you only the opening: "I've just finished a disappointing week's tour as the local Medical Examiner—three uninteresting autopsies on Monday and Tuesday, then five consecutive days without a dead body. Death takes a holiday." Witty, don't you think? Once again he cautions me not to publish excerpts from my journal, diary, or letters. Says it can only injure my reputation. Perhaps he's right, after all. But what is there that I haven't already revealed?

This morning I revisited Luis in an effort to tell of his childhood—what he left to come to the municipal dump. It is not yet successfully done. Meanwhile the entire manuscript grows more and more illegible as I scribble it over. I shall hang it on a wall and title it *Frenzy*.

The Japan trip is off. The publisher is unable to find a sponsor and "laments the one-eyed view of the Japanese medical world as well as Japanese society." I heave a giant sigh of relief. Hayashi-san says he is thinking of another translation of my work. If that takes as long as the first one, I'll be able to observe the proceedings from the Great Beyond. I am cutting short this dull letter to go for a swim at Richard Sewall's pond. Perhaps there'll be a last thought when I return.

There, that's better. An hour exactly like Adam in the Garden of Eden prior to his rib resection. I've poured myself a gin (there is no vodka) and am preparing to type the morning's hieroglyphs. What with all the brilliant novels being published weekly, why do I bother?

Til the next time

R

AUGUST 25, 1989

Dear Peter,

It was with Luis that I spent the day. The scene takes place in a room at the clinic where a doctor is attempting to explain to Luis and the girl the "truth" of what happened. I am pleased with the way it came out. Now there is the task of filling in a few gaps in the story, arranging the episodes in order, retyping, rewriting. But perhaps I see a faint light at the end of the tunnel. I have decided *not* to sign the contract with Random House until the story is finished. It was a bad idea that served only to cause me anxiety. I await disapproval from Random House and Borchardt, but I must have time to write this piece without pressure. I have enough inner demons afflicting me without asking for others from outside.

An article in the *Times* about Nabokov's letters today has me thinking about *Said*. Nabokov refused to be interviewed unless he had the questions beforehand

and was able to compose and write out his answers. He hated the impromptu, spontaneous interview, said that his responses were invariably stupid and poorly expressed. As a writer, his style was all he had, and he meant to keep it. And so he conducted his interviews formally, treating them with no less precision than his novels. The same went for his letters, which are to be published soon. Reading over the two excerpts of *Said*, I begin to wonder if he is not, after all, right. Many of my answers are quite tossed out without the least regard for style. More than once I cringed at my carelessness, my injudiciousness. All of which leaves me feeling rather naked and insecure. Do please tell me what you think of all that. I know that I am prone to let everything come spilling out, carried along in the enthusiasm of the interview experience. I too have always detested the printed interviews I've read after the fact. But perhaps I am not the one to judge, and should listen to those who know better—you, in fact. Bill Ober called today—full of cautionary advice which didn't help. I have no thought to be difficult or obstructionist, or an old scaredy-cat either. But I'd also hate to be misunderstood, or appear like an asshole (my least favorite word).

Did Keats hint at the process of evolution when he addressed the sky children: "So on our heels a fresh perfection treads"? He had a sense of nature that was as keen as it was exquisite. I've been noticing how the flowers of my pea plants, which are shaped like Spanish galleons, turn their backs to the wind whenever it blows strongly enough to endanger the delicate parts upon which the seed depends. There is a holiness in that which Keats would have intuited.

Love
R

August 27

It is a perfect day and I am planning a walk in East Rock Park with the field glasses. It is time to look for hawks. There ought also to be a V or two of geese arrowing overhead. Right about now the hawks begin to gather in kettles to ride the thermal updrafts all the way south. It is curious that hawks insist upon solitude for their time of hunting and nesting, but prefer company when traveling. Unlike the warblers whose gender is readily told (the male has all the colored plumage and song), hawks do not reveal their sex. They all look the same to me. I suppose the best way to tell would be to offer a hawk a mouse. If it is a male, he will eat it. If it is a female, she will.

I see that Annie Dillard has a book *On Writing*. Everything she says is so sensible and companionable. I plan to read it when my spine needs stiffening.

Like everyone else, I am awed at the photographs of Triton, the moon of Neptune—even the very words with all those *n*'s are unearthly. And to think of that tiny instrument hurling out into interstellar space where the imagination cannot go. Let's hope we won't be punished for our arrogance. It takes an act of will to rearrange the mind for the rhythms of *this* tiny world.

AUGUST 28

Spoke only to Luis, did everything but blow into his ear until finally he spoke back to me. I am now at that point where I must take an entire week and retype these pages so that I can have a clean copy to work with. Which week shall it be? The Random House contract came today but I've decided not to sign it until Luis is actually born. If then . . . If ever . . .

I loved that story about Samuel Johnson meeting the King at the library and the lovely interest of his buddies. Camaraderie *is* hard to come by. At least as hard as love.

Last night I reread (after thirty years) *How Green Was My Valley* by Richard Llewlyn. It is a lovely moving novel of the sort that wouldn't get published today. It contains a powerful rendering of a bare-fisted boxing match, a moving impression of sexual congress (f—ing to you), and a description of a nightingale singing that is truly magical. It is all written in a kind of Welsh religiosity and it seems to me better than anything by D. H. Lawrence, which it resembles. Also read two long letters by Henry James to William and his father about his (Henry's) constipation while in Italy. What he didn't know is that everyone gets constipated in Italy—because of those intimidating *gabinetti*—holes in the floor over which one is expected to squat. It's all described in my memoir of Italy. The word for squat in Italian is *accocolarsi*. It's something Americans can't do.

How many words have we written to each other? It seems many thousands. The correspondence is one of my few pleasures.

AUGUST 30

I am allowed only one more day with Luis and then I am off to West Point—in a tumbril on the way to the guillotine. The library is closed Sept 2–4! What shall I do? Go to the Green, I think, and sit with the other elderly unemployed of my ilk. It has become intolerable to be locked out of my nest, my cocoon for even one day.

This afternoon I babysat with granddaughter Becky. We had a good deal of old-fashioned conviviality during which one of us was incontinent. I leave it to you to decide which one.

September 1

Such a racket on the terrace today. Dogs are barking, a cement-mixer is grinding next door, nails are being hammered. It is a day such as to envy the deaf. (No! No! God! I didn't mean that. Stay your thunderbolt!) But I'm not Thomas Carlyle, who roared from his study for Jane to shut that damn door. To which that delightful woman took no offense, knowing that a man's roar, unlike a lion's, is neither here nor there. Where *are* those women who knew?

I was distressed by the note of sadness in your last but one letter. How hard it is sometimes to stiffen the spine and even make sweet use of adversity. But I am buoyed by your determination to soldier on. One of your many attributes is the very intensity with which you approach all of your diverse works, as though there were a generator in your mind that drives the whole mechanism. Let us work on and look forward to a glorious autumn. Another of your assets is your great good health. It is enviable. At my age *il y a toujours de quoi*—there is always *something*. At the moment it is toothache, headache, and fatigue. Bah! I shall ignore them and even call out for yet one more affliction if Fate has the nerve.

September 2

Bart Giamatti's death dealt a blow. I remember our monthly lunches over a period of ten years—so much riposte and wit. He was a delightful companion, altho' the day he became President of Yale was the last time we visited, other than a howdeedo on the street. Too sad for words. He was a strange mixture of refined scholar, wit, and practitioner of realpolitik (a pol). I couldn't really concentrate today—it all seemed frivolous somehow. And then came a lovely visit by Varkas Kinoian—Armenian extraordinaire—who teaches English at Fairleigh Dickinson. Very learned and extraordinarily beautiful of soul. We sat in the yard for two hours and talked about the modern Greek poets, Arabic literature, etc. He is medicinal. Helen, his immense wife, is an antiques dealer. She is an enormous blob of love. She supports Varkas and their two sons in grand style. A wife like that is worth rubies and sapphires.

In lieu of writing, I read a stupid detective novel by Michael Innis and am cured of him forever. Went to East Rock Park, but left five minutes after having been accosted by a cop who asked me: "What are you doing here?" I said I'd been coming there before he was born. But I shan't go again. The park is full of drugs and cruising gays and that is all now in the past. Nothing lasts forever. But I'll miss the hawks this year, with the sun shining *through* their wings. I'm about to crawl into bed, rather whipped, and will read: Shakespeare—open to any page and rejoice.

SEPTEMBER 4

I had awakened last night with the idea of introducing a third character into the story of Luis. And so I have. He helps tie up a number of loose ends. It is all very exciting at this point. I cannot keep my hands away from this story to work on the West Point speech. But that time has come. It would make you laugh and cry to see the chaotic process by which I make my pieces. It involves endless repetitive acts and triplication of effort while all the great writers are whipping their word processors and producing 1000 pages to my one.

I spent an hour in the park—taking part in the September hawk watch. But not one hawk showed up in the area to which I was assigned by our leader. I did meet a quite lovely gay man who was *not* on the hawk watch. We tried hard to understand each other's reason for being in the park. I sincerely hope he had better luck than I.

The penmanship of this letter, wilder and more unruly than usual, is due to (1) absence of tobacco; (2) presence of vodka; (3) four cups of espresso coffee. So shut up about it.

SEPTEMBER 6

I am misbehaving all over the place by not getting down to the West Point gig. Instead I am scratching away at Luis—which I'd love to read to you in its embry-

East Rock Park in New Haven, Connecticut, Richard Selzer's favorite site for birdwatching.

onic form. It is exactly like one of those anencephalic monstrosities I showed you at Yale. Perhaps I should put it in a jar of formaldehyde for a year.

September 10

It is time to leave off Luis. I am mired in plot, character, point of view, dénoument, and *deus ex machina*. I swear this is my final piece of fiction—ever! It is just too damn hard. I'd cast it to the winds right now had I not signed the bloody contract. Your offer to read the manuscript (pile of disjointed turds) was rash and I won't hold you to it, but I'd be grateful, I don't deny.

I am presently reading a most unusual body of work by Guy Davenport. A genius, without a doubt, and a lore master. Unfortunately the work is fatally flawed by his cleverness. Still, it is instructive and fascinating.

Now I've told you that West Point ain't what we thought it was, haven't I? So we must both create a dream of West Point and visit *that*.

I must say that I personally have no objection to the presence of a convent at Auschwitz. In fact, it seems to me an act of immense sympathy to put it there. How can prayers to whatever God be a source of resentment? Who owns death?

The reason you're having so much trouble painting my face is that I don't have one. It is a countenance. Or a mask. Or something that resonates from one to the other.

Today I picked the rest of the tomatoes in my pot garden. All but one—a beauty—to which I bowed deeply and then left on the vine as an offering to Priapus, the God of Gardens and the Erector of Penises, in order that He will provide a generous crop of vegetables and hard-ons next year.

Most of my time has been spent on Luis lately, with things taking shape. I need a week in a cave with a typewriter. A clean typescript would be a sign from Heaven.

I must tell you about Ron Pasquariello—age forty-two—Ph.D. from Columbia in Education—dying of AIDS. I visit for conversation. He's reading *Moby Dick* for the first time and is sure he will stay alive to the last page. I have rarely encountered so sweet a person. It is moving to watch him suffer and smile.[37]

October 2

I am the knight of the woeful countenance. Janet is again plagued with kidney stones and depression. I spend most of my time in attendance. It is hard to watch her suffering without the inner resources necessary to keep it in perspective.

At the moment, Luis seems like the Myth of Sisyphus. I've got the bastard typed—or as good as—and am trying to make sense of it. I shan't forget your true and generous offer to give it an editorial glance.

I can never stop thanking you for the Cathedral, Museum, and Battlefield at Princeton. I loved every second of it. That blue window, the majesty of the great nave—and Remington's four riotous cowboys. The horrific Golgotha with the feasting dogs at the foot of the crosses—you can almost smell the stench. And that painted ass we couldn't decide the gender of. Makes you wonder just how rigidly set our sexuality is. In me, you have the perfect pupil—as you can see, I am curious about *everything*.

OCTOBER 3

Among Janet, Gretchen, and Becky, I am engulfed in femininity—two-thirds of which has opinions with which I am placed in daily response. I refuse to sell the house and suffer a dislocation worse than death. So we embark upon refurbishing the Ark of St. Ronan. It is a balance that is yet subject to capsize. I need not tell you how it all detracts from my peace of mind. It is Luis who suffers most. But I shall make it up to *him*, I promise.

This morning at the library I was interviewed (yet again) by a young reporter from Associated Press, so I suppose my stupidities will be printed here and there in due course. This afternoon the phone rang eight times, so there was no work done. I ought to follow in the footsteps of Flaubert and go into seclusion. And the typewriter died—probably of despair, so I shall have to take it to the fixer. A man introduced himself to me at the library—he's Alexander Theroux. We have read each other's books. He once wrote a highly flattering review of *Mortal Lessons*. He is the most genial guy and full of lore. We'll meet again next Tuesday.

And now it is Saturday. I read through Luis. Tomorrow I begin to type, and will for the next two weeks at the least. Then, Sir, for your sins, you shall be required to read and suggest and pencil. This evening I spent lolling about the terrace with Janet. We are like two old lions whose claws and teeth have gone blunt. The worst we are capable of is a paltry cuff or two.

OCTOBER 7

Three lovely days in a row—and a week free of renal colic. Whatever could Jehovah be thinking of? Should this keep up, He risks losing His reputation for severity. But the weather affects me not. Of all New Haven, I alone hunker at my indoorities: this blasted Luis and, more immediate, a long promised essay on the body for Drew Leder, former student and now editor of a philosophical journal. The typewriter is being discharged from the hospital tomorrow, so I shall be under the oval window in the attic all week.

Yesterday I spent more hours taping *atonement* sentences for a friend incapacitated by Obsessive-Compulsive Disorder. I had to say—with immense accuracy—

such things as: "You do not live on a hundred fortieth street." He made me do each one several dozen times until I got it right. But it will be worth it, as now all he has to do is play the tape and he'll be free of the need to *atone* which has been taking up all his time. Here's another: "You will be alive on May twenty-seventh." That is virtually impossible to say in accordance with the requirements of his OCD. But I finally got it right. There but for the grace of God go I.[38]

As for the Light House, I am thinking of having the narrator be a sufferer of OCD. He has retreated to the Light House to escape the world to which he has become painfully hypersensitive. The rest will be a descent into madness. I shall ask my friend for the details of his affliction. I may change my mind about this tomorrow.

OCTOBER 9–12, 1989

Dear Peter,

I have actually typed the first four pages of Luis, and now I see that the opening is quite different from my other stories in its architectonics. I'm not at all sure yet, as the plot has not begun. That may be too long a wait for the reader. Today I'll do the next segment, which is to be interrupted by the pleasure of Miss Becky's company for a couple of hours, as I've been dragooned into babysitting while the women of the tribe are hanging out the laundry.

Yesterday I picked up one of the notebooks lying around this study and read some of the things I wrote therein a few years back. It is like visiting with an old and silly friend I haven't seen in years. After which, I lit a cigarette and turned the world into transcendental vapor.

Okay, it's noon and another four pages typed. The three characters have been introduced, the dump described, and I begin to relate Luis's past in the village of Araguaia. Ouch, it is slow going. But art, I am told, is supposed to be laborious. By the way, what are *you* up to? I tell everyone I have a friend who can do *everything*, so you'd better not make a liar of me. This afternoon I have a date with writer Alex Theroux at the Elizabethan Club. He's going to show me a piece of bone that is a relic of an eleventh-century saint. Shall I steal it for you? Your grand letter came today and I am thrilled to think of you hanging from those scaffolds. May you hang so until you are dead! Rather like Christ *and* the two thieves, in which case you are a version of the Holy Trinity—all by yourself. I'd like to ferry over and see all three. You are entering your time of glory, I just know it and I rejoice.

Well, I did have tea with Alex Theroux and you'd like him—a most delightful man—full of lore and wit. But complicated. We are to be friends, as he'll call me next week for a reprise.

This letter is taking days to write, as, to my horror, it is October 12! Alex Theroux asked me whom I should like to visit in the hereafter. Swinburne, I replied without a moment's hesitation.

AT: "Swinburne? But why?"

RS: "I should like to give him a spanking."

AT: "Again, why?"

RS: "First of all, he'd enjoy it. Second, he deserves it for having written all those naughty poems."

And *that* was the high point. The rest of the conversation was even worse.

I like to think of you painting in public—out there in front of Gawd and everybody, like Michelangelo in the Sistine Chapel. Will you be on a ladder?

R

October 12, 1989

Dear Peter,

Two masterful letters from you today, any line of which would lay a Walpole or a Lamb mad. Truly, in the matter of the epistolary art you have no living rivals. My own puny chirping replies make me cringe. But what can you expect from a brain covered with lichen? If ever you take it into your head to publish this correspondence, I'll be ruined by your glory.

I have now typed sixteen pages of the dullest prose ever written. It goes by the name Luis, but its real name is shit. I loathe it and for two cents . . . but no, I won't, I'll go on typing to the end and then start over.

I remain flabbergasted at the news that seventy Josyphs are pendant on Long Island.[39] The whole peninsula is your gallery. Tomorrow, the world. Daub on and on to renown. If further proof of your brilliance were needed, it is there in your suspicion that Thucydides's plague was AIDS. At the conference in France two years ago, a historian rose to give evidence that the disease has probably always been with us, that it has outbroken here and there over the centuries, but never so widely as now when international travel and anal intercourse are *de rigueur*. What doesn't fit is the disappearance of the birds and dogs.

I too keep thinking about West Point—the sterility of the place. Uncontaminated by life. Rigid, fierce, robotic, and utterly beautiful. Yet for all its muscularity, a core of cowardice that one can smell if he has the right shaped nose. I suspect that despite our lack of "leadership," you and I lead braver lives.

Generous of you to group me with Robert Louis Stevenson—one of my beloveds. From *A Child's Garden of Verses* to the unfinished *Weir of Hermiston*, I have been in his lifelong thrall. Much the same as with Poe. Actually, I am quite full of myself this minute as it has been relayed to me that the *poobahs* of the Yale English Department have informally decided that some of my prose will be read "as long as books are read." So now I don't have to finish Luis or anything else. Break out la vodka! Let us swill!

I am wallowing in *The Sunset of the Splendid Century* by C. S. Lewis's brother, W. H. Lewis. I love all that gossip and intrigue at Versailles and the lovely dirtiness of it all. Like my dump, it was the very delta of Hell.

Like the Lewis boys, I shall initiate myself→   Love

R. A. Selzer

P.S. I am sending you the lyrics of two songs—"Just Before the Battle, Mother," and "Just After the Battle, Mother"—that my mother used to sing in her heartbreaking frail soprano. They never failed to wring from Billy's and my eyes a flood of tears. Which, of course, she well knew. And sang them anyway. Now you know where I come from. It is amazing that I am as good as I am—intact, that is—considering. But she was a sweetie. One day I'll play them on the piano and sing them for you.

R

November 1, 1989

Dear Peter,

All right, all right. So I have, under humiliating circumstances, fallen and broken four of my best ribs. It doesn't matter. If ribs were plates, I could still entertain at dinner twenty of my dearest friends. It has been an afternoon of what I can only call my bliss. To be a little bit sick—there is no pleasure like it. To lie in bed propped on a thousand pillows, strewn all around with books, notebooks, pens; in cahoots with one's body:

"We're in this together," you tell it.

"Aren't we, though?" it replies, and sinks six inches deeper into the mattress. I had an aunt who loved nothing better than to be "sick in bed with the doctor." Now, fifty years later, I know exactly how she felt. Heaven is *not* a place; it is a state.

Today I learned that the Italian poet Leopardi—a contemporary of Byron—lived in a great drafty palazzo. There he spent all day inside a bag lined with feathers, from which he would emerge now and then looking like Papageno (ask your sister "who?"). I learned also that Samuel Johnson liked to carry an orange peel in his pocket. Is that what you meant when you asked about the medicinal properties of orange peel? Also, that Aristotle had a hot water bottle made of leather that he filled with hot olive oil. So—they were no different from the rest of us with our tahini and our vodka and our other peculiarities.

It is a lovely feeling to have finished a draft of Luis. Now, should I die during the night, you will be able to slap it into shape.

Alex Theroux phoned to ask would I read to his writing class. I've broken my ribs, I replied. Either he didn't hear, or wouldn't; said how much it would mean to him, what a favor etc. So I gasped yes—yes. And now I must get a ride to Yale and back and hold forth for friendship's sake. It will be trial by ordeal all over again. Writers, like all distracted schizophrenics, are oblivious to the woes of others. But with me friendship comes first. I'll let you know if I died.

Love

R

November 6, 1989

Dear Peter,

You will know to what state of ruin I have sunk when you see that I am not writing with my Mont Blanc, which needed a slurp from the well and I too feeble to lead it there for a filling. The pain is altogether marvelous. I am made aware of every part of my skeleton with each breath. A sigh has the force and velocity of a gale among my ribs. A hiccough would lay me mad and frothing. Still, there is no better teacher, as each pang is a philosophy unto itself, a learned commentary on the frailty of man. The matter is not without humor, as I must laugh when confronted by such Herculean tasks as lighting a cigarette or wiping my ass. And so I creak from bed to chair—a distance of twelve miles. Never mind. It is all proof that the body is an expression of fate. Some are perfectly constructed, others deformed from birth, still others undergo obesity or emaciation during life. Then there are those who faint in restaurants and splinter. Proof, too, that we are prisoners of our anatomy. Except for the imagination, that is. As Hamlet put it: "O God, I could be bounded in a nutshell and count myself a king of infinite space, were it not that I have bad dreams." Just so do we faint and learn.

Worst is that Luis the Neglected gives me glances of reproach. I shall have to make it up to him next week. When I am not stuporous from codeine I read one of my favorites, *The Aunt's Story* by Patrick White. It is an unreadable book—written by a madman. But on every page a strew of rubies.

The Houston trip was especially wearing, somehow. Very hospitable and friendly but I couldn't quite bridge the gap. Everyone born again and going around with the Ten Commandments on his face. What do they do for sin in Texas?

Okay, that last spasm did it. I'll sign my name

Pity Me

November 7, 1989

Dear Peter,

Morning at last. And with it, the incompletely welcome news that the old cadaver stirs and waves its clackety graspers feebly. And such a night it was. I longed for that kindly old soldier of Paré's with his gentle knife. To be awake in this house all night is truly to be left to one's own devices. I and that mouse who has taken up residence in the piano, the one who picks at the bones of Chopin's mazurkas. His nest is built of two of my beloved pieces of sheet music: "Take Back the Heart That Thou Gavest," and "The Gypsy's Warning." Just as well. Had I *not* survived, they would have lain unplayed forever. Who else would quiver and throb o'er so tropical a repertoire? But I may be getting better after all, as I no longer have to shriek and sob so. More than one visitor has glanced up the staircase as if he had come upon Mr. Rochester's terrible secret right here on St. Ronan Terrace. I could very easily have been *she*.

The man from Albany was dashed at my news. All those posters, those announcements, those thousand palpitating hearts. As an actor, you must tell me precisely *why* the show *must* go on. Valorous as the gesture may be, there are times (fractured ribs, for example) when it had better not, or are you of the Captain Bligh crowd that is duty bound? What is the sickest *you've* been while standing on a stage? Have you vomited into Yorick's skull? Coughed your way through *Pygmalion*? What with the narcotics I am full of, I can read and grasp nothing. Except for an article on Margaret Thatcher. Why has no one deposed that woman? It is a lapse.

A final coincidence. At the very hour when I fainted and cracked my ribs, my poet friend was hit by a car and broke two vertebrae. What can it mean? I much regret that I can't go to take care of him. You are mystified by my taping his sentences of atonement? But it works. He needs only to play the tape once a day to be free of all need to carry out the ritual, and so has been able to work on his poem. I'll explain it all when I see you.

Love

R

P.S. Barbara is a saint to help with *Said*. But of course you know that.

November 8, 1989

Dear Peter,

The Conservatives have lost! I am referring not to yesterday's electoral shenanigans but to the bloodier tho' less dirty politics of my chest. The score is 12 to 8, with *four* of the right wing ribs broken. It is my body making a political statement, that's all, and one *ought* to suffer for one's beliefs, don't you think? The x-ray is daunting—all those bony fragments and even a little lake of blood above my diaphragm. So I am strapped up tight and settling in for the long haul. It is comforting to imagine all the fibroblasts invading the blood clots to lay down a nice scar and all my osteoblasts gearing up to produce new bone to bridge the gaps. It is also good to know that I am beyond medical help. Either I will heal or I won't and without any medical meddling that would transform a mere injury into an illness.

I am once again studying the prose of Patrick White, and marveling. On every page he offers a hint as to the future of Luis. But he can get away with anything. Who would dream of taking him to task for an eccentricity? He is not for everyone, I know, but for me he is catnip. My next project will be to read all the sonnets of Shakespeare—one per day. I have never quite understood many of them. Since I can no longer sling ink, I must read the works of others. It ain't half bad either. Here is the sum total of my writing for one week:

(1) For his part, Luis received the ribbon of rum into his throat and felt the dump spring closer. He sat up, or half.

"I was sleeping," he murmured.

"You who never sleep," she indulged him.

"I have seen things," he told her.

"What things have you seen?"

But Luis did not say. For in his dream he had seen again the body of the man lying where it had been flung—turned to wax by the moon, congealed among pools of silence. When he looked again, there was only the imprint of it on the ground.

(2) And this (about the doctor):

Here he was at last, then, in this dump which had been expecting him, and where his clothing was no longer a guarantee of privacy. Kneeling, he fastened his ear to the ground as if to suck up sounds. Where are they? Where could they be? For he sensed their presence all about him. In whatever direction he looks, he sees the same fever-dark eyes in an amber-colored face and that girl—like a battered bag that one would throw away.

And that is it. Shame on me. Fainting is for sissies.

Love

R

NOVEMBER 10, 1989

Dear Peter,

Your pair of winners came today—both so full of histrionic woe and declaimed as from the apron of La Scala. I enjoyed you immensely. I cannot bear to read any other mail these days—it makes my fragments scrape together. This morning, out of sheer mulishness, I walked to the Divinity Library with my briefcase and had to be carted home by Theodore, the maintenance man of those holy premises. He actually said: "Yo' a caution an' a damnfool, Doc." But I managed to jot down a half dozen phrases before I died. I won't copy them down here, don't worry.

My friend Dorrie—ht. 5'; wt. 260 lbs.—dropped by with a bag of butterscotch drops "from Austria" plus four books to read: *Five Hundred Dollars* by Horatio Alger; Iris Origo's autobiography; *The Hours of Mary of Burgundy*; and *Lark Rise to Candleford* by Flora Thompson. So I am in the books. And there is a daily phone call from my friend Ben Ivry from Paris, who charges it to the French *Newsweek* where he works off and on and mostly starves. I particularly enjoy ripping off that magazine.

Your friend [the actor] Earle Hyman sounds just fine to me. I'd love to meet him. Imagine learning Danish and Norwegian! One is humbled properly. And please tell your sweet mom that "Doctor Selzer" is on her team against the whole race of rock throwers and muggers. It all raises the killer in me. I'm pleased that you've elected to paint Poe over the others in the list. Oh the copious fecundity of your mind. Will it never run dry? I also like the idea of replacing *The Legacy* at Stony Brook with six American writers. The one authentic photo of Emily Dickinson shows a quite plain girl with walleyes. You must see it before you do her.

Yes, we'll go to Troy in December for sure. We'll cremate then or bust. The Harvard visit is put off, I think I told you. From where I lie, flung and spattered, the idea of speaking aloud to anyone is ludicrous. Let us hope that in three weeks I'll be repaired. It is cold in Troy in December. We must rag ourselves about, wear newspaper inside our shirts, stamp and beat each other's circulation with fists. I have only enough left to sign

Your Chevalier without fear or reproach
R

November 11, 1989

Dear Peter,

Why don't you come December 3 and we'll drive up the morning of the 4th. On the 5th we can prowl. What fun! I've written to Bill McQuiston at the Newman Foundation to warn of our arrival, and I'll let Pat Quinn at RPI know. Both are superb human beings. But then, they're Irish and *ought* to be better than anyone else.

The ribs are feeling better. I only have to scream now and then, and can tie my own shoes, so you won't have to tote the carcass around. I've been staggering over to the Divinity School Library each afternoon and have managed to scratch out the first draft of Luis. I'll tinker for a week or two, then ask you, please, to read it and be severe with me. There are a thousand rough edges yet to be planed smooth. I'm off to Divinity Hill. The very words cause my atheist's heart to swell.

Love

Richard

NOVEMBER 15, 1989
OR IS IT 1589?

Dear Peter,

If spasms were orgasms, I could call this a day of uninterrupted bliss. Fourteen so far and it is only mid-afternoon. They are caused by the rubbing together of the bony fragments. Who says I can't take a ribbing?

Today, a letter from Myra Sklarew asking if I'd go with her to Merck Pharmaceutical Co. when she persuades them to establish a Yaddo fellowship for science writers.[40] So I shall. And perhaps you'd like to drive up to Saratoga when we are in Troy? I'll take you both to lunch and we could walk once more the hallowed ground. Remind me to show you Myra's small prose gem *Like a Field Riddled by Ants*. It is a knockout. And a call from Toronto—a woman who makes documentary films—she's doing one about surgeons (not me) and wants to come to talk about it, but she hemmed and hawed when I asked for the thrust of her film. She had heard I was to be at RPI and wanted to go there too. That I have nixed, although I wouldn't be surprised if she were in the audience. But no horning in on our *Say* and that's final. Tomorrow a man comes from the American Medical Association newspaper to, yes, interview. Why? Folly is the right answer. But I told him he had to read all five books first or he'll have come in vain. There is more madness: a shrink with the evocative name of Victor Bloom (a bellicose flower of large and smoking pistil) phoned to say he'd read about *lunaqua* and *aqualune* and is

A street in Troy, New York.

sending me a photograph of a path of moonlight on the water for my comment. Will they never stop?

You are a marvel. And the best epistolarian alive. Your *show must go on* is a classic; but then your [letter on a] yellow napkin is a scandal of equal proportion. And here come Gretch and Becky to call forth my last smile.

Love
Richard

November 16, 1989

Dear Peter,

Tell me straight out if you're sick of these unletters and I'll quit pestering you. I feel like a swarm of gnats around your head.

I'm just back from teaching Alex Theroux's writing class. A two-hour stint that a curious Fate has permitted me to survive. With a pain pill, a cigarette, and a vodka, I am resuscitating. It was, however, sweet to see fifteen teenage faces cloud up with compassion each time I had to holler out and clutch my ribs. Maybe, even, I screamed once when I didn't really have to, just to see them wince with sympathy. Such tiny illicit pleasures as an old splinter takes unto himself. Alex Theroux is someone I'd like for you to meet. He's grand and congenial and humble. Remind me to give you his novel *D'arbonville's Cat*. It's, in its way, a phenomenon. I like your idea of a sequel to *Said*, called *Wrote* [*What One Man Wrote to Another*]. But do give yourself a break of ten or fifteen years. You deserve it.

The damned voodoo witch in my study has just let out another rip. What could it mean? When I look up to see, she is as opaque and expressionless as ever, but I know she means me no good. Reminds me of a story, "The Blue Room," by Prospère Mérimée, the guy who wrote the story on which the opera *Carmen* was based. It's all about a statue—jealous—who steps from her pedestal to strangle a man on his wedding night. This painting was done by a Haitian named Prospère. Believe me, I am in the grip of a malevolent force. My ribs have not sated her lust; it will be my liver or my prostate next. God! There she goes again! You must promise to burn her up if I am found one day disemboweled on the floor of this room.[41]

And now I go to my chair. You would die to see how I arrange each pillow, the footstool, the glass of water, my books and pen. And there I spend the ten hours of night, dropping off now and then, waking up to read a paragraph or two before sinking once again into torpor. Nice pass I've come to, right? And to think that I rode a horse into a canyon last June. How the mighty have fallen.

Love
R

November 17, 1989

Dear Peter,

The dogs still gnaw at my ribs. Every half hour or so I must give forth a Hoo-Hoo. That is exactly the call of a screech owl. There are those around here who split their sides laughing each time. Marry in haste; repent at leisure. But I have discovered my own deep-seated (!) passion for chairs. There is a story by a Japanese writer named Kobe Abe about a man who lives in an overstuffed chair in a hotel lobby. He actually gets inside it, sleeps and eats there. People come and sit on the chair and he listens to their conversation, feels their buttocks, etc. Now that is my version of Paradise, and I am planning to follow in his footstool.

Today I reeled to the Divinity Library where, for two hours, I planed the rough surfaces of Luis, then translated a page of the *Aeneid*, then did the *New York Times* crossword puzzle, and so the morning went. Each time I run through the story it seems to assume a bit more heft. I do hope the whole thing is not an enormous miscalculation.

Tonight is the first chamber music concert at our house. Sixty people have signed up to hear the Wall Street Players. I shall remain as upstairs as Emily Dickinson. When the applause has died off, the audience will hear the feeble clapping of hands from on high, like the ghost of Mozart.

As you may have noticed, this letter is typed, a violation of my principles brought about by the Mont Blanc having once again run dry. I swear that thing has diabetes insipidus (a disorder of the pituitary gland characterized by excessive thirst and urination). By the time our correspondence is over, you will be fully prepared to join the barefoot doctors of China.

I begin to feel rather like the CBS Evening News. This is silly letter #4000.

Love

Richard

November 17, 1989

Dear Peter,

Here I sit, deep, deep within my chair, with my pillows and blankets bestrewn, while from downstairs wafts the music of the Wall Street Chamber Society—Wall Street, New Haven, that is. The chink of coin does not intrude upon these premises. And downstairs, the *crème de la crème* of Yale sits entranced. For the first time I am excused from carrying coats upstairs and opening bottles of wine. It is exactly as tho' I have died and am looking down from on high. I have only to wait til 10:30 before I flush the toilet, which would not go with Brahms, I am told. The pipes in these old houses exaggerate each bowel movement. Despite your philistine approach to music, you'd love to be here, I know, taking notes and writing a sardonic piece for the *New Yorker* on provincial pretensions to society. Never you mind. There are two Nobel Prize winners and a clutch of Pulitzers and Nat'l Book Awards weighting down the furniture, so you needn't be so high and mighty.

My buddy Bill McQuiston at the Newman House in Troy just called to assure that we are welcome to stay there. He's a peach. So it looks like a good time. Gary, the priest, has quit and opted for a life of sin for which he was more than ready. We'll see him too. We shall have to woo the new cleric. I told Bill about you and doubtless he'll be asking *you* to come up and perform. Say yes. It will start your life all over again.

Somehow it has gotten to be Friday, despite that time has gone viscous and slow in this rubbish heap of a study. In the mail today, your lovely gift—the old birdwatcher's book. It is a gem. The drawings so good; the verse so bad. I love it. And your apologia for fainting. So I am in syncope with the immortals after all. But Lee! At Appomattox? Never!

Daily report on Luis: He is ready for typing. That onerous task begins tomorrow and I plan for it to take one week. I am in awe of your tireless and efficient management of manuscripts, tapes, envelopes, erasers, all the contraptions of the writing life that stand as boulders in my path. I have the wrong-shaped head for all that. Also, I'm horribly spoiled.

And now Saturday too has passed during which I discontinued the pain-killers. Tonight I shall abandon my chair—my ankles have swollen from the excessive dependency of sitting all night—and take to my bed. I've been rehearsing the act in which I get out of it. Or try to. Meanwhile, outside my window, New Haven goes on being New Haven, heedless of my aches and pains. Ah, the cruel indifference of brick and asphalt.

Love
R

November 21, 1989

Dear Peter,

I'm better and better each day—the ribs no longer poke so. Mainly I'm bowed down with fatigue—an old adversary, only now compounded. By Troy-time I'll be right as rain. I plan for us to drive up leisurely, stow our gear at Newman House, and arrive at RPI at 3 p.m. The lecture is at 4. The next day is *ours*. We will go to the Crematorium, perhaps twice, and roam the alleys of Troy. *Saying* all the time. That *will* wrap up the book, won't it? Praise be!

The men have come to take away the piano. You can't imagine what a crunch that is. But there is the need to raise some ready cash, and so it is off to be rehabilitated and sold. Again, not my idea, but it is no good to become too attached to *things*, and best, I suppose, for it to go. So I shan't be playing "Fair Elise" anymore. The world of music will not mind. When you come there will be a large empty space in the livingroom. Don't notice. I went to the Yale Library this morning. Janet drove, and picked me up at noon, by which time I was moribund. But I'm better each day and only hope I won't annoy you on our trip to Troy.

In the mail today a psychotically wrapped, framed photograph of an *aqualune* from Victor Bloom, Chicago shrink. It is a lovely photo and I'll have it up over my desk when I can nail again. You would not believe my lecture schedule from March 22 to April 6. It would kill a lesser man. I am to be in: Chicago, Milwaukee, Utah, Little Rock, and Connecticut. Let's hope the socks and underwear can handle it.

Love

R

November 26, 1989

Dear Peter,

The other 3 o'clock in the morning, awake and aching, I stumbled to a bookshelf, pulled out the first I could reach, and found myself in a state of enchantment. The book is *Joint* by James Blake—which will be yours to read and memorize on December 3. He was (is?) a convict who spent most of his life in the pen, but a gifted writer whose letters to Nelson Algren and others make up this volume. I am devouring it avidly. Vulnerability has rarely been so transformed into the hieroglyphics of language. It is prison raised to the level of literature. Don't let me forget to give it to you.

The infamous ribs ache on and on. I reel, I stagger, I shout. Whatever will you do with me in Troy? But never fear, I come and go as usual. Today to the Sterling Library—although it means asking Janet to give me a lift, pick me up, etc. Demeaning and undignified. To her credit she is only slightly resentful.

I wish I had heard your talk, seen the Venetian red dripping between your fingers. It would have done me good. I met here an obnoxious little bitch who lives in Cedarhurst. When I told her (a painter) that you were showing at Smithtown, she allowed as how she too was showing there on the first floor. When I suggested that you two meet, she was suitably distant. At which I said: "Let me not press this upon you," and walked away. She is AWFUL. If one such comes up to you, fend her off. Her husband is a monetary twit of the worst sort—a little shrew of a man (impossible). On the rare occasion that I enter society, I am nauseated and am reinforced in my intention to stay solitary from now on. But now the piano is gone. To be refurbished and sold from under my clumpy digits, so I have nowhere to play "The Golden Links of Love Are Broken." Never mind, I'll play it in my mind. I'm so looking forward to December 3 when you arrive. Troy awaits! The topless towers of Ilium and all that.

Love

R

NOVEMBER 27 OR SO, 1989

Dear Peter,

    I can now rise from my bed in just over ten minutes. It is rather like slithering uphill on my back, achieving crest after crest of pillows until I am sitting upright. Then to shift to the edge; one foot drops searchingly for the floor; a backhanded push with the opposite arm coincides precisely with a torque of the torso, then comes the moment of truth. Will the other foot seek and find the floor? or will a sudden spasm lay me mad and screeching? You will be vastly relieved to learn that my asshole is within reach of my left hand, so you will be free (robbed?) of the burden of wiping for me. As a matter of fact, I am mending and every sign points toward survival—my version of the Resurrection of the Flesh, tho' I'm not sure yet why. This ordeal—I hesitate to call it an ailment—has come to represent a longish tunnel into which I crawled a young, vital, robust fellow and from which I shall crawl a beaten-up old man. Perhaps it is time to dye my hair? Wear a gold chain? Reeboks? Or, better idea, when Tom Gibson opens the door of the Crematorium in Troy, just give me a shove, like the one Hansel gave the wicked witch, then watch the cadaver melt. A grand finale to *Said*. Call it *Gurgled*.

    Yesterday I got a lift to Sterling Library, where I took a lovely nap and got nothing done. Waiting outside for my ride home, up comes this famous academic who claims I stood him up for lunch. "My ribs," I tried to explain, but he'd have none of it and commanded me to apologize and kowtow. "Fuck you," I replied, just to be congenial. A friend more, a friend less, what does it matter? And *this* one a man for whom I have interceded over and again in matters of family illness. This morning I wrote him a note calling off our "affair." A Dear Alan letter. Doubtless he will bend his considerable intellect to getting even. What shits these academics are.

With "Luis" in the can, as it were, I spent the day touching up a segment of the diary—the Italian stretch—but really thinking of E. A. Poe's Light House and how to go about it. I *must* do it.

                                                                  Keep the faith

                                                                  Richard

---

NOVEMBER 27, 1989

Dear Peter,

    One of the complications of MRF (multiple rib fractures, as the Index of *Trauma* puts it) is that the acreage of one's house increases by a factor of ten for each FR. I have figured that these once snug environs now measure six miles in length and width. Rising from bed at 7 a.m. I begin to journey with might and main toward the kitchen, stopping in the hall (halfway) to water the horses, then arriving for breakfast at noon. After coffee, toast, and juice it is time for the return voyage, so you can see that I am on the road all day long. Or, on the other hand, is it I who have shrunk? And then there is Janet tiptoeing into the room to see if I am still breathing. Today I *drove* to the library and am quite full of myself.

    Your last two letters are perfect specimens of the genre. I think you the best epistolarian extant. In fact, I'm quite ashamed of my puerile scrawls in reply. Thanks for all the good bits and pieces: Pope's *Essay on Man* which I love and will begin to read again tonight. The pictures of Whitman—who had to be the handsomest man in North America. I love his face. If I were lying wounded in an army hospital and he bent to kiss me, I wouldn't lift a finger or an eyebrow, as I am sure those poor soldiers did not either. I am enthralled by your struggle to render Poe in paint. I've just read again Patrick White's *The Vivesector*, which is a great portrait of an artist. It made me think of you. When I get mobile, I'll look for a copy to send you. My friend wrote the enclosed which I am passing on to you. He is Alex Theroux of whom you have heard me speak. Alex is a fine fellow—spent three years in a Trappist monastery, fell afoul of two monstrous women, and, I think, now lives for his art. Which isn't a bad thing to live for. As, what else *is* there?

    I'm seriously worried about your poverty. When you can, try to stay here for a while post-Troy. You could use the break.

                                                                        Love

                                                                         R

SUNDAY THE 10TH OF DECEMBER, 1989

Dear Boswell,

The day has passed with the Light House blinking reproachfully over a thousand miles of churning sea—and no rescue in sight. I am, as usual, stranded. Perhaps this time I gamble *beyond* my means? Damn this writing! But then there is vanity to deal with, and I am once again that admiral who says, on the eve of a naval battle: "Never fear, I have taken the depth of the water, and when the *Venable* goes down, my flag will still fly." Or, better still, that Cockney star of the English music halls who, on the night of her retirement from the stage, says: "I 'ope I may h'allude to my past triumphs with *bigotry*." (Did she mean braggartry?) Well, Boswell, Destiny was in a mood of mischief when she introduced me to *you*.[42]

Miklos Pogany has just phoned to suggest that we go to New York on Wednesday. Considering the inertia in which I now swim, it will require an act of the *sane*—will, that is. For the first fifty-five years of my life I lived with the intensity of a puppet—every movement and gesture exaggerated, jerky, frenetic, and made in obedience to the Ten Fingers on High. At fifty-six I reached up to snip the strings and ever since have lain floppy, sprawled, and contented in an overstuffed chair. But then, I think, *Miklos*—what a wild delightful character—and a Hungarian! Yes, I'll go. A grand letter from Patrick Quinn today. About you he uses two adjectives: *appealing* and *enigmatic*, and ends by insisting that you return to Troy with or without me. So go.

Just returned from an opening of a gallery of prints collected by a friend who wants to sell them. Met there the whole of the Yale Intellectual *Establishment*. You'd have laughed to see the collection. The people, I mean. One woman who, when she heard that I own a Jan Matulka, dissolved into a "loathsome mass of detestable putridity"—Poe. And steered me to a dealer at 50 West 57th Street—Robert Schoelkopf. So I'll go there and say: "Listen, Buddy, I have. . . ." And then 6 St. Ronan Terrace will be safe for another year. And another woman so blonde I could hardly see her. A novelist would have soaked in it. Myself, I couldn't wait to leave.

I think I'll close this letter, altho there are three-and-a-half inches left of blank space.

Love

R

SUNDAY, DECEMBER 10, 1989

Dear Jamie,

Here at last is a letter with a purpose other than to divert (or numb) your sensibilities. And that is to thank you again and again for your many acts of kindness and generosity this past week, not the least of which was to lug the cadaver to Troy and back. I think I could not have gone without you to prop and bolster and fend. All in all we had a fine, exhausting time—so full of warmth and conversation and a pocketful of new friends, which in itself is a miracle. I have written nothing all week, preferring to lie on my bed and bask in the recollection of our visit to Troy where, I am glad to see, the city's blood still runs romantic, swift, and at high tide. I am pleased that you were able to partake, even if you had to choke down a plate of salmon. By now you have purged with a thousand cups of hot water? I imagine your large intestine—it is squeaky clean, which, as you know from my theory, will do wonders for your creativity.

I have begun *Israfel*, the biography of Poe by Hervey Allen. But it is too sad, and I must read it a verse at a time—like the book of Ecclesiastes—or I shall despair. It helps to read it at the library where I can look up and see the beautiful Yalies perspiring at their copies of Milton and Virgil.

My excursion to the Ladies' English Literary Club in Fairfield was great fun. Imagine twenty dowagers, each one smart as a whip and rich as Croesus, sitting in a circle in the center of which I stand oozing charm. The club is 150 years old, has only twenty members. One of them has to die before a new woman can be taken in. The waiting list is over fifty long. Afterwards there was sherry and macadamia nuts (three each), then lunch at a country club with only one urinal and a great view of Southport. It was a lot of fun, and I made some new friends there too. I only wish you had been there to see. Tonight Janet is giving a dinner party in the diningroom—a rare, if ever, event these years. So I have lit a fire in the livingroom and set the table. Don't sneer. It is how the bourgeoisie carries on. Myself, I could happily go to bed at 6 p.m.

I am reading a fascinating book on lighthouses for—you know. In January I shall begin. What with the curse of the voodoo painting and daring to tamper with Poe, I have a feeling it will be the end of me.

              Love

              ~~Richard~~ S. Johnson
              Esq.

P.S. It is high time I thanked Barbara for working on *Said* and for lending you to me for these excursions. Do, please, kiss the hem of her garment for me.

December 13, 1989

Dear Peter,

  Well, I can almost hear your wild malevolent laughter when you learn that I am sinking deeper each day into Poe's Light House. Once again, having sworn

NEVER AGAIN, I am chaining myself to the cruel pillar of fiction. It's no use my crying out NEVERMORE! The raven has perched and there he stays. It's all your fault. By whatever dark and obscene witchcraft you have come to take absolute control over my mind. I am helpless as a cockroach beneath your upraised shoe. My only resource is to write the damn thing and hope that will slake your lust. Somehow I doubt it. For three days I've been making notes, setting the scene, reading Poe and books on the history, architecture and archeology of lighthouses. For the present, I'm focusing on the style and tone of "The Domain of Arnheim," trying to absorb it into my fingers. I don't want to write a conventional horror story—a la "The Pit and the Pendulum" or "The Tell-Tale Heart"—but something more psychologically complex. While I shall bend every effort to retain Poe's three-page beginning exactly as it is, I have already departed somewhat. My idea is to let Poe tell his opening verbatim, then give an aside to the reader: "And here the Master lay down his pen." Then go on as if nothing had happened.

As I may have mentioned, the narrator is a young nobleman suffering from Obsessive-Compulsive Disorder which is thought to be a demonic possession. Actually it is a severe form of the condition known as La Tourette's Syndrome in which the sufferer is compelled to shout curses and filthy words at seemingly inappropriate times. To spare his family disgrace and himself shame, he goes to live as keeper of a lighthouse erected on a rocky reef in the middle of the North Sea. "As no other man save an eremite, by the force of personal circumstance and by my wish to retain what is dearest to me—my dignity—I have been thrown back upon myself." That sort of thing. He is not, however, alone. With him is his dog and a manservant who is a deaf-mute. Communication with the mainland is by homing pigeon. Every few months the cutter makes the perilous voyage to bring supplies. Twice the cutter has foundered with loss of life. You get the idea. Why don't *you* finish it? Which brings to you once again my immense gratitude for playing Figaro, the barber, to my *Black Swan*—now *our Black Swan*.

I have been interrupted by the Library Lamplighter—a man about my age who replaces the dead lightbulbs in the Main Reading Room. Armed with a grabber on the end of a long pole, he unscrews the old bulbs, then fishes a new one from inside his shirt where he carries them all around his belly. Into the grabber it goes, up goes the pole, screw round and round and—presto! A new day dawns. During the procedure he tells me that he has to go home and study, as he has a final exam tonight. Turns out he is a night student at a local community college, taking a course, Death and Dying, for which he is reading Elizabeth Kubler-Ross and the *Tibetan Book of the Dead*. Even the lamplighters at Yale are dabbling in philosophy and the other arcane mysteries. "Lots of luck," I said, whereupon the bulbs inside his shirt clinked like glasses in a toast.

Reading Room of the Yale Sterling Library.

So now I can return to Arnheim, or else descend into the maelstrom in search of the genius of Poe.

Love

R

December 16, 1989

Dear Peter,

Today I spent the morning reading on the lighthouse. Then walked to have lunch with Ferenc Gyorgyey. He applauds you and Norma for the possibility of the Lam Qua Grotesques being shown at Smithtown. I remain a bit edgy over any unpleasant fallout for Norma over the pictures, but perhaps I underestimate the Long Island stomach. Frank told me more about his seven year imprisonment, the torture, beatings—only now that Hungary is becoming free can he bear to talk about it. After lunch we went to read the original account by Gilles de la Tourette of the disorder which bears his name, La Tourette's Syndrome. It was published in 1885 (French). The narrator of Poe's/Selzer's Light House will have suffered from this horrible condition—characterized by manifold muscular tics (facial and bodily), echolalia, and coprolalia. Echolalia is the compulsion to repeat the words of the speaker as though to jeer. Coprolalia is the compulsion to say obscene, dirty words. The outbursts are sudden and unpredictable, causing shame to all present. It is to avoid the humiliation that my man will go to live in the lighthouse accompanied only by his dog and a deaf-mute manservant. That's about where I am. You must suggest to me a dramatic and critical denouement. I am mulling over your thought to include Light House in the new collection. Perhaps I'll write to Ms. Saletan at Random House.

In the mail today, a copy of *MD* magazine with, on the cover, a portrait of Anton Chekhov. His is the most beautiful face I have ever seen. I shall paste it on the wall over my desk. A photograph of Chekhov with his family confirms his extraordinary physical and spiritual beauty. I see now how Pygmalion fell in love with a statue.[43] I have written for another copy of the magazine to send you. Bill Ober has a piece in it, too. On top of everything else, my poet friend called—he of the fractured spine and obsessions parvificent (opposite of magnificent)—to ask if I can do some shopping for him. The list has but two items: toilet paper and something even more personal. Rather a narrow focus, don't you think? But, then, what do I know about romance?

On the way back from the Medical Library I dropped in on Rothko [at the Yale Art Gallery] for an hour. All alone in the museum—not another soul. I sat there until the interface between black and orange began to flame up, and that between red and black to hemorrhage. Am I beginning to see?[44] On the fourth floor, an exhibit of early nineteenth-century daguerreotypes (American). Eerie, powerful, moving—what faces! I surely wish you could see it. Speaking of old photos, of course I'm glad I showed you the ones of my mother. For that they have sprung to life. It is little short of a resurrection.

Love

R

December 19, 1989

Dear Boz,

One of the troubles with Christmas is the avalanche of "greetings" from every part of North America where I have stood myself up at a lectern for the past decade. Why do I feel it necessary to answer all of these good wishes? For my sins, for my black urges. And so, for two hours each evening, I inform my public of my hitherings and thitherings.

Today I awoke at 6 a.m. and, after a night of pulmonary congestion, declared the day smokeless. It worked until 4 p.m. when I lit up. It is unjust, to say the least, that I cannot inhale smoke without paying the price of dyspepsia and guilt. I went to lunch and saw, at a nearby table, two young Italian men—smoking with such casual grace. It broke my heart. I could not take my eyes from them. How they reveled in the act, while I had to steel myself to a cruel abstinence. But more and more, each day, I hear "Time's winged chariot" drawing near, and must go to my eternal reward. You can guess which I've chosen.

Tomorrow I begin to type the Lighthouse, having no firm idea where it will lead. On Wednesday I go to New York and will have lunch with the editor at Random House, to whom I shall propose that we delay the book til I've done this piece. Will she or won't she? We'll see. As she is twenty-eight years old, I can guess at my disadvantage. Old age is considered a vagary by everyone these days and I must pray only to be *indulged*. Or thought eccentric.

Do you not think it time for me to read *Said*? I promise to keep my hands off. Only to read.

Love
R

December 22, 1989

Dear Peter,

Another day at the lighthouse and a problem (I think) solved. The problem was: how to use Poe's entire fragment verbatim and then go on to finish the story in what must be a different voice. The solution: Introduce the story in the voice of J. J. Moran, the young resident doctor who attended Poe during his final illness at Washington College Hospital in Baltimore in 1849. During a period of lucidity, Poe tells Moran about an unfinished story that he regrets will never be written now. Moran asks Poe to tell him the story. Poe does. Moran writes it down. Thirty-five years later, Dr. Moran, still haunted by the story and by Poe, finds himself compelled to complete the tale. What follows is "The Light-house" by Edgar Allan Poe. The reader is left to wonder at what point the master lay down his pen and the doctor took it up. J. J. Moran is the real name of the young doctor. From the letters he wrote to the family and friends of Poe, we know that he was a fine fellow, although, as he admits, no writer. Anyway, that's how it stands at present. It all has a strangely coincident note. Perhaps I am the reincarnation of Moran?

I was pleased to see the Mills Pond House—it's quite beautiful—and to read the announcement of your—and Kevin's—duet. What with all you have to contend with, it does seem from here that you lead the most interesting and multifaceted life—at least the part I know about. As for the other parts, well, one day you'll tell me and if not, not.

Love
R

December 26, 1989

Dear Bos,

Your letter today was itself a work of considerable mastery. When the correspondence is collected (by you), it *must* be included verbatim. Hereabouts, we wallow in blissful exhaustion. Such all night hilarity and confab. Last night we laughed so hard a picture fell from the wall and smashed! And tonite, daughter-in-law Rossi-cum-fetus arrives. Only missing is Regine the Rhinemaiden. I am blessed. But weary. And no writing—except that Larry, to whom I told the story of The Light House, came up with twelve ideas for it. One or two are most appropriate and I'll follow up just to see. He *is* a clever dog, that boy, and terribly loving. He loves to manhandle his "famous little papa." As for my reading *Said*, I shall, with pleasure, and never utter a word, I promise. So fear not, it is *your* book, after all, as will be Lauderdale.

You're dead right about Bill Ober. His soul is not visible in his work. A sad life, a sad case. My friend Leon Lipson, Yale Law Professor, who grew up with Ober, told me that he was a ferocious bully. I just can't believe that, but who knows?

Peter, I am more than grateful for your attending to *The Black Swan*. You know I'd never, never have touched it again. In regard to our literary ancestry, I learned today that Johnson only reluctantly changed his "underlinen" every few weeks, and so the adjective for dirty drawers was *Johnsonian*. I hasten to set it down for the record that I change *mine* every day. On the other hand, I do not know how many times you have contracted a dose of the clap. Put that on record, if you dare. I *did* have *the crabs* once, but, I swear it, I got them from a young woman I treated in the Emergency Room. That Janet did not instantly divorce me is to her everlasting credit.

Love
R

Toward the end of December, 1989

Dearest Bos,

The bosom of one's family turns out to be an inexhaustible Amazonian tit, merely to cling to which for a space of two weeks is exhausting, however nourishing. We laugh, sing, play, dance, joke, tickle and *eat*. If I did not die of RIBS,

I shall surely die of this—but with a smile on my wizened face. To bolster my flagging strength I have put on my blue Troy shirt and poured a large vodka. What with Becky molesting me—a regular Lolita—and Rossi (daughter-in-law) two months gone, as we say, I am permitted to smoke only in my study, where I sit writing to you in a swirl of burning tobacco. As I must keep the door closed and the window open, it is exactly like the hibernaculum of a bear. You are the only one I know who would enter undaunted, or at least *senza rancor*, as Mimi puts it in *La Boheme* (ask your sister about that).

"Luis" arrived today from the typist in Milwaukee. It reads, I dare to think, rather well. Now, to correct it and add the dozen or so inserts. So it is, by God, *done*. This morning Jon the Beloved and I went to the Science Library—he to *compute* and I to wield a listless pen on The Light House. It begins to take shape. Pray for me in my hour of need. Please, Boz, stop referring to me as a genius, which I am most determinedly *not*, only a poor wretched scrivener with no blood in his veins. But with a heart full of lust to keep him going, yes indeed.

Thank you so much for Henry Miller on Rimbaud [*The Time of the Assassins*], which I shall dig into with delectation this my bedtime. You certainly know exactly what I adore to read. Does anybody else know me so well? By the way, your last letter but one—on Louis Kahn and Philip Johnson—is a winner. No, I never met either one. Nor did I meet Eero Saarinen—bad luck—who lived at 10 St. Ronan Terrace for a decade just before we moved here. His widow had just departed. It was *that* house I had wanted to buy, but $59,000 was way out of my reach, and besides, Yale sneaked in and bought it first. So that is why we live here. Yale sold it to Brustein at a pittance just to get him here. It was in that house that I dined with Gielgud, Irene Worth, Claire Bloom, Philip Roth, Jerzy Kozinski, Mildred Dunnock, Robert Penn Warren, Kathleen Nesbitt, and a dozen other notables. But that is all in the dim past and, as you well know, I see no one and haven't for fifteen or twenty years. And so much the better, as I never knew what to say to them. I *did*, I think, tell you about my gaffe with Frederick March.[45] It happened there, or at Maury's, I can't recall now. And to think that I've outlived them all, or some of them. Claire Bloom and Mike Nichols are still around. Nor even was I really a part of all that—just a curiosity for the others to glance at briefly. And poor Janet, who had to endure those painful evenings of not fitting in, wishing she were elsewhere, and *me*, not sensitive enough to know better than to subject her to the "great and the famous." Shit, man. I am no better than a Cossack. So now you know.

Love

R

P.S. Larry has read "Luis" and: "Well, no. . . ."!!

Almost 1990

Dearest Bos,

Happy New Year! Today I went grocery-shopping for my friend the poet of the four fractured vertebrae. Having delivered the orange juice, bread, milk, and sundries, I was treated to his *Ode on Masturbation* which is how he passeth the days til he knits and can once again go aprowling away the girls of Yale. At sixty-one, masturbation is rather more a noun than it is anything else, tho' I do vaguely recollect . . . I haven't looked it up, but I might be not far off in the translation: *Masturbare* = the verb meaning to pull, which would seem to make a bit of sense. It is my friend's *violon d'Ingres*. Okay, I'll elaborate. Ingres, the painter, really didn't like to paint; he'd much rather play the violin, which he did badly. All France laughed at the idea of its greatest artist cleaving unto an art that was not *his*. And so the word for hobby in French became *le violon d'Ingres*—Ingres's violin. I'll stop there and leave you to wonder at the vagaries of the human mind. Or hand.

Meanwhile, I have been assigned the job of putting Becky to sleep. As I am the only one capable of administering discipline in this house, I am the court of last appeal. Five minutes of faked anguish having been ignored, she is now fast asleep. Fascism is not without its charms. Besides, I will not be bossed around by yet another woman and that's that!

I am looking forward to your visit in January. You, will I deposit at the Beinecke Library to cut your teeth on Lauderdale while I slouch through Sterling Library in search of beauty and truth in a light-house. The hyphen should tell you that I am your most obedient servant

S. Johnson

P.S. I made the mistake of reading this letter before enveloping. It occurs to me that I am obnoxious, bestrewing all this Latin and French over Wheatley Heights. I'll make every effort to quit, but, as with tobacco and vodka, I am likely to backslide.

A letter today from the Baylor Medical Center in Houston full of praise and thanks for my near-fatal efforts there, and closing with a crescendo of disgust at my shameless smoking. Which makes me wonder what vices he, the great professor of medicine, performs in the dead of night while looking over his shoulder. "And I thought you were perfect," he wrote. Which stirs in me the suspicion that the concern for others' health and immersion in the sickness and death of his fellow men—so much the role of a physician—is an attempt to avoid his *own* mortality. At the very least, *I* know that *I* am going to die; while I do not wish for it, neither do I shrink from the expectation of it. Van Gogh died at age thirty-eight or so. The only thing I would have wished for him is the carnal love that was denied him and that comes so easily to ordinary men. I would gladly give him a decade of my own. Make that two.

Love
R

into the cave of aeolus

1990

JANUARY 1, 1990

Dear Peter,

    Did you know that the executioners (there were four) of Louis XVI wore breeches and three-cornered hats with large tricolor cockades? They executed the king of France with their hats on. And one, named Samson, without removing his hat, seized the severed head and held it up to the crowd—by the hair, letting the blood drip on the scaffold. While, in the mayor's carriage, two infamous priests laughed and spoke in loud voices. At least the head did not bounce beyond the leather basket onto the pavement—which often happened. Most touching were the words of Abbé Edgeworth who stood next to the king on the scaffold and said: "Son of St. Louis, ascend to Heaven!" Which all causes me to hope that if the Vatican releases Noriega to the Panamanians, they *won't* kill him. No matter that he so richly deserves punishment, that he is so detestable. History can't bear the affront of another guillotine or firing squad. Leave the bastard to Heaven, I say.

Just so do I open the year in a mood of religiosity. Now we'll see what happens. Last night an endless party at which the guests were forced to enact the roles of suspects in a murder. A more convoluted plot was never contrived. By midnight it had not been resolved. Janet and I and Jon drove home in a dense fog that was an exact exteriorization of the climate inside my skull.

About *Said*, I've become quite neurotic and now have qualms about *reading* it. Maybe I shouldn't, til it's published. A great shyness has come over me. The notion that I've said too much. Above all, I don't want to interfere with your work. I have too much respect and regard for you. Perhaps *after* you've gotten a contract. What a shivering mass of uncertainty I've turned into. Let's blame it on the ribs. I used to be a toughie.

I've almost finished the corrections and additions for "Luis" and, as usual, have developed a big disgust for the story. I think now it is just awful. But it exists, and I won't burn it, I promise.

I do wish you could meet Jon. He is as close to human beauty and innocence as anyone since Billy Budd. There is no guile in him, only generosity of spirit and kindness. To think that he is mine—and that I have him for another week. Think of Eden and you'll have the idea, almost.

Love
R

January 3, 1990

Dear Peter,

Any number of delights today. Jon, Larry, and I hiked down to the Yale Co-op where I bought three haircuts, a copy of Dick Ellmann's *Golden Codgers* (Joyce, Yeats, Wilde, etc.), a 1990 calendar, and a pack of Camels. Home for lunch and a German lesson from Jon. Now they've all gone off to ice skate and I have some hours alone in the sunroom, where I've just enjoyed your letters having to do with a slave anklet, your underlinen, and the rigors of *Said*. About which last, stop worrying about my reaction. I've said I *won't* smudge out so much as a single comma. My only demurral is that I doubt that anyone can possibly *say* what he *means*, or *mean* what he *says*. One of the potentials of the book might be that it reveals something of the process by which the "fiery clay" becomes the "wrought jar," if there is anyone out there who is interested enough in my work.

Yikes! A letter from a doctor in Cote St. Luc, Québec, admonishing me for not offering better advice to the graduates of the Mayo Medical School. He also took a rather ignoble pleasure in letting me know that the word *vaccimulgence is* in the Oxford English Dictionary, although he is willing to accept that, after Coleridge, no one has been apt to use it. So, I am scolded. Just wait til your Lauderdale appears and you too will receive such missives. Meanwhile at the Light-house:

Through the narrow window a pallid light casts upon the face of Mathias a stricken, rather a frozen look. Then he turned to see that I was there. And his face widened in a smile. He licked his lips before speaking.

"Did you sleep well?"

I nodded and opened questioning fingers at him. His eyes told me that he had, too. Unaccountably, my heart began to pound, as if I desired something I could not name. All at once I knew what it was. I wanted to embrace . . . to caress him.[1]

And so the plot thickens. My wretched pen goeth where it listeth without asking my permission. May the ghost of Poe forgive me for what I am doing to his Light-house. And won't the psychiatric crowd have a field day with it! Perhaps you will be the only one who will still speak to me. But then, I may just change the whole thing and behave myself. Do you the same, Boswell. By the soilage of my drawers, I swear I am your friend

                     The Doctor

January 6, 1990

Dear Peter,

The days are running through my fingers. I can't hold on to them. And up ahead looms Monday the Dreadful, when Jon must be surrendered to Germany. Larry and Rossi leave on Sunday. Then it will be only the Light-house to burn off the excess of feeling. I shall become like a monk who, assailed by impure thoughts, doubles his prayers and his labors. Today, we three men took up saws and hatchets to cut wood for the winter's fireplace. *Touching* is the word for the solicitude of those boys engaged in keeping their little parents warm through February and March. Touching, too, the little sidelong glances they exchange whenever I light a cigarette or pour a vodka. It is enormous to be loved so by one's children into old age. Fate owes me nothing.

A phone call today from a Methodist minister in Maryland informing me that 500 (!!) ministers have been writing sermons on my work. Then came the cagiest of questions: "Am I correct in assuming that your heritage is Judaic?" I tried to explain, but couldn't quite, and so must go to Johns Hopkins this spring to try again. *500 Methodist Ministers*, like Bartholomew's 500 Hats, will be there to diagnose my persuasions. Also, a letter from one Sam Vaughn at Random House asking if I'd write him a book. Obviously, the R hand knows not what the L hand do'th at RH.

Love

R

January 6

At 2:30 a.m. I read *The Murder of Gonzago*, the play within the play of *Hamlet*. His instructions to the actors are wonderful. But I would not have liked Hamlet much, I think, nor any in that play. The characters seem to me rather devices upon which to string his—Shakespeare's—enormous lingo. In fact, I confess: I've never laughed or cried in the theatre while watching Shakespeare, except maybe during the English lesson in *Henry V*, and the Pyramus and Thisbe bit of *Dream*. And, oh yes, at the sight of Lear cradling the body of Cordelia. I can relate to *that*. I'd rather *read* than see when it comes to W. S. But then I am a true peasant of Troy. The subtleties escape us every time.

January 7

And now Jon has left. We are awash. These departures are getting rougher for both of us, but harder, I think, for Janet. I have my work to console me, but she will be at sixes and sevens for a while. It is only now that I envy my bachelor friends. Damn. And then news of your piles! Honestly, it is worse than Job—what with our ribs and assholes out of whack. But I pray that by now your sphincter has sheathed its sword and you are once again able to enjoy a decent sit-down. If all the hemorrhoids I've treated were tossed into a heap, it would reach to the stars. To be betrayed by one's very own anus is a deceit beyond words. What a Judas of an orifice you have.

I love the photographs of Chekhov with whom I am hopelessly in love. I shall cherish the playbill which you can retrieve from the left top drawer of my desk—somewhat wrinkled and smudged with the tears and fingerprints of this inferior insect of a scribbler. And *Between Chekhov*—it is a little gem. I laughed out loud a dozen times. To think under what circumstances it was written—and you as Chekhov. You are a phenomenon.[2]

January 8

This has been a week dominated—it is the only word—by the Luis-Peter affair.[3] My second visit left me in tatters, with resolve shattering, and thinking, with Macbeth—"If it were done when 'tis done, then 'twere well/It were done quickly"—or I shall run out of courage for the deed. The complexities are yet to be unraveled. Next visit—Sunday at 4 p.m. I've jotted it all down in my notebook—not to write, but to try to convince myself of the wisdom of the act. Or perhaps it is the condition of my soul that worries me? How I should like to turn this one over to Mailer or Wolfe or any one of the assured literati. Perhaps I should ask Susan Sontag? February 10 is the day Luis has chosen, and I must see that through. O that coincidence of names! Or is it Providence telling me something I cannot hear?

As for *Said* and my letters to you—*protegge ma*—protect me. I am so effusive and lacking in restraint that only you can keep me safe from harm. So I am at your mercy. Cover up all the lies I have told you, all the flights of fancy, the bullshit, too, lest I not lie peaceful in my grave.

Sidewalk chat with a notorious Yale prof today. He said: "You are the one *authentic* writer I can name today" !!! And another long stupid telephone interview—for an American Medical Association newspaper. "Do you consider yourself a great writer?" "For heaven's sake, NO. I am a grace note that shall remain unheard." But the deal with Whittle is set. I only have to write 1200 words and get paid a Bastard's Ransom.[4]

January 11, 1990

Dear Peter,

I am still reeling from my encounter with Peter and Luis (the namesakes of those you do not know), and for one of whom I am called upon to be the Malach-ha-Mawis—the Angel of Death, if fifty years has not obliterated my scant knowledge of Hebrew. It is pronounced: MAWLOCH-HA-MAW-VISS, but you'd have to ask a maven to get closer to accuracy. All of which cleverness is obscene in the face of the tragedy.

At precisely four o'clock I knocked on the door. It was opened by Peter—exceedingly handsome (perhaps too?). Altho' we have never met, we recognize each other as presences on campus. He has made use of my writings in his teaching at the Divinity School. I am at the end of the AIDS underground. Luis sits stiffly on a sofa in what is called an invalid cushion—he has ulcerated hemorrhoids due to his intractable diarrhea. Luis is a short man, surprisingly unwasted, but pale as this paper and in obvious discomfort. A brilliant brave smile, even white teeth, close-cropped hair, a neat lawn of beard which does not quite conceal the black tumors on his face. He is a Mexican doctor, speaks with an accent. His hand is delicate, just-this-side-of-dead in mine. The eyes do not take part in his smile, only the mouth.

There is a plate of cookies on a table. Peter pours mugs of tea. For a few minutes we step gingerly about the secret. All at once the veil is rent and we are engaged. The air in the room is charged with impending death. And love.

I need to know how sincerely he wants to die. "Don't you have moments of happiness?"

"Only when Peter embraces me, kisses me. But in a moment that is gone and I am longing for death."

He says this calmly, without the least emotion. Two hours later, I am convinced. I would want it too. A lethal dose of barbiturates has arrived in New York City from Mexico. It will be sent here. They want to be sure it won't fail. They are curious about the "process." Luis wants only Peter to be with him, holding him. He wants Peter not to cry.

Me: "But that is too severe. Of course you must permit him to cry. He loves you."

Peter is afraid to be alone when the time comes. He is afraid he *will* cry. He is afraid that they will be found out—their "crime"—and that he will face legal action.

Me: "I'll be there, helping. But I don't want to intrude."

I want to be only the man who moves the scenery on and off the stage. I'll put diapers on him, add my bit of narcotics to the dose, retire behind a screen and wait, dark wings folded. Afterwards, I will *pronounce* death, call the authorities. And hope not to be caught. But it doesn't matter. I can finish Light-house in jail.

We speak of Death as Best Friend, not enemy. We deplore the denial of death which is the legacy of the Christian and Jewish religions. We remember that the pagans were far more civilized. They had the sense of return to Nature; that, no matter if a member dies, the tribe lives on. Luis wants to retain his dignity, and the control of his life—which now means choosing the hour of his death. But then there is Peter's grief. What to do with that? I wish only to be the instrument they may pick up to heal themselves. But there is the *LAW*, and we must be furtive.

Me: "Put it in your will: NO AUTOPSY."

Luis: "Si, si. That is best."

Love

R

January 12, 1990

Dear Peter—O Thou!

And so I am to be shorn of my *All at onces*? So be it. I bow to severity and will be the better man for it. I shall take up *Suddenlys* instead.[5]

Becky Saletan [at Random House] phoned. She's full of *Said* and *The Wounded River*, told me she called Borchardt and asked for the manuscript of *Said*. I urged her toward Lauderdale. You *must* come up now and transcribe a few of his letters to give to her. I swear I'll keep you busy so that you don't worry about your piles. Come to New Haven, copy all the Lauderdale letters, take 'em to Yaddo and perspire. When that's done, I'll cook up something else to keep you off the streets.

Philistine! Swine! You dare to write to me from the upper reaches of the Concert Hall? To the 7th circle of the Inferno with you. Have you no couth, no couth at all?

Worked today on Light-house and it begins . . . slowly. I have til mid-March (Becky says). J. J. Moran features in the story. Take care. I may need help putting Light-house together in time for the publication date.

Thine

R

January 12, 1990

Caro Pietro,

Cattivo Sogetto! (Nasty man!) What have you done to my swan but wrung its beautiful white neck? Ah well, perhaps it will sing once and die. I am consumed with curiosity to see it. I long to tell you dat you are all vet. With the library closed this weekend, I am forced to begin typing my notes on Light-house. Here you are in the well:

Holding aloft a torch, I descended the steps into what seemed the dark wet gullet of the Light-house, a grotto bursting with malignant energy. In the damp saturated air I could scarcely breathe. Even the torch struggled to stay alive, and burned low. The darkness here is utter, or would be were it not for a pale greenish gleam from the sweating walls. In the subdued light, strange shadows break apart, collide, fuse, chase one another in a wild metamorphosis. I saw that the walls are not vertical here but have been constructed as an ever-narrowing cone. And it was silent, for I no longer heard the buffeting of the sea, only *felt* the pressure of its immense weight. What could have possessed the builders of this tower to place at its core this horrid submarine well—like the lowest circle of Dante's Inferno where Satan weeps "with six eyes"?[6]

What do you think? Selzer truly in his element? Or derivative hogwash?

In the mail, the bound galleys of a collection of essays by a doctor—Gerald Weissmann. They are utterly brilliant—full of lore and learning, and so well crafted. I wrote a lavish blurb for the dust jacket. But I gnash my teeth in envy. He is much too good for my good. And, no, I will not write the introduction to a book on Chinese medicine, not even for the Emperor's favorite concubine. Sometimes I feel like a storekeeper whose shelves are bare but who is besieged by customers all the same.

AND IT IS MONDAY.

First thing, I read over what I had typed yesterday. Not a wise move, as now I must begin yet again.

By God, it is Wednesday. Yesterday, I had my second visit with Peter and Luis. I see now just what a dangerous project I have adopted. There is every likelihood of exposure, in which case I'll be the one in the dock. Peter is, he tells me, incapable of lying. So, if asked, he would have to tell the truth—that it was an "assisted death." The best I could hope for would be manslaughter. And a martyrdom of publicity. Yet I just can't abandon Luis to his fate. He is altogether too sweet and lovable.

                                                        Love

                                                        R

JANUARY 12, 1990

Watashuki-no-tomodachi Peter-san,

    It just means Dear Friend Peter in Japanese. The impulse toward Japanese comes from having discovered, in the attic, a box of letters I wrote to Janet from Korea in 1955. I have rescued them from the thrower-out-of-memorabilia and they will be yours to use as compresses for your piles. I read two of them with mounting horror. There is no sign in them of the writer that was to be. Lauderdale's are better. But, I doubt not that you will peruse every one of them with your gimlet eye. I was so very *normal* in those days, before the explosion in my brain. I also rescued a half dozen letters to Larry, my second son, who seems to have saved every scrap. I bequeath them to you. When I have gone to my reward you can expose me for the jerk that I was. Not before.

    Today in the mail, three essays by graduate students of Chuck Schuster in Milwaukee. Two of them are quite extraordinary, especially an interpretation of "The Hartford Girl." It is right on the button, and I have the extreme happiness of an author: that of being completely *understood*. When you come, they will be yours too. What a lot of work you will have when I have finally gone to my rest. Serves you right, you blackguard, for sentencing me to complete Poe's story. Somehow all Yale has gotten wind of the fact that I am doing this story, and just today I was asked if I would read it to the Ezra Stiles Fellowship. And *it* not written. I begin to feel rushed, and that is not good, so I must exercise caution and not yield to the blandishments of the academy.

    Janet is on the third floor clearing things out. I estimate it will take her six months to make a path through the rejectimenta up there. I've been reading in French all day in preparation for Poe. Only the French understand his genius. For

Americans, he is an outcast, something surplus. How wrong of us. The French know that he must be read through ultraviolet light or not at all. You must read Mme. Marie Bonaparte on Poe. She was a student of Freud and a member of that family. Very acute indeed. By the way, I've decided to call the doctor John Jacob Moran instead of J. J., which is a bit callous. The denouement must take place in the well. But how? Why aren't you here to discuss it with me? Ungrateful boy! I don't like being thrown back on my own resources anymore. I like talk. In any case, the journal will be encased in wax from melted candles in the hope that it will be found one day. In case you don't know, if you seal something in paraffin it is waterproof and it floats. So, even though the Light-house must topple and both men die (THE DREADFUL WELL!), there is hope that the log will be found one day. And so it *has* been, as here is the story. Very strange and difficult to execute. I'd rather play checkers on the Green.

Love

Junichiro Tanazaki[7]

January 19, 1990

Dear Peter,

About Canaletto, we see eye-to-eye. Once, while in Venice, I went to a palazzo, now called the Cinefondation, where a large number of Canalettos had been assembled. It was quite thrilling to turn from a painting to the city and back again. After a while I could not be sure which was real, which depicted. Or had I stepped *into* the paintings? The Cinefondation is next door to San Giorgio Maggiore, and constituted the totality of my sightseeing in Venice. You already know what I did the rest of the time.[8]

Light-house has twenty-five sheets of paper to its name, and racing. Every little while the pen bursts into flame and burns my fingers. Still, I am avoiding the climax, circling it instead with description of the tower, of Mathias, the well—and hoping for revelation.

In today's mail—in addition to your Canaletto masterpiece—two letters from friends each suggesting that someone collect my letters. Whoever would that *be*? And where, I wonder too, did Robert Louis Stevenson write this: "Life finishes with a better grace foaming in full body over a precipice than miserably struggling to an end in a sandy delta." Which brings me back to Luis and Peter. But of that, no more for now. Tonight, fatigue notwithstanding, I hope to hear the great Protestant historian, Jaroslav Pelikan, find the origins of the New and the Old Testament. He is an encyclopedia unto himself and a superb speaker. It begins at 8:30 though, and I may have gone to bed half an hour before. That's what happened yesterday when I intended to hear a lecture on the Greek Idea of Death and Beyond. So I'll be left to my own devices as to the Hereafter.

Something strange about writing Light-house. In every other story I have identified with the characters. In this, I identify not at all with the characters but with Poe himself. He has interPoesed himself between the story and me and will not get out of the way. Doubtless because the narrator *is* Poe? Who has become a fiction in my mind.

The notorious Richard *Seltzer* has struck again.[9] This time in the current *Harper's* magazine. Everyone wants to debate me on what *he* wrote. My only recourse is to write a scurrilous piece of libel, insert a *t*, and let *him* fight off the dogs for once. But his fame is spreading wildly and I am becoming more schizophrenic. Where is the man who will rid me of this pest? But here comes Becky and wants to play.

                                                 Love

                                                 Richard

JANUARY 22, 1990

Dear Peter,

Around a coffee table, 'tho it was tea that was served, Luis, Peter, K, and I. A moment of shock at the door when I see that K is a woman I used to know—at thirty-eight extraordinarily beautiful; at forty-five, not at all, but hard, etched. It is *my* failing that when she came forward to kiss me I stiffened and shook her hand. The meeting had a certain formality—each of us to speak in turn. Luis first. He has obtained seventy additional pills of levodromoran, an opiate. The phenobarbital has arrived. It is in the bedroom.

"A great many pills," he says. "Will I be able to swallow them? Will I vomit? Will they be *absorbed?*"

I'm next. "February 10 is too soon. You are not ready. Neither is Peter. I advise you to wait."

Luis covers his face with his hands and groans.

"I can't wait."

Peter: "Why do you say he isn't ready?"

Me: "Because he hasn't already done it. Because he has chosen a method that might well fail. A gun, a jump from the roof, yes, but pills. . . ."

K: "We are going to be found out. Your fame, your eminence—the press, the media will love it. You don't have what it takes to be a criminal."

In fact, I *did* ask a former colleague the other night what the lethal dose of barbiturates was. He *looked* at me. To Peter I say: "And you are unreliable. You can't lie."

Peter apologizes.

Me: "Don't apologize for virtue. It's stupid."

Peter: "But I'm letting you all down."

Me: "Christians always have, always will."

And so we conspire, plot, whisper, hypothesize. . . . What if they. . . . What should I say if they ask. . . . And I wilt. I'm afraid to go to jail and, even more, of the blaze of notoriety. But I can't abandon Luis and that's that.

Meanwhile, the Light-house proceeds. I see now that it will occupy me for months, not weeks. It shows promise, but not much more. On the 13th I will speak on "The Crematorium and Other Places" for the Philadelphia Institute of the Arts. Yesterday I attended the unveiling of a portrait of the first black man to receive a Ph.D. in this country. It hangs in the great hall of the library. It was immensely moving to be in the small crowd of people who listened to the president tell the story of this man who came from poverty to eminence in the face of all odds. The black students who were all about me wept and so did I. But then, I am a notorious piss-head and my tears must be discounted most of the time.

                                                  Love

                                                  Richard

JANUARY 24, 1990

Dear Peter,

So many riches amidst the poverty! You are that draggletail puppeteer working so many strings whilst falling out of his shoes. The man from the Pollock-Krasner Foundation [VP Charlie Bergman]—did you examine his scapulae for folded wings? And what about *Legacy* at the capital? I am blown away by the vision of it. And O! Albany! And *Said* and *Swan* and Lauderdale and *Town*. I shall make a pilgrimage to the cave of Aeolus, God of the Winds, that he will send a zephyr to waft some of these ships to harbor. You go to church, I'll invoke the Pagans. That way we'll have all the bases covered.

This day spent rummaging in my study for what to say in Plattsburg. Let other travelers bring a change of underwear; I shall bring two or three pairs of manuscripts in case of incontinence. *MD* magazine came today with "Desk," therein gussied up with an execrable piece of "art work." But a sweet apologetic note from [editor] Gerald Weissmann, who claims to have fired the poor wretch because of it. Too severe a punishment for so small a misdemeanor, I think. Where is Mercy? I know where: in apartment 17-D at University Towers in New Haven! And a letter from a doctor insisting that I place the accent on the first syllable of *lunaqua* because the dactyl is the "most beautiful foot" in all language. So it is to be *loo*-nah-kwah. Far be it from me to turn my back on a beautiful foot. I do vaguely recollect one or two whose toes were edible.

I have re-stashed the 1955 letters I wrote to Janet from Korea. They are puerile, if not downright insipid. I disown them and I spit on the callow moony crybaby who wrote them. Now I am off to the library to arm-rassle that Lighthouse to the mat. I shall try the toe-hold on it and see.

Love
Richard

January 26, 1990

Dear Peter,

I'm just home from the Lizzie, where I visited with Stan Levy—psychoanalyst, editor of the Freud/Lou-Andreas Salomé letters, author of tons of erudite books. He's just finished a long essay on a French writer I much admire, Alain Fournier. I have a translation of Fournier's only novel and will lend it to you. Then you too will kneel and kiss the hem of his garment. Fournier was killed in battle during WWI. There is a fascinating five-volume correspondence with his boyhood friend of whom he was dearly enamored, and who became his mother-in-law, which is the next best thing, I guess. Stan, at age seventy-six, is rereading Proust—an act of sheer optimism. But there's no quenching these intellectuals' spirits once they are on fire. The vault was opened at the Lizzie, it being Friday, and I examined a wonderful book on tithing by one Selden, an eighteenth-century lawyer. Also a thumbnail-size almanac printed in 1837 in honor of Queen Victoria upon her coronation. You'd have loved it.

Next day.

I think I must diminish the role of Mathias, the deaf-mute. He must be not a friend so much as a manservant—but one of utter purity—a kind of blank white page before which the narrator is seated—in awe. Perhaps he is an angel? As the pain of writing this story increases, "It's a game," I tell myself. "Relax." But I don't believe that for a moment. It is a matter of life and death. Lightning has struck the dome of the tower where the two are "toiling redly" at the lamp. Mathias runs out to the gallery. "I did not see him fall, if fall he did. But heard the calling of a single clear note—like the blare of the last trumpet—that lasted only for the time it would take for a man to plunge to the reef."

Tomorrow at 4 p.m. I visit Luis and Peter for the third time. Nothing in my past life has prepared me for this. It is terra incognita and fraught with peril. And

Tearoom of the Yale Elizabethan Club.

no one to ask. Only to be borne along on my own blood. I long to absent myself from this city for a while. These distant appearances will come just in time. I am getting mired.

Love

Richard

January 28, 1990

Dear Peter,

    I'm just home from Luis and Peter. What prevails there is a conspiratorial atmosphere. We go over the details, finding fault with each scenario, then starting over, but now bound together for life by the act. We meet again on Saturday. I fear and believe that it will boil down to *me*. The others are worried about my "fame," that I will be the lightning rod for publicity, the press, police, etc. What holds it together is our covenant with Luis. How will we behave toward each other—the surviving three—afterwards? I have nothing of the criminal in me and am bound to make a mistake. If caught, I shall write a *J'accuse* that will rival Zola's declaration in the Dreyfus Affair. As it may be written in prison, Oscar Wilde's *De Profundis* may be a more accurate comparison.

I am increasingly worried over your poverty. What is to be done about it? Can you hold out til one of the ships comes in? I gather that *Swan* is giving you fits. You will rue the day you offered to put your *cygneture* on it (look it up). You'll have heard about the letter from Sundance. So, as soon as you have a bird in the hand, we can find out if it's worth two in the bush. But already my lilied liver wishes you would go without *me* to be dragged along on your coattails. Don't worry, if they say yes, I'll go. But not without *you*.

Love
R

January 31, 1990

Dear Peter,

If there is anything more boring than being interviewed, it is reading interviews of writers. I have just read an interview with one of our celebrated writers in the *Paris Review*. Frankly, I'd rather sit in on an AA meeting. My one New Year's resolution was to quit being interviewed—cold turkey. I've already broken it once and am about to again—this time over the phone for the *Albany Times Union* prior to my visit in March. The only advantage of telephone interviews is that you can fidget and scratch away.

I was perked up yesterday by a good long chat with Alex Theroux at the library. If he isn't the sweetest man, who is? I'd like to put you two in a room for an hour or two with my ear to the keyhole. Alex is teaching writing at Yale and pounding out articles for *Art & Antiques*. Which reminds me that I have done nothing about *my* assignment there. May never, as I am up to my old evasive tricks these days. I've quite run out of discipline is what. I can't even bring myself to request from *Art & Antiques* a xerox of the piece I wrote on the anatomical drawings of Casserius and Leonardo—which of course I have lost. Alex read it and swears it is damn good, but how do I know?

I am elated that *The Legacy* will be in Albany while I'm there, as I surely want to see it at last. I imagine you must feel a soupcon of pride at the notion. If you don't, I do. About Sundance, do send along to [director] David Kranes the finished version of the *Swan* and your own credibilia (I made that up). But your idea of retreating to the former version! Is it a failure of nerve? Come clean. Which brings me to the graffiti in the Men's Room at the Sterling Library, where my favorite stall has been newly decorated with a long curved penis burrowing in an ass. Hallucinating over Luis on February 10, I sit there telling only my beads. "Ora pro nobis," I say to myself, and go upstairs to write another line or two of the Lighthouse. Perhaps the artist of the stall is only kidding? I somehow doubt it.

Which brings me to mull over the wisdom of attaching your name to anything, lest posterity, that dreaded beast, get hold of it. Somewhere in the nineteenth century a doctor first described the curious phenomenon of a crooked penis. Anatomical dissection proved it to be due to a scarring down of one of the "corpora." I can't recall whether it's the *corpora cavernosa* or the *corpora spongiosa*, which fill up with blood and thereby produce what is known among certain tribes as a hard-on. Anyway, due to this selective scarring, the corpora are asymmetrically filled and, when erect, the penis will bend so as to prevent intromission and to cause pain. The doctor who discovered all this was named Peyronie. Ever since, it has been called Peyronie's Disease. How would you like it if 100 years from now, whenever people heard Peter Josyph, they thought of a bent pecker?

Your Slut,

R

FEBRUARY 1, 1990

Dear Peter,

It occurs to me that there is a great hole in the portrait of myself which I have given you over the span of our friendship. Issues are skirted; elisions and hiatuses abound; secrets kept. Which brings me to wonder about the validity of the autobiographical statement. I only know that there are some paths of confession that I could never take. What cannot be told must therefore be divined. Let's, however, go on.

For Heaven's sake, will you stop apologizing for *Swan*? I am certain that I will see the justice and wisdom of your treatment. I am the most malleable of men, and can be bent to fit, I assure you. You are correct in your amazement at the lack of courtesy in editors. They haven't the least idea of quality. But there you are, and I am hoping that you will at least get some money for *Said* so as to be able to go on with your work. Here it is Friday and tomorrow at 4 p.m. my penultimate meeting with Luis, Peter, and K. February 10 is the day. Or night, rather, as Luis prefers to die at night. I fully understand that it is harder to bid farewell to the sun than to the moon.[10] No one can imagine what this is costing the four of us. I can only hope it passes unrecognized, leaving us three to suffer the torments of our action in private. It is no easy thing to kill. There is no thing harder to do. Meanwhile, I scour the newspapers for word of a miraculous cure that will save us from this—that is both folly and wisdom at once. And the boy is *so* sweet, *so* beautiful, hardly older than my son Jon. Have another vodka, Richard, and get hold of yourself.

This afternoon, a walk in the park where I met a young homosexual who asked me if I were a married man, said he was looking for a husband. As I said goodbye, he called over his shoulder: "Am I adorable?" "Yes," I said, "yes," like Molly Bloom, only I didn't mean it. What is it—life—all about? You tell me. I begin to think that I am living too long.

Love
R

FEBRUARY 3, 1990

Dear Peter,

Final meeting with L, P, and K. On the way home in the car, by one of those mysterious correspondences of life, the opera matinee was *La Gioconda*. Flicking on the radio, I listened to the aria called *Suicidio*. I begin to think that all I have done is go from Doctor to Witch-Doctor.

Not to argue you away from your beloved vegetarianism, but the vegetable kingdom itself scorns it, what with carnivorous plants such as the Venus Flytrap. So have a lamb chop. New Haven is the location of this year's big cat show. So *tout le monde* is walking around carrying one of those loathsome creatures. I am convinced that people who adore dogs and cats hate other people. I have the eternal satisfaction of having once eaten cat in the form of *kimchi* in Korea. And for two cents I'd do it again.

That phone call was from agent Denise Shannon. "Georges [Borchardt] and I both . . ." With sinking heart I gathered they will not do *Said*. You were right. A direct approach to the editors is next. It is most depressing, but you are not to yield. Life is to slog on. I just can't write another word about this, Peter, but you know how I feel. And that finishes this that I put in an envelope out of sheer habit alone. It is *not* worthy of the steadfastness of the U.S. Postal Service.

Love
R

FEBRUARY 7, 1990

Dear Peter,

I am still smarting over the Borchardt Agency's decision against *Said*. It is hard to accept. I did ask Denise Shannon whether she would write the contract if and when you sold it. She said that she would, but then so would any agent. Word has come from Laurence Baudry in Paris that a tiny theatre has contracted to produce her adaptation of my French books [*La Chair et le Couteau*, directed by Philippe Ferran]. Although the theatre, called Théâtre Du Guichet Montparnasse, is small, she assures me that it is "famous known." She wants me to go over for the first night, but I shan't. My mind, every chamber of it, is filled with Luis and Friday night. I am quite unable to write, but I'd better try, as work is massing and advancing upon me like an "archipelago of clouds" before a storm. I have to pay for the redecorating of St. Ronan that is now in progress. Grub Street's what it is. I do have a sort of typescript of the Light-house, but only a bare-bones affair. I'll show it to you when you come.

The day was saved by learning that Colorado means reddish. I trust that you are using Colorado among your other pigments? The only other real pleasure was obtained by sharpening a pencil and inhaling the smell of woodchips. And look what I found! In the Autumn 1955 issue of the *Sewanee Review*, an article by Dick Ellmann in which he outlines the very tale he suggested I write: "The Mirror: A Tale of Aran" [in *Confessions of a Knife*]. Told to friends by James Joyce. I'm glad I hadn't seen it before I took up that particular pen. I'd never have had the nerve.[11]

Love

R

FEBRUARY 7, 1990

Dear Peter,

Another tossy-turny night left me in no condition for such a thing as a Light-house this morning. Instead, I read the poems of Seferis—a Greek poet—which were of benefit to my soul. If they are that good in translation, what must they be in the original?

Are you hung in the Well [of the Legislative Office Building] in Albany? Bill McQuiston phoned and I told him about it. He will spread the word in Troy so that our friends there will journey 'cross the Hudson for a look.

How did it get to be Wednesday? An emergency lunch with Peter and K. She had confided in a sympathetic lawyer who advised that I stay out of it. The pathologist would know the time of death. I would have been seen entering and leaving the apartment. I'd get *caught*. So, I have been fired and given a reprieve. What do I feel? Relief. And shame that I will disappoint Luis. If it doesn't work, he'll be brought to the Emergency Room and resuscitated. Yet another martyrdom.

The photo of *The Legacy* is gorgeous. Your account of the hanging in Albany is riveting. I can't wait to see it. What a superhuman feat.

THURSDAY.

Awake at 4 a.m. shuffling words on a page til dawn. Discovered on my walk to the library that some of the trees are leafing out! The times are out of joint, all right. Tomorrow at this time, Luis, with any luck, will be dead. And I not there to see him safely aboard Charon's boat, put pennies on his eyes, stuff a rolled fiver in the oarsman's cowl.

I gave your name to *Newsday* to review Gerald Weissmann's book of essays [*The Doctor with Two Heads*]. I hope they call you.

Love

R

FEBRUARY 10, 1990

Dear Peter,

It did not work. As I knew it would not. The old father did not go to make sure, and the poor children lost their way in the thickets. Luis would not die. He is in an Intensive Care Unit with a tube in his trachea and a needle in his vein. It is no easy thing to leap off the planet. That he did not take all of the pills—did he hesitate? Peter, unable to lie, had told Luis that I would not be coming. Imagine the boy's disappointment, his feeling of betrayal. Imagine then my shame and self-disgust. Imagine Peter's turmoil—relief that Luis has not died, pain over the miserable fate in store for his lover, and the fear that Luis will not forgive him for initiating the resuscitation. And K's horror at finding Luis, not dead but deeply asleep, breathing like a tree. None of us will emerge from this unscathed. What malevolence stage-managed this cruel fiasco? Surely not God. Somehow the notoriety that would have been my dessert, and probably imprisonment, seems a lower cost. To have the prize slip from our grasp, and to feel utterly responsible—that is mine to chew from now on; to be left to grieve over life instead of death. Well, it is to weep over the days of martyrdom to come for a sweet, innocent man, and to be confronted by my own failure of nerve, which is the same as a lack of manhood, as I see it. There is relief in other quarters here—Janet and some friends—but I don't share it. They are not equipped to get beyond my personal safety. And Luis, all the energy for suicide spent, will have to drink down not the poison he loved, but the fullest cup of physical degradation. I shall go on Monday to beg his pardon. What I have taken in this is my own measurement. And I am not so tall as I might have claimed.

R

FEBRUARY 19, 1990

Dear Peter,

I've been mulling over [a photo of] *Science and Charity* at the Yale Art Library.[12] Ought one to consider it at all? Would anyone, if it had not been painted by Picasso himself? I surely doubt it. First, there is the dead, static quality of the four portraits, lacking in inventiveness and quite grotesque, at least in the obesity and misproportion of the child, and the coarseness of the nun who is another of those religious who could "strangle a wolf with her rosary." In the hypocrisy and absurdity of today's art market, I doubt not that some sharp barker at Sotheby's could get 250 million yen for it, but I would price it more realistically—at a tag sale—for ten bucks, and that for the signature alone. To me, the painting shows an adolescent understanding of people and objects. It is entirely lacking in the gusto which characterizes Picasso's mature works. In fact it is sentimental, if not downright bathetic. Heresy, you say, to denigrate the very deity of modern art. Still, it is time to be honest. I, frankly, find it difficult to step into the story of this painting. It is too much a cliché of Spanish Death. Still, I am well aware that Picasso was sixteen when he painted it and that I am also six and one (reversed) when I see it.

Well, then, what is there to celebrate here? The wall, the contrast between the hands of the doctor and the patient, perhaps the pleats of the counterpane. But that's it. The woman's face, originally turned toward Science, is now toward Charity. She seems preoccupied with her pain and shows little real interest in the child or in the cup that is strangely suspended from the nun's fingertips. Well, I'll look some more and then write the piece. Oh, one thing: There is the greenish yellow smell of the sickroom, the odor of decay hidden beneath the sheets, and the utter silence. But perhaps that is Selzer, not Picasso. I suppose it is evidence of Picasso's condition as child prodigy, but I've never been moved by the prodigiousness of children. It is a phenomenon, but quite lacking in meaning of life. So speaketh an ordinary ignorant viewer of paintings. From such a painting, who would have imagined the explosion of genius that was to come?

Don't fret over my reaction to *Said*. I'll read it again, and again. Life is interesting, if nothing else. The fact is that I don't like myself very much any more is a kind of bigotry that is self-directed.

Love

R

FEBRUARY 21
DALLAS

From the restaurant (two vodkas helped) to a reception for wealthy benefactors. Then the talk. First the dean spoke and thanked the donor family. Then the dean delivered a fifteen minute oration. I could tell the exact instant of climax. Then my friend introduced me at length, invoking Apollo and half the inhabitants of Parnassus. By now it was 8:30. It was either die or go to the podium, and as I refuse to die in Dallas, I had to soldier on. This morning I took a walk in the traffic and among the debris. Every house is guarded by a burglar alarm and a dog. Pansies, tulips, magnolia in bloom. Even they are ugly. I learned that I am the third to give this lecture here, preceded by Vann Woodward and Leon Edel, biographer of Henry James. Poor Vann. So he too came to Hell and back.

February 25

I learned in Dallas that Luis died. You can imagine my tangle of feelings: Elation that it worked; dejection that he *is* no more; relief that *I* did not kill him. It is over.

March 17

The play—*La Chair et le Couteau*—opens in Paris on April 24. The woman who will play the role insists that I be there. It is her big chance, and the publisher is also eager. Press interviews have been arranged—the literary and medical establishment has been mobilized—receptions, lectures, parties, etc. But I DO *NOT* WANT TO GO. The only real reason to do it will be that I can take the train from Paris to Stuttgart to see Jon. I just today put the finishing touches on "The Lighthouse." I am modestly satisfied. I surely do owe *you* the inspiration to write this story, and I am immensely grateful, as you can imagine.

March 21

About the piano, you will be amazed to learn that it is coming back. My first win in thirty-five years. I tell you—the tide is turning! And it only cost me six grand to pin her to the mat.

I dispatched "The Light-house" to Random House in disgraceful condition, as I insisted on scribbling all over it up to the last second. Nothing really ever gets *done*, does it?

April 7

I've just read all your lively brilliant letters that had accumulated in my absence. What a virtuoso epistolarian you are! And I revel in your progress with *Town*. But Peter, dear Peter. The editor of *Medical Humanities Review* sent me a copy of the excerpt from *Said*. I read it, and shriveled up. I see that its publication would be quite inappropriate *and* injurious to me. It is just another example of my saying *yes* when I mean *no*. A lifelong defect. In any case, I have written to *MHR* and so expressed my reluctance. I can only hope they will choose not to print it til after my death. It is extraordinarily hard for me to disappoint *you* in any way, as you are so close a friend, but I *know* this would not redound to our benefit. Let's set it aside.

April 10

I am fully engaged in convalescing from my lecture tour. All 208 of my bones are fractured and my softer tissues have rotten spots all over. This house, upon my return, was piled high with manuscripts of books, plays, poems, sent by hopeful writers, and invitations to do book reviews. Are you interested in another hand-me-down? I am mighty anticipatory over your *Town*. Just tell me when I can come to see it and I'll be there reaping secondary gratificatio.

Façade in Troy, New York.

The editor of *Medical Humanities Review* was suitably downcast over my reluctance to see the excerpt from *Said* printed there, but caved in to my paranoia. Forget it. I just could not see my remarks about female surgeons, other surgeons, etc.—all very condescending—come to light. I don't need any controversy and should learn to close my mouth on the pill of silence.

Man, I'm weary. Surgery was a snap by comparison. To hell with retirement. It's a delusion. Forgive my epistolary lapses. They have nothing to do with affection.

April 12

Such a lot of nice weather—and it has been congenial to my pen, as I have been writing six pages a day. All in the memoir of Troy. The book takes on its own life and I begin to have zest for the enterprise. Zest for anything at my age is a miracle.

Poor Laurence Baudry, the brave actress who is producing and acting in the French version of my books. The Paris publisher will give her no help whatsoever, which is what they gave me, the bastards. So she is on her own against the snobbery of Paris, which is monumental. I've decided not to go to France—it's just too much. And I am now quite fully engaged in the memoir of Troy, and I don't want to leave it.

APRIL 14

The only good thing about poison ivy is that it is not terminal. My pecker itches for you. (Editor's Note: Not to be taken either literally or figuratively, but as in "my heart aches for you.")[13] By now, the worst will have passed. I'm pleased to hear that the *Times* is taking note of *Town*. I long for your success.

Here's a story of treachery: I learned on my recent lecture tours that *Taking the World in for Repairs* could not be obtained anywhere—this from five of my hosts. Viking/Penguin did not return my calls until today, with the news that the book was out of print and that Morrow had requested reversion of rights so that they could reprint it. A downright lie! Morrow knows nothing about it. Viking had not even informed Morrow, much less me. Another lie: of the 12,000 books printed, 6000 were sold and 6000 returned *damaged*. I called the editor a liar, he took offense, I reiterated it. And so I am left in limbo by yet another unbeatifiable publisher. I must now try to get the rights back myself and find another publisher. See what I mean by the esteem in which I hold these vipers? I'm going for a walk in the park.

APRIL 18

By now, I pray, you are no longer itching. No god in whom I would believe would create such a plant as poison ivy, therefore I have no choice but to remain an atheist. Poison ivy is just further evidence, if any were needed, of the sublime indifference of the universe to the plight of man. As for *Said*, your letter pricked me much as the blisters did you. I agree: the sound of my voice is disgusting to me. I can't bear the silliness of my utterances. When I read my remarks about female surgeons I all but vomited. How could I have said all that? Except out of a wish to acquiesce, to say *something*. In any case, rest assured that I won't nix publication of *Said* when the time comes. I'll just put my hands over my head and duck.

I did go to a seder, but unwillingly, as my sympathies are only partially with the Israelites. Also, I do not approve of the way Jehovah handled things. Doubtless He was the God who thought up Poison Ivy.

This week I am beginning to add my memoirs of Troy to the diary book. I am thinking of casting it in the manner of Rilke's novel/memoir *The Notebooks of Malte Laurids Brigge*, without the least attention to story line, unity, cohesiveness, and all those virtues. It will be instead beautifully disjointed and carved like a roast chicken.

Here's another book I won't write: for Macmillan, *My Sojourn in Surgery*. This time I said *No* and meant *NO*. The wretched man is coming anyway to blandish me with money, praise, and the promise of immortality. Cut out the first *t* and I might waver.

APRIL 21

While waiting for *Imagine a Woman*, I've tried working on the diary (Troy), remembering all sorts of dark happenings. Being molested in Proctor's Theatre on Saturday afternoon. Being told to take a pail and scrubbing brush to the sidewalk to wash off the bloodstains where a whore had been beaten by her pimp in front of the house on 5th Avenue between Jacob and Federal. Of what exactly *am* I a product? In other words, who am I? About *Said*, I remain abashed, hangdog, shamefaced, guilty. And alarmed.

APRIL 26

Yesterday I trained up to Boston—how I love the train—and saw numerous birds along the shore. I sat in on a writing class where two students read their essays aloud for me. One by a girl with bulimia—and about just that. The other a boy writing of his suicide attempt. I was wrung out at the end. Both astonishingly powerful pieces by nineteen year olds, so we don't have to worry over the next generation of writers—if they live to grow up. Then I read to the faculty—about fifty writers—an extremely fine group. They are all teaching my work in the composition department, had a thousand questions, to all of which I responded by lying. After that, dinner at a lowdown restaurant where I ate goat balls. Yes indeed, my first swallowed testicles of *any* species. They were shockingly tasty, so now I'm wondering about my sexual persuasion. I felt extraordinarily virile on the train home this morning.

A letter from Harvey Ginsberg at Morrow: "The Civil War letters sound intriguing, but I have to doubt that they are for an allegedly generalist imprint such as ours." Now really, is that human speech?

APRIL 27

A night full of mares. All having to do with Jon, whose surgery for a hernia has been complicated with a testicular thrombosis. Poor boy! How we fret and berate ourselves and bewail the vast distances between. Parenthood is a never-ending tribulation. That *anything* works out is a miracle.

Last night, dinner with Dorothy Horstmann, the *real* discoverer of the polio vaccine, and Dan Wilson, a historian I met at Muhlenberg College who is writing a history of polio. He is altogether a superb human being. As he will be in Paris in May, he promises to see my play there and report back.

Where, by God, did April go? It is beautifully hot in the garden and I read about Joan of Arc, the poetry of Milosz, and the stories of Nabokov until it is time to come in and take a shower.

April 30

Your review [in *Newsday*, of *The Doctor with Two Heads*] is superb—just what I would expect from you: thoughtful, balanced, and perhaps a wee bit generous. Don't expect gratitude from the likes of Weissmann. He has an immense ego that will have been pricked by your few gentle words of demurral.[14]

Word from my Paris agent and witch, who went to the opening night of *La Chair et le Couteau*. She pronounced it "excellent." It is in a very small theatre, she writes, and doubts there will be much press coverage. But Laurence Baudry, the actress, has arranged for coverage by the medical press. I want her to succeed, as she has spent all her time, energy, money, and talent in this venture.

May 2

As I have no wish to be bopped on the head, I shall not hinder publication of *Said* any further. I am having a cross erected in the backyard and will be rehearsing my crucifixion thereupon. You must come up and ladle a dipper of vodka into my parched mouth when the time comes. Despite all good intentions, I have written nothing for two days. I'll charge back into the ring this afternoon and hope for the best. Anyway, *you* are accomplishing enough for the both of us, so my conscience is, if not clear, moderately opaque. I've changed the title of "The Light-house" to "Poe's Light-house." After all, it is *his*.

The William Morrow book will require a superhuman effort. Part of the problem is that I cannot find the pages of manuscript that I need and have to keep hunting in my study. I've just about decided that this is to be my *last book*. Oh I'll keep scratching away, but no more books. Too old for books. *You* write books. I shall follow the advice of Epicurus: Love Obscurity. But I've just been taken on the Board of Incorporators of the Elizabethan Club. Didn't have the heart to say no, so now I run the place. The others on the board are over ninety years old.

May 6, 1990

Dear Peter,

Well, it has finally happened. I have fallen in love. With a book. Ah bibliophilia—the dark vice. What torment it engenders, this filthy habit which separates one from the fellowship of decent men. Oft and again have I left a bright room crowded with handsome athletic surgeons to slink off to my solitary pleasures and my shame. O God, I wish I were dead. The book for which I have tumbled is Volume III of *The Book of Knowledge: Jay–Mortmain* (one needs no further alphabet—thou art all in all to me). Volumes I, II, IV, V, etc.—they are as the planets of the void, undiscovered and perhaps undiscoverable save by some bookstall serendipity. Oh there have been other, casual *affaires d'amour*. One, a spineless Spanish-English dictionary with whose pages I had been altogether too flippant. And a dog-eared uriniferous edition of *Household Medicine*, a giant compendium of poultices, plasters, unguents, counterirritants, charms, amulets, incantations, and gesticulations all designed to ward off disease. But never a grand passion such as this. Herein are:

Anne Caldwell Marsh, 1798–1874, born at Lindley Wood, wrote more than twenty novels, one called *Mordaunt House*. And:

Locri Epizephyrii, where there is a temple of Proserpine. In the battle at the River Sagras, 10,000 Locrians defeated 130,000 Crotoniants with great carnage. And:

Samuel Marsden, a missionary who wrote a discourse on *Intercourse with the Maoris*. Oho! Marsden, so that's your game. Do as I say, not as I do! And:

J. Proctor Knott, who earned notoriety by making humorous speeches ridiculing Duluth, Minnesota, and Marschner's opera *Der Vampyr*. And:

The county of Marmaros, where I would die to live. And:

The fate of Marquette's bones. And:

Kingfish. See Opah, it says. Alas, I shall never see Opah. Perhaps my children or my children's children? And:

King George, a county in Virginia, the valuation of whose real and personal estate is $1,511,329. *Here* is the stable, rocky, unwavering worth of man.

So now you know my secret. Reveal it only *after* my death. I shall meanwhile offer *Said* to Macmillan as so directed by you, whom I obey in *almost* all matters.

Love

R

May 8, 1990

Dear Peter,

Nothing ever works out. David Kranes phoned to ask me back to Sundance, then hastened to tell me that he is going to assign the play to another director to whom he is absolutely committed. I begged, wept, entreated, but—no soap. So I must either go alone or not go at all, the latter being my preference. I told him I would confer with you and let him know. He made no comment on the revised play. It is ironic, to say the least, that had you not restructured the damn thing and coaxed me into writing to Kranes, I would never have gone, or be in the position of deciding *whether* to go. The only reason to go would be in hopes of a later production which *you* might then direct somewhere else. The whole idea of Sundance gives me fits of anxiety.

My son Larry and I went birding for five hours this morning. A heavenly time. We tramped and climbed and saw everything with wings except an angel. He is the very best companion in the world. So kind and caring and *normal*. I could spend the rest of my life's mornings just that way and never write another word. I begin to think of retiring yet again. But first I must finish *The Book of Troy*. Meanwhile, the news from Paris is favorable. Everyone likes the play. I congratulate myself again and again on not going to see it.

Love

R

May 16, 1990

Dear Peter,

I like the announcement for *Town* very much. You and Kevin look quite bloodless, like things seen on x-ray: Knights of the Living Dead. One day in June I want to come see. I'll ferry over from Bridgeport. I did spend Monday in New York. I arrived to find that the editor from Scribners had *forgotten* and was at a sales conference in Florida. The big shot from Macmillan knew that he wouldn't be there, but never told me for fear I'd call it all off. I surely would have. He dragooned the editor's assistant for lunch, and they are all eager for me to write the book. I therefore set impossible terms. I also told them of *Said*, described the process by which it was written, the format and content. They said NO. I then told them that perhaps some of the material in it would find its way into the projected book. "What then?" I asked. Whereupon they said that if I agreed to do the book, Scribners/Macmillan would pay you handsomely for use of that material! Next I went to see Borchardt, who had already been phoned by the forgetful editor from Florida, who made him an offer (not enough) for the book. Again I discussed *Said*. Again he turned a deaf ear. His principal objection is to the dialogue format, which he says won't (except for Bill Moyers) sell. I told him that Scribners would offer to pay you for use of the material in it. He lifted a finger and purred: "He'd be wise to take it." He then figured it out in dollars and cents. I'd keep trying to get it published if I were you. If I do decide to do this book, however, and if you haven't had any luck, I shall put in the contract that you are to be well paid for any such usage. So, if all else fails, there will be money.

I next went to Becky Saletan, said what about *Said*? She said NO. What next? The six stories are now completely edited, with only a bit of pulling and hauling at [the title story] "Imagine a Woman." The dust jacket is grotesque and ugly. But Random House looks on it with favor so far. Yesterday I gave your name to *MD* magazine as a reviewer of a book on Louise Nevelson. I hope they call you. Keep daubing.

Love

R

June 13

What a project, your *Town*. Has it killed you? I fear it has. I am bowled over and over, tumbled, bestrewn, spattered, and riven asunder by the magnitude of your accomplishment. The list of paintings in itself is a *Do*-cument—and three sold already! I pray for reviews, fame, riches, sex, and truckloads of tahini to come your way. Now I long to come and see for myself. I know you are now in Washington making arrangements to be hung next to the portrait of John Foster Dulles, so we'll see when you return.[15] The pamphlet you wrote is just a little gem, nothing like it ever seen before.

With Janet in Germany for ten days, I am staying home to work on Troy, lowering a bucket to the dead and hauling it up full of cries and whispers. It is strange, and there is danger in remembering too much.

The *New York Times Magazine* may print the "Malpractice" piece, but I am concerned about being sued by the plaintiff and his lawyer. Altho' no names will be used, the case may be recognizable. The *Times* lawyers will decide.

June 18

Keep me posted on the numbers and enthusiasms of visitors to *Town*. And although I don't know the Cannon Office Building, it sounds fine for your *New York Signatures*. Think how many people will view it this summer, and perhaps the *Washington Post* will take note. The titles of your short stories give me indigestion. Whatever could they be *about*? Intriguing and smile-producing.

The manuscript thickens a bit each day. I hope to do the final writing in July/August, then hand it to Harvey Ginsberg with a flourish. Then with a huff and a thump I'll sink to the floor and the rest of the proceedings shall interest me no more.

My Allentown friend Dan Wilson returned from France, where he and his wife went to see *La Chair et le Couteau*. The theatre seats thirty people, the curtain is a sheet of clear plastic, but the performance was excellent, I'm told, and the reviews favorable. Afterwards they went for coffee with Laurence Baudry, the actress, and enjoyed it all. They spent all next day looking for a copy of my book and finally went to the publisher, who excavated a copy from the warehouse. I am not exactly a household name in France.

June 27

You just can't imagine the delight I feel in the success of *Town*. It's nothing short of thrilling. Demur however you will, I'll have none of that and will just set up here on the Terrace smiling and basking in reflected glory. You must send me every scrap of news. Here there is no such sense of accomplishment these days. Troy goes on being Troy. This afternoon I'll stay home and type some notes. I see that it will take through the fall to deliver this baby. But I am not suffering—it is a pleasant sort of masochism to stalk with patience one's childhood. And with *Woman* now behind me, I'm free to do just that.

Sundance looms and I'm filled with misgivings. I am too old for Summer Camp, and then there is the problem of *Swan*. Damn that Peter Josyph, who would not let sleeping *Swans* lie. The director—or is he the dramaturge?—phoned yesterday. He'd read the story in *Repairs* and raised the question of the shifting of focus from Rosalie to Anna and Ken. I agreed to send him the original, i.e., Williamstown, version. I think I shall be typing all night in Utah just trying to acquiesce and placate. Don't worry, I'll bring my lucky stone.

Macmillan will not leggo of my leg. There are daily phone calls from Ken Warren—mastermind and polymath—and from Robert Stewart, editor of Scribners. And look out! They insist on coming *here* for the capture. At least I'll be safe for two weeks among the Mormons, so the trip will have some use after all.

July 15, 1990

Dear Peter,

    Home. And what a time it was. I have rewritten the play yet again, keeping what seemed to work from both earlier versions, writing new material, adding, subtracting, tinkering until what there is—is a play. I have retained your beer drinking experiment as I do love it. The earring is back, and altogether you might not recognize the creature. I was assigned a director, two dramaturges and four actors. All but the one who played Anna were superb, and even she came along in time. We rehearsed, restructured, rewrote right up to the reading at 8:00 p.m. on Thursday. These readings are really quite tense, a high value placed on them. The audience consisted of seventy actors, directors, dramaturges, and sundry visiting firemen. I was fully prepared for disgrace, full of self-loathing. Why had I come? But to my astonishment the thing actually rose into the air and flew. Even the dogs and cats wept. At the end, a standing ovation. And a multiplicity of plans for productions. I remember only Playwrights Horizons. Circle something. Louisville. In the excitement I've forgotten the others. I've told everyone about you, your plays, and everyone expressed interest and curiosity. Come September, it is hoped that you will show your work. I'll give you the names.

    A huge part of the success was due to the actors who played Rosalie and Ken. Really gifted, those two. The director is a sensitive man, an actor, who drew forth all the nuances. And best of all the two dramaturges, one of whom sat down and restructured the play, did every bit of the detail work, and picked me up each time I flopped down. My instructions are to type, cut and paste, and send it off. Even I can handle that much. Peter, I really have trouble believing that Thursday evening really happened. Perhaps I made it up—another one of my fantasies. I do owe it to *you*, without whom, as well you know, that play would have lain dormant for keeps. So thank you. My dream is that you will one day direct it and we will work together.

The new version of "The Occasion Fleeting" is just fine.[16] Send it off with my blessing. A good idea to approach the university presses with *Said*. Maybe one of them will bite, as the academics do know who I am. And I like the idea of taking Poe, Whitman, et al. to Washington. Leave *Legacy* where it is. You'll hang in two capitals. Now you need to get back to *The Wounded River*. And we need a visit.

Love
Richard

July 20

I've a few letters from Sundancers requesting copies of *Swan* which, in its newly typed version, looks more like a cygnet than a swan. So little! There is a man named Andre Bishop at Playwrights Horizons, whatever that is, who will read it too. So I am doing secretarial chores instead of working on *Troy*. Meanwhile, my tomatoes are ripening on the vines and the heat is satanic here. I go to swim at the Yale gym every day at 4 p.m. Swimming, I have decided, is boring and odious.

I long to hear about your paintings. When you come I shall listen with every one of my ears. And what are you doing each day? Thinking? Writing? Daubing? When do you go to Washington to be hung?

August 10

Troy inches and swells. I continue to type my notes and think perhaps it will be a book of its own, as you have wished. I have already started to save the money to pay back Harvey Ginsberg for the second book. I don't want to do it and that's that. Also, I finally nixed Scribners, so I am rid of all obligations and can scratch away in peace.

August 12

It's been a struggle. Trying not to smoke—because of the tracheitis. Lovely nights of coughing, wild dreams. But today—only one cigarette! That's a return to the state of virginity.

This morning I reread your play *The Last Colored Lightbulb in Louisiana*. The humor is grand. "Chop and save" and all that quick wit. Very Beckettian, right? Now you must write to tell me whether it was ever performed, and how long the play runs. It is fifty-three pages. Is that a full-length play? I'm asking out of ignorance, of course. You must also help me out with the play's meaning, the duel-like dialogue in which Paz and Greene reverse positions. Why "brother pig"? What about the mumbling girl? The blood bread? It is all fascinating and mysterious. Do enlighten me, and do also forgive my being obtuse. My mind has *not* many mansions.

I need to establish the tone of the memoir. I surely do not want it to be gloomy or elegiac. Intimate, yes, but with a certain reserve for dignity's sake.

No word from anyone on *Swan*, save for a NO from Robert Brustein. I have ceased to anticipate any. Which would be all right. I don't seem to have a lot of faith in it myself, so how can I expect others to? Really, it's not first rate, I know that. I have concluded that the "success" at Sundance was not the play's, it was mine, a measure of my popularity there and having little to do with the quality of the work. It's what comes of being adorable. You can't believe a word that is said.

August 20

Janet and I are in the midst of a nightmare that will have no end. I'll tell you about it, *but*, please do *not* write to me of it or mention it to me in any way, as I *cannot* hear it spoken of. Our daughter-in-law, [Larry's wife] Rossi, about to deliver her child, had the sudden onset of a rare blood disorder that is usually fatal. She has recovered somewhat. The baby, Hank, is profoundly damaged. We flew to Virginia to give support, but now are back at home. We are devastated to the point of sitting and staring. I bleed for my kids. Can't eat or sleep, much less write. Everything seems trivial. The suffering is extreme. Okay—not a word. One *can* live too long, I see. Those who do not involve themselves with others are safe from such calamities. I won't mention it again. Do you the same, *please*.

Hope you get funded somehow for *The Wounded River*. Met Vann Woodward today and mentioned it to him. He is *pleased* you're doing it. If I can help by getting his say-so on those grant applications, let me know.

August 28

What keeps us going? As for me, I am quietly winding down—like a music box that hasn't a note of melody left. The Marquis de Ginsberg phoned to ask me to fork over the manuscript. I told him it wasn't anywhere near done, so he has given me until Columbus Day. I need another year. Can they put you in jail for tardiness? I hope so. Nevertheless I shuffled the desultory pages all day yesterday and again today. It's like the Augean Stables—it would take Hercules to flush it clean. Presently I am grouping the pages into headings (more or less). Troy, River, Father, Mother, School, Saloons, Crematorium, Trojan Whores, Me, and Return. As is my wont, I am running out of patience with the thing. I alternately like and loathe it. Mostly the latter. But I've found a way to use parts of "Malpractice," "Crematorium," "Desk," and "St. Mary's Hospital." It is bliss to think that I am writing my very *last* book. I am already casting about for a way to be of some use thereafter. What fun to think of beginning again. Also, I want to study Greek so as to be able to read Homer and Sophocles. Just the thing for an old man. I hope you can tell I'm writing this with my Mont Blanc. The luxury of it. But don't tell everyone or they'll bring back the sumptuary laws which imprisoned people who dared to display their wealth.

SEPTEMBER 16

I don't know if I told you that Arnold Schwarzenegger's brother-in-law, Robert Sargent Shriver, called. His mother Eunice had read the *Redbook* version of "Whither Thou Goest" [in *Imagine a Woman*] and decided it would make a TV film.[17] The son is a lawyer who does venture capital, whatever that is, and one of his companies has to do with film, so he is buying an option on the story. He is sure it will be done. Borchardt says the other stories are being looked at, so who knows? And so what? I am utterly uninterested. The guy from Macmillan calls daily now, the latest with an offer to take out life insurance on me for the amount of the advance so in case I die, my heirs won't have to pay it back!

The *New York Times* is a huge pest over "Malpractice" and I heartily regret selling the piece to them. Also, it makes me nervous, as I imagine someone will sue me. I don't need that and would doubtless die of it. For the same reasons I gave up surgery, I shall now give up writing. Bah! to both of them.

SEPTEMBER 20, 1990

Dear Peter,

So, McFarland is willing? That's fine to have in your pocket—the hole in your pocket—but the lack of advance is cooling. On the other hand, it would ensure a good library sale and they would keep it [*The Wounded River*] in print a long time, which the trade presses would not. Will they wait? I am delighted about the Vietnam Memorial Gallery show.[18] Lots of exposure plus a good spot. Good work.

No news to report except for sloth, idleness, and melancholy. I do not write. Did I ever? Some of it due to the presence of the Germans. We sit in the garden speaking that gargle of a language and drinking beer. But Jon is an angelic presence. That boy would lend grace to Paradise. This afternoon we are to be joined by my brother, who will stay a few days on his way to Troy. Neither one of us can keep away from that haunted town.

Here's another job I will turn down: Whittle Communications, a publisher in Tennessee, plans to issue a series of books related to medicine, each written by a big shot, each about 100 pages, each containing ads from ITT, Federal Express, etc. They're to be distributed free to doctors, paid for by the ads. They sent one dreadful example on how to sway opinion to get ahead in business. I am asked to be the General Editor of the series, not to write a book—which is a new twist. The lady will call back on Monday for a yes or no. I'd rather hustle my ass in Harlem than be *that* kind of whore. No final news on the option of "Whither" for TV, nor any on *Swan*. Just as well, as I wouldn't be up to participating in any theatricals. I have enough of them around here. "Malpractice" will be in Sunday's *Times*. I will not read it. I'd break out in hives if I did. Let us pray that I not be sued. The *Times*'s lawyers promise that I will not, but I fear the worst.

The very next book I want to read is Harold Bloom's *The Book of J*. Beyond his eccentricity, Harold is an original and great fun to read.

Becky at one and a half has learned a new word: *Fuck*. She says it all the time to make us split our sides. Of course she thinks it is *Fox*, but we know better. *Fuck!* she cried at supper last night, then joined in the merriment with a sweet smile.

              Richard

SEPTEMBER 26, 1990

Dear Peter,

Congratulations on the award! Buffalo is a fascinating old city, rather like Troy only with the lake instead of the river, and bigger, of course. There is a black lesbian bar there you might want to visit. Bring your own tahini.

The first advance review of *Imagine* came out in *Publishers Weekly*. It was most favorable. I am "a truly talented practitioner of the storyteller's art." So now you know. Never mind, it will be yet another worst-seller. I've been through it before. Dozens of letters about the *Times* piece, all rather comforting. I wait for the boom to fall, but I am no longer sorry to have published it. The *Salmagundi* [excerpt of *Said*] looks great. The interview is superb, thanks to you. We are in print *together* after all.

Last night at 1 a.m. the mansion in back of the house caught fire. Janet and I were awake all night watching the conflagration and wondering when our house would be next. The most enormous, frightening fire. But today all is still. And dead, the building a corpse.

              Love

              R

October 10, 1990

Dear Peter,

I had a brawl with Harvey Ginsberg, but it is patched up—sort of. He has taken the book off the spring list, so I am free to poke at it *ad libitum*. It *seems* to go well, but then I discard 90% of what I write each day. A friend gave me to read Russell Baker's *Growing Up*. It is so good that I have lost confidence in *Troy*. *Imagine a Woman* will be in your hands the end of this month—the first copy. It has to be out this week, as I am, in the end, forced to Book and Author it after all on October 18. George Plimpton, Jonathan Spence, and Moi. I dread it—250 educated ladies reeking of toilet water. Let Plimpton carry the day.

No real news about *Swan* except a phone call from one of the actresses at Sundance who was at Louisville and reported it is "under consideration." The *Times* piece has gotten around, so now I am the darling of the malpractice crowd. It is to be reprinted all over the place. The publisher whose editor job I nixed now wants me to write a 25,000 word "book" on five doctors of my choosing to show Medicine in a good light. They'll pay $70,000 to turn me into a whore. That Ginsberg poem conveys *my* physical reaction—but not *his*. I can't quite imagine the pleasure of getting screwed up the ass, no matter the artfulness with which it is done. It has *got* to hurt. So, no, I won't do that either.[19] I'm delighted that you will go back to the theatre. You must. Those plays just have to be done. Let me know when you will appear at the Beinecke.

Love

R

October 12, 1990

Dear Peter,

The clutter in this study has reached the stage of submersion. Hercules, where art thou to cleanse the stable of horseshit?

Having turned down the editor job, I must now say no again. What they want are four upbeat profiles of heroic, saintly doctors to stir the hearts of the several hundred thousand physicians to whom the book would be sent *gratis*. Any profit to Whittle comes from the ads with which the text would be punctuated. The whole idea would be appalling were it not for the seventy grand for 25,000 words—a mere eighty-five typed pages. Comes to $3 a word including *and* and *the*. Tempting? Well, yes—but, I think not. Besides, there is still corn in Egypt. If I finish the memoir I can collect it. The memoir has transformed itself from centipede to slug, but one is fiercely determined. *The Black Swan* sleeps on with his head buried under a wing—no longer even interested in his own reflection. It has been turned down by almost all the theatres to which it was sent. They are all having money troubles, so I guess that will be that.

The rain is falling in dollops and slathers as I write. Only missing is a guttering candle to turn this place into Otterholm—the light-house of Edgar Allan Poe.

Love
R

October 23, 1990

Dear Peter,

So proud of you, that I am, for those prizes. Rothko, look to your laurels. Tremble, Motherwell. Here comes Josyph! And I'm delighted with your decision to return to the stage. Commit armed robbery, highjack a theatre, hold the audience hostage and make 'em watch *Rue Picasso, Adventures of a Red Ball*, all the rest, under the threat of grenades. I'll guard the stage door.

Your notion of how to accomplish the Whittle book ain't half bad. I probably would have to do *some* of the interviewing, though, just to break down any reserve toward the *laity* on the part of the *clergy*. I have two physicians in mind. One is Frank Lepreau, a great man and surgeon who spent ten years at a hospital in Haiti, came back and worked in Appalachia, and is now practicing in Three Rivers, Massachusetts. The other is a young woman who graduated from Albany Med the year I gave the Commencement Address there and got an honorary degree. She had been a prostitute, drug addict and, virtually uneducated, got turned around and eventually became a doctor. She does family practice in the rural Midwest. I haven't picked the other two or three yet. I don't have to say yes or no til November. I'm still leaning to NO.

Imagine a Woman has arrived and I'll get a copy in the mail pronto—maybe even this afternoon. The dust jacket is ugly, but I didn't paint it. I did do that Book and Author after all. Plimpton was a colossal bore, read for one hour an unfunny piece on football to an audience of 200 *ladies*. I walked out in the middle to smoke a cigarette. Calvin Trillin didn't show up, so Jonathan Spence, the China man, filled in. I was frantically amusing in a room that was hot as Nebuchadnezzar's oven, and with a microphone that you had to insert in your mouth in order for anyone to hear you. Dreadful. But all the ladies reminded me about their gall bladders and varicose veins, so it was nostalgic. And they all bought books. Well, I told them to.

Love
R

October 29, 1990

Dear Peter Prize Winner,

I now have sixty typed pages of the memoir. Each morning, instead of going to the library, I go to my study and type. It is infinitely boring and depressing. Meanwhile, Sundance has invited me to write a children's play. Can you imagine? They've got the money for a new children's theatre program—lots of it, so doubtless I would be one of many dredging up notions. Of course I'm not going to do it. And of course I'm not going to write the Whittle book either. When the man phones on November 1, I shall fend him off. Not refuse, quite, but say "I prefer not to" a la Barlteby the Scrivener. The money would be nice, but I have the wrong-shaped head for this stuff, and it is not my fate to be rich. I'll get by . . . ♫. Ditto for Macmillan, so that's that. I am free, free at last—only to finish the memoir. Isn't that nice? I can stroll and swim and go to the Lizzy and chat with Harold Bloom. Heaven. This Thursday I must speak at the opening of the new New Haven Library. Couldn't say no. To a library? Never!

The Yale Co-op has 150 copies of *Imagine a Woman* and is actually selling some of them, so the recession couldn't be that bad.

                                        Keep the faith

                                        R

November 5, 1990

Dear Peter *Joseph*,

Once again I tell you how pleased I am with your burst of creativity in painting. The article I thought grand. Where will you stay in D.C.? How will you live? Do they sell tahini there? Is it possible—you *will* finish the portraits in time? And your sale—I like that the best. Far as I know, you've sold three or four or five this year. Not bad. Best of all is the one-man Viet Nam show. You are on a painting roll. Don't stop. Forget the writing for now and keep daubing.

The boom was lowered on me today. Apparently, many months ago, I agreed to write a critique of one volume of *Literature and Medicine* for their retrospective issue. Of course I forgot or had no intention of doing it. A call from Anne Jones, editress and friend, insists that I perform. So the Troy book and everything else is to be set aside and I am frantically at work on this unwanted job. A rather wimpy pilgrim came on Saturday, an internist at NYU who desires to be a writer. I tried to foist it off on him. He was eager to do it, but Anne said NO. Janet wouldn't let the wimp in the house, so I had to take him to Yorkside Pizza for lunch. He introduced himself as *Doctor* Voigel. Can you beat it? His handshake gave me the willies. Damp and limp and any other four-letter words ending in *mp* you can think of. Thursday I must speak at our new city library. All the ladies will come. I must get a haircut and be charming. The haircut will be easier. The Whittle man is miffed. The Macmillan man phones every Monday, Wednesday, and Friday. Perhaps I'll yet take the money, run, and hide.

I am in daily contact with Myra Sklarew [president of Yaddo] by phone. They want to hire one John Nelson, my friend, to run Yaddo while Myra goes around to raise money. I hope he takes the job. I hope Yaddo survives. When do you go there? Cheer everyone up. They need it.

Love

Richard *Seltzer*

November 25, 1990

Dear Peter,

Your letters from Washington are simply marvelous. I love the idea of you back *in* the closet.[20] It is good to know that you are making the most of the National Gallery.

The *New York Times* review [of *Imagine a Woman*] was quite disappointing, but my spine is too stiff now to cave in over it. Three other reviews were most favorable. The manuscript of *Troy* is now up to 190 pp. I am beginning to think that I should go somewhere for a couple of weeks in January to wrap it up. Perhaps Yaddo if there's room. Perhaps Troy. Much of my time is spent drafting that review of *Literature and Medicine*. I couldn't get out of it. Painful, as I have little good to say about it and will doubtless lose six or seven friends in the process.

You must tell me every detail of your exhibition in Washington. How does it look? What are people saying about it? It is *too* exciting for words. This will be a short note as Becky has just arrived and insists that we play piano together.

Love

R

December 1, 1990

Dear Peter,

Your review [of *Imagine a Woman* in *Medical Humanities Review*]! I should really die right now, as I shall never be so ready to enter the Kingdom of Heaven.

Saying thank you seems utterly inadequate. But, thank you just the same. I haven't seen any other reviews save for the *Times* and the three publishing magazine reviews, the last three being most favorable. Unfortunately, it is the *Times* that will squelch it.

I simply *must* get away to Troy to finish the memoir. Lassitude is a problem I shall surmount. Meanwhile, I inch along. February will be the cruelest month. I go to Halifax for three days, then to Kauai for five, then to L.A. for three, then by night-flight to Albany for Troy/RPI. The whole idea of it stuns me. No use farting against thunder, however. Have I told you that your letters are really first rate? I'm saving them all to return to you for posterity. Let her deal with them, I say. Tomorrow a young female pilgrim arrives at the library from Hartford to worship. You, I feel, would make the most of it. I, the least. After that I go to a ritual circumcision up the street. They're still doing that against all common sense. As for me, I prefer the penis neither cut nor uncut. But it seems to matter mightily to some.

I hereby take you on: I'll write the Prioress's Tale and you take it from there. But I've quite forgotten what I am to do. Please write and tell me again—the point of view. It will be my next project after *Troy*.

Love

R

P.S. The abyss of despond. Just heard our little Hank has *no* pituitary function. How to grapple with *that*?

P.P.S. Just reread your review. I have *never*, nor ever shall I, receive a more sensitive and intelligent one.

R

DECEMBER 2, 1990

Dear Peter,

A sleepless night—full of horrors of a pituitary nature. At 11 o'clock I met with a pilgrim from the University of Hartford who is writing a "psychobibliography" (whatever that is) of Richard Selzer for her class. And in the mail today, a turn-down of *Swan* from Playwrights Horizons. "Too symbolic for us." But I am enjoying the short stories of V. S. Pritchett. You *must* read them. Not at all like mine. I met him at Bellagio—a grand lark of a man—now ninety years old. This afternoon we went to a ritual circumcision down the street. Quite barbaric and unpalatable. We all stood around and watched the foreskin come free. We have not advanced at all from 5000 B.C. The circumcision was performed by a former

A street in Troy, New York.

student of mine, a silly giggler. Do you suppose the terrible myth that Jews drank the blood of a Christian child at Passover (shades of "Little Saint Hugh") arose from this replica of human sacrifice? Only missing was the stone slab of an altar and a priest in a long robe.

Yesterday and today, despite (because of?) my despair, I have written honestly and well in the memoir. Walking the streets of Troy in my mind, I find myself encroached upon by shadows. I peer at them long enough and they draw near and begin to moan and sigh. You see why I cannot permit myself to be rushed to *produce* this book. The process is unfinished; it dilates like pupils—slowly, as twilight deepens—to admit more light. And to hell with every other project. It is this one that consumes me. I could write it for years. For the first time, I begin to see my life as out-of-the-ordinary, its crucial moments, the wild excesses, the humiliations, the fires with which I have been singed.

Sitting here in my study at 6 p.m., I listen to an owl hooting nearby. It is the loveliest sound, so mopey and disconsolate. I hope he gets a mouse tonight. I hope *I* get a mouse tonight—or tomorrow or the next day. Not bloody likely.

Love
R

DECEMBER 17, 1990

Dear Peter,

Fate has dealt her cruelest blow. My little grandson is blind and deficient in pituitary function. There is nothing to be done. We are plunged into black despair. Whatever else I am, I am primarily a father. The rest does not matter at all. Janet fills the house with her wailing. I prowl all night in silence. There are two acts I am ashamed to commit. I am ashamed to cry and won't. I am ashamed to die with anyone watching—the helplessness of it, the ugliness. Let's not write to each other about this. I couldn't. Only to say that Lear was lucky to be able to give out his four howls. I continue to believe that there is some purpose in affliction. Else, why did Christ get up on that cross?

                         Love

                         R

DECEMBER 29, 1990

Dear Peter,

    I'll be waiting for you in the basement of Sterling Library, and you must know how much I'm looking forward to it. My God! You and Kevin are truly embarked, or is it unleashed? No less than the *Lives of the Saints*.[21] I do hope the Manhattan space comes through.

    As for the reviews of *Imagine*, I am trying *not* to read them. Well-intentioned friends insist on sending them to me. Janet devours them and puts her thumb either up or down. L.A. and S. F. ↑, Washington ↓, that sort of thing. But the book is not being ignored, as everyone, it seems, wants to take a poke at it. What with the huge new expenses related to my poor little Hank, I have caved in on the book for Whittle and Co. I wrote a letter of intent and, if they are still interested after my turn-down a month ago, I'll peck out the damned thing, but now toward a good purpose. That will take care of 1991 so far as any real writing is concerned.

    I've just finished the C. S. Lewis letters. They are really quite wonderful, altho' the Christianity is rather labored and convoluted at times. At others, it makes excellent sense. The truth is that I envy his religiosity. It is no cinch to endure life without love *and* faith. To say nothing of good looks and a dog.

    See you soon

                         L

                         R

lazarus rising

1991

JANUARY 1, 1991

Dear Peter,

   Happy New Year. I know part of it will be, as you will be at Yaddo. The Troy book is as good as done. I also finished a 1500 word article for *Newsday* on books by people who have had serious illnesses and lived to write about it. I've used Fanny d'Arblay's mastectomy as an example of neurotic exhibitionism—but gently.[1]

   The holidays were tough. Daily phone calls to and from Larry. We are terrified of the future. The baby is flourishing—perhaps too much so—he is very fat, and I wonder has it to do with the pituitary deficiency. The thing is attached to my mind like a leech and cannot be pried off even in my dreams. Worst is the lack of faith in God before whom one could lay this. Janet is inconsolable, although I try. I have told her that she mustn't compare the child with any others, that he is unique, piling grain upon grain until what there is is a life. And perhaps each tiny milestone—a word spoken, a laugh, some vague proof of recognition—will gratify more than were he normal. I say all that with great stage presence and then my own courage leaks from me and I leave the house.

Well, you'll soon be here, so perhaps I'll hand this to you rather than mail it. I try to imagine what it is like to begin to make a collage, when the canvas (or whatever you make it on) is still bare. Makes me think of when Adam was but a red outline in the soil of Eden.

Love
R

JANUARY 6, 1991

Dear Peter,

What a grand visit, so long overdue. I've corrected the typescript of two and a half tapes of Troy. I am shocked to see what a slim little volume it will be. Harvey Ginsberg will surely feel short-weighted. I shall resist any impulse to padding.

I've spent two days on my neighbor, who fell while chasing her cat and fractured her humerus. She is garrulous to a fault, the opposite of Keats's "still unravished bride of quietness" (from the "Grecian Urn" ode). My nerves are shot from the breathless flow of her drivel, my sanity only saved by vodka and tobacco. There's no use your flinching. They *are* my best friends.

On January 18 I lose my virginity. Not only will I have signed with Whittle, but Macmillan/Scribners phoned and I said yes to a book on surgery. I go to meet the publishers on that dreadful day. I understand fully that I am surrendering my art, but the baby's medications amount to $30,000 per year. I can't hope to raise that, but will spend whatever time I have left pitching in. Strangely, the sacrifice of my writing is the only thing at all consolatory. At least I can be a man. I'll close by remembering one of the letters of Horace Walpole, who urged his correspondent to tell him about all of his *movements*. Even unto such peristaltic minutiae does my own curiosity toward you extend.

Love
R

JANUARY 8, 1991

Dear Peter,

Up at my usual 5 o'clock to escape the agony of the bed. Read the *New York Times* with mounting disbelief and horror over the stupid war that is coming next week. Is it possible? Damn Bush and Sununu et al. They are mad. In the afternoon I went to the gym but had no heart to exercise. Instead, I steamed. There, I met a former colleague, an oncologist who collects American daguerreotypes. It is his passion. He thinks Eakins our greatest artist. I tend to agree.

I'm terrified about signing the two book contracts and won't do it without taking out life insurance for the advances so that my heirs won't be saddled with repayment. It is awful to think that I won't be able to write what I want to, but only what I *owe*. Never mind. It's the least I can do. Poor Janet. What am I to do about her? She is demolished. We sit up all night and murmur to each other. Ironically, she is the only human being I can talk to anymore. Our suffering is equal.

Many reviews of *Imagine*—all referring to it as a collection of horror stories! They are *not*.

Love

R

January 11, 1991

Dear Peter,

I am overjoyed at the news that Michigan State (excellent) will publish *The Wounded River*. Wonderful news! I phoned Harvey Ginsberg to let him know that the Troy book is being typed and that he should have it in two weeks. His question: "How long is it?" Answer: @ 200 pages. HG: "Oh dear me. That's too short." I explained that it was longer than Eudora Welty's *One Writer's Beginnings*, which I had used as a model. "No," he said, "that won't do." And sighed. I am quite disheartened over that attitude. He is far too rigid and nunish for me. I'll send it off to him and expect the worst, but I won't put up with a good deal of negative comment from one who publishes the shit that he does. What's wrong with these guys? If he, in the end, doesn't want to publish it I'll go elsewhere and gladly.

Much positive response lately about *Imagine* from all around. Thank goodness for my 15,000 readers. And a grand letter from a pastor at the First Church of the Nazarene in Galion, Ohio, telling me that I am his favorite writer, quoting chapter and verse—the way they do. I mailed him a copy of *Repairs*, as he can't find it anywhere. One reader like that is worth a thousand Ginsbergians. Don't you love the word Nazarene? I shall henceforth think of myself as the Trojene. It has more *cachet* than Trojan, which will always be a condom.

Swan has now been returned from the last of its exploratory sorties and I shall shelve it for good. For the good of the American Theatre, I am convinced. Janet is fretting over the heavy snow, as guests of ours expected tomorrow won't be able to make it up the driveway. I shall have to get out the ropes, pitons, and crampons to hoist them aloft.

I keep writing you letters, then failing to mail them. What's the sense in that? Your offer to help with the two grubstreets is mighty sweet, and doubtless I'll take you up on it, but only on a *business* basis. We shall *both* profit and that's that. I'm reading the letters of Maxwell Perkins. Now *there* was an editor.

Inconceivable, our plummeting to war with Iraq. Bush *and* Saddam Hussein should be shot.

Love
R

January 22, 1991

Dear Peter,

The *New Yorker*! Wonderful. You have *arrived*. Let us hope that the cognoscenti will descend upon the bank and buy up all your paintings. January 28 or thereabouts would be fine for you to come. Janet says yes, *but* you are *not* to bring *anything*, e.g., bagels or other ratshit food into the house. *You*, she likes; your edibilia, no. So come and let me bake you twelve potatoes.

Yesterday another lost day—a damned photographer kept me posing for five hours. And today I am writing the deadest prose of my life. The end of *Troy* keeps receding farther and farther. I hope I can get out of this rut. I just hung up from a telephone interview with a guy at Associated Press. He is doing yet another article on Doctor Writers. It all stems from Oliver Sacks's fame over *Awakenings*, which I haven't yet read or seen as a film. So I am but a minor character. On January 31, I go to Troy overnight to boost St. Mary's Hospital. There'll be lots of nuns and Irishmen, so I'll be happy—they're my favorites. Tonight I'm dragooned into going with Janet to the symphony. I shall have an attack of the sleeping sickness after ten minutes, but we are keeping company with each other lately for reasons that you might imagine, all having to do with Hank, our grandson. Let me know when you can come and I'll sharpen my wits.

I met with one Robert Stewart of Scribners on Friday along with Ken Warren, the Macmillan man. I outlined the proposed book and they showed a good deal of optimism, so I guess I'll be offered the job. Never was writer more loath, but I'll get over it. There will be a two-year deadline which I can drag out to three. By then, who knows?

The Iraq war is disgusting. We are all a bunch of barbarians. I'd have preferred single combat between Saddam Hussein and George Bush. I imagine the slaughter in Iraq and Kuwait—horrible—and more to come. My friend Saad says they will never give up but will fight to the end. He says we do not understand the Bedouin mentality.[2]

A photographer is here to take my picture for *Entertainment Weekly*. Never heard of it, have you? She has blue eyes and is pretty. Just your type.

Love

R

FEBRUARY 9, 1991

Dear Peter,

Arrived in Halifax with my cold in full flamboyance, quite sure that I would infect all the maritime provinces of Canada, as if they were not already sufficiently afflicted with poverty, gloom, and a sense of impending doom about the secession of Québec. This, I am told, would isolate them from Ontario and cause even more insularity and closed provincialism. The symposium was attended by 350 people who came from all the medical schools of Canada. It was dubbed *Medicine and the Humanities*. There were many fascinating papers. One on the Jake-leg Syndrome caused by drinking an adulterated booze: 35,000 were paralyzed. Another was about Jacques Ferron, a French-Canadian doctor-writer who is a real discovery. I read this morning, with the usual reaction. You'd have thought I had written Revelations or the Gospel of St. Mark. The people are almost all Scottish, fiercely devoted to Nova Scotia. The medical students sang in Gaelic and everyone wept shamelessly. This afternoon the dean picked me up for a sightseeing tour, but on came the cough and I had to return to the hotel where I'm writing this letter.

There are only two statues in the city—one of Sir Walter Scott, the other of Robert Burns. Monuments to poets! Very civilized, don't you think? The inscription on the Burns pedestal is "A man's a man fo a'that," which ought to give the feminists a spasm or two. I suggested a third statue—of James Boswell, the best of the lot. They said, "We'll see." Such polite, kind people, these Nova Scotians. Hardworking, egalitarian. It is one of the many places I could live contentedly.[3] There is a hill called The Citadel atop which is an eighteenth-century British fort, now a museum. In 1917 a ship blew up in the harbor and leveled the city: 2000 dead. The dean's mother-in-law still carries bits of glass in her scalp from that. The big difference between Halifax and New Haven is that in Halifax the plastic surgeons operate to make breasts smaller; in New Haven they make them bigger. That's it, really, in a nutshell.

Love

R

February 16

When I don't hear from you I think perhaps you have taken an overdose of tahini and are being disimpacted somewhere. But I imagine the Herculean grunts over *Lives of the Saints* and *The Wounded River*. There was a wonderful portrait of Oliver Sacks in today's *Times*. I surely would like to know him. Apparently, a most lovable mess—just my type.

I'm trying to put the finishing touches on Troy and am grateful for your suggestion to include "Mask on the Face of Death in Haiti," "St. Ronan Terrace," and the AIDS piece, which is now as finished as can be. About that, I feel I must show it to the survivor to see if he objects to its publication.

March 5

It is strange. My entire life has focused on my poor blind, hypopituitary grandson, an infant whom I do not know but who has become the target of all my efforts. It is as though I were born precisely to harbor him—now and after my death. I think of little else, as though I had been an arrow shot to that point. It is the single extraordinary event of my life.

March 8

I have reread Mann's *The Black Swan*, and the reason why I *had* to rewrite it is clear: there is an immense chasm between the powerful theme and Mann's execution of it. The poor sad little novella is festooned with page after page of formal, stylized, and unnatural dialogue between Rosalie and Anna. The symbols go off like landmines in Kuwait. They are lying buried everywhere. Now I'm supposed to stand up and celebrate its publication in this fancy edition? Then, too, there is my friend John Hejduk, who illustrated it. I'll have to work it out somehow.

Yesterday I drove up to Amherst to teach a class in a course called "Reimagining the Human in a Technological Age," taught by two superb men—one a physicist, the other an art historian. Before and after, we chatted and I came away uplifted and impressed. Lucky Amherst to have those two. Then I stopped at the Dickinson House just down the street. To think that she really did live on this planet! The students had all read *Mortal Lessons* and spent a week talking about it before I came. Next Friday they all go off to an anatomy lab in Worcester to see cadavers being dissected. "Should I eat breakfast?" one eighteen-year-old asked me. They are terrified of being confronted with their own mortality. I wish I could play Cicero and lead them there by the hand.

March 11

I have returned to Troy, tying paper leaves and dried apricots to the branches of a dead tree to give it the appearance of life.[4] Honestly, I had not meant to love and pity so. Nor had I meant to go back like Antigone to bury my dead—only to find all of them lying where they had fallen half a century ago, waiting for me to cover them with words. It is a painful book to write. I've about finished the talk on *The Black Swan* (Mann's) and am dreading the occasion. Janet is coming to make sure I don't drink vodka *before* I rise and clear my throat.

I spent an hour at the library this afternoon to little avail. At a *working* desk, a young man with a long full beard which he played with while reading. Combed it with his fingers, lifted it, let it fall, turned it in his voluptuous fingers with automatic libidinous verve. Come to find out that he was reading the history of the Peloponnesian Wars! What do you make of that?[5]

MARCH 16

Yet another note from Harvey Ginsberg. *Where* is the manuscript? Where, indeed? It languishes while I read *Far from the Madding Crowd* and know once and for all that I am a mere hack. You are right about Hardy. Terrific. I imagine your huge paintings taking shape. And you dwarfed and daubing. Paint on, for your sins. I am presently battling an intestinal varmint that keeps me gushing from one or the other spigot. Better get over it by Limited Edition Day. Wouldn't do to appear in a diaper.

MARCH 20

Your letters are so full of work, arduous lovely work. Yaddo was never so well used as by you. Thanks for the photo of Kipling and for the news of Melville's house. He also lived for seven years in Troy, that part called Lansingburgh. There, he wrote much of *Typee* and *Omoo*. The house is still standing but in disrepair and with no memorabilia. So I am not the first writer to roam those streets. Perhaps, even now, there is a future Shakespeare living in South Troy. There is something about that town.

Yesterday I worked on *Troy*—hardly dented the corpse—so much yet to be done. Today I finished the *Swan* talk. There will be an audience of 200 with only 100 chairs. Half must remain erect while I speak. To give to so many an erection, it is a blessing. You should see the Limited Editions version of *The Black Swan*. It is huge, black, soft leather, paper the feel of which is erotic, and decorated with John Hejduk's lithographs. They are dark—abstract, I guess—triangles, circles, other shapes. Nothing to do with the story. That is best, I think. The whole thing is a bit much, and way too much for that poor bird with both its wings broken and incapable of flying. I only hope not to offend the audience with my utterly frank assessment of the novella. One can't ignore the defects nor the influence of Mann's suppressed homosexuality lately revealed in his journals. He *is* Rosalie von Tummler.[6] I've been reading John Cheever's journals as printed in the *New*

Detail from the Tiffany mural at the Troy Public Library.

Yorker. About the saddest story in the world. All that pain—it's a wonder he wrote at all. I'm sorry to have rebuffed him at the end. Kindness would have been called for. But I was stupid.[7]

MARCH 24

A great miracle here. For a month the parents have noticed that little Hank reaches for things held out to him. Wishful thinking, they said. But then he began to turn his eyes as if to follow movement. And yesterday the neuro-ophthalmologist confirmed that there is *some* vision. Perhaps there will be even more improvement. We are limp with joy, dare not speak of it aloud lest the angel be scared off. Just to think of a ray of light, however pale, piercing the blackness—it is what a week ago I would have died for, and still would, gladly, to hold on to it. But the shock has catapulted us to new heights of exhaustion. We totter about, leaning against walls, forgetting to eat. Is it a dream?

My overnight in New York was a great success. I stayed at the Algonquin—all those literary ghosts. I walked up to 72nd Street and found Limited Editions at six o'clock. Some 200 bookish folks, a barful of good vodka, and a string quartet of pretty girls. At 7:30 I spoke, the audience most appreciative; at 9 p.m. to 63rd Street for dinner; at 11 p.m. I died, a hearse arrived, and the corpse was delivered to the Algonquin.

MARCH 29

It appears that rarely in optic nerve dysplasia some development of the nerve occurs *after* birth. It has happened with Henry. He sees! However little, he sees. It is beyond all belief. Perhaps he will be able to walk without a cane or a dog; perhaps he will know day from night; see red or blue; gaze into a fireplace and see flames. I tell you that I am altogether joyful. It is exactly as though a dawn, however pale, had diluted a black universe. My heart is so full of this that I can think of nothing else.

Whittle: I have decided against it. Any number of reasons, the main one being that I just don't want to do it. I haven't that much time left, after all. I'd rather write the story of Charles and Mary Lamb, the fourth segment of *Little Saint Hugh*, anything but "profiles" of doctors. So that is that. I hope you are not too disappointed. *I* am vastly relieved.

MAY 1, 1991[8]

Dear Peter,

Here's a crooked little note to show you that a version of handwriting has been returned to my atrophic, tremulous hand. I now go downstairs for my meals, and hope to be in the garden as soon as the sun comes out. Otherwise, I am in my room reading or resting. I finished the Hardy novel [*Under the Greenwood Tree*] yesterday. I loved the re-creation of village life. I am enjoying the book of letters, too. You surely do know what I enjoy reading.

Regaining one's health is humbling in that one must wait for the body to make its decisions. I have no say in the matter. I do, however, exercise when I remember. There are all these therapists (physical, occupational, etc.) to placate. My spirits are fine—can you tell? I still remember nothing of my sojourn in Hell—altho' I shall recognize it the next time, I'm sure. Perhaps I've left my fingerprints on a shovel there. I still have no energy to think of writing. That will come in time and, if not, I shall quit and read the rest of Hardy, the new Josyph stories, and other masterpieces. John Nelson [new president of Yaddo] visited, said how much he admired your work, and how thrilled he was at the invitation to visit your studio. I've had letters from everyone you know in Troy, Albany, etc. John Hejduk sent a bilingual edition of Rilke's poems. I couldn't be more touched by everyone's concern. No sense in posing as a hermit anymore. I've been found out. Janet had fun canceling all my speaking dates for this year. I can't imagine how I did all of that stuff.

My hand is tired.

Love

R

MAY 12

I love "The Borning Room." It is so well-wrought. The suspense and sense of horror are paid out to the reader most devilishly and to great effect. Your rendering

A street in Troy, New York.

of the Whitman house is evocative—I could just *see* it. The story is also funny in the narrator's manipulating of the seating arrangements when visited, and the inspection of the man's buttocks. A good touch. One small carp: when you use the word *someone*, you can't refer to him/her as *them*. *Someone* is singular. I'd correct that in two places. Otherwise the story is superb. Bravo!

Today Janet and I went to the hospital to give copies of my books to the nurses who looked after me. While I was duly celebrated like Lazarus after his raising, I experienced no nostalgia for the place. I am just beginning to realize how lucky I am to have survived. Now I must find something worthwhile to do with my new life. Give me suggestions. Perhaps it will have nothing to do with writing.

May 31

Like Cicero, I cry out against injustice: How long, O Catlaline, will you continue to perpetrate, etc. I'm referring to your unimaginable homelessness. Will there *be* no end to it?

This afternoon I am in the great Missionary Room at the Divinity School Library. I read through the manuscript of *Troy* and am thoroughly disheartened. Never will I be able to sort it out and put the pages in the order of narration. I have the barest inkling that it is a worthy book, but I am baffled for now. I've developed a miserable cough that plagues me night and day. An x-ray shows an abscess in my right lung—small, and one hopes it can be treated with antibiotics, although the very idea of further treatment appalls me.

A woman I met at Sundance—Alyssa McGuiness—she took the role of the daughter, Anna, in *The Black Swan*—called a night ago. She has just "built" (?) a new theatre on the 8th floor of a building in Lower Manhattan. She also teaches acting at NYU. She wants to produce my *Black Swan* this fall in her little (seventy seats) theatre. I'm supposed to journey to New York City as soon as possible to discuss the matter and see the theatre. I asked her for three weeks. By then I should be better—or dead.

I am *so* curious about your *Saints*. Can any of them match that sanctified, beatifiable nurse—Paddy Cunningham—who gave me a bath at the hospital? I doubt it. Ah—it thunders—I'd better get over to St. Ronan Terrace.

JUNE 8

I've been jotting down a "treatment" of my illness. Not easy, as I was unconscious during the best part. To top it off, the hospital has lost—perhaps forever—my record. It has disappeared. You can imagine the turmoil over there. I had asked to read it in order to write my account. *Therefore*, I am inventing the chart in my mind, noting when "his" blood pressure fell, "his" temperature rose. In my version, "he" did die and remained so for four seconds, after which the something that had left him came back, and he went on to make an uneventful recovery. It is perfectly logical that during that four fatal seconds "he" heard and saw the sounds and sights of the other side. Is the coma and amnesia Heaven's way of protecting the secret? Or does "he" know and remember and, like Lazarus, say nothing? Or has "he" been forbidden by the Angel to speak? As you see, no ordinary hospital record will ever match the record of the mind once that organ has been unleashed upon the poor facts.

JUNE 16

I'm getting better bit by bit. The cough is less prominent and perhaps I am less tired? I can't tell. I have finished the first week of penicillin. The hospital did locate my lost chart and, foolishly, I read it—or *in* it, as I could not bear to know everything. I suppose I should be grateful to have survived, but all I feel is a vague horror.

The trip to New York City all but killed me. 48 West 21st Street turned out to be a tall dreary building with a minute "lobby" and a single rickety elevator. My heart sank, but once on the 8th floor I felt much better. It really is a theatre. Half a dozen workmen were still putting on the finishing touches. There is a large high-ceilinged area at one end of which is the "stage." At the other end, space for three rows of fixed seats. One large problem: between the audience and the stage there is a large structural pillar. They will make "creative" use of it. Alyssa is peppy, pretty, and ambitious. Apparently she has obtained backing, has a partner, etc. *The Black Swan*, if all goes as planned, will be their opening event, possibly late October or November. My enthusiasm is dampened by the news that I am expected to attend rehearsals and participate in the "development" of the play. Now you know I can't do that. Anyway, we talked about casting, a director, public relations, all those weighty subjects. I tried to look sophisticated, but at 1:15 I had to announce that I had to go home, and did. Considering that I arrived at noon, it was anybody's quickest trip to New York City.

JUNE 29

I experienced a CAT scan of my lungs on Thursday. Nothing dire, but still residual pneumonia, which explains the cough and fatigue. I walked to Sterling

Library and back one day just to act up. I had a reunion with my cronies at the guard stations and elsewhere. Everyone at the library was shockingly well-informed as to the particularities of my illness and could discuss it with ease and confidence. However *did* they find out about my diarrhea, though?

I read *Dr. Jekyll*, thanks to you. It's great fun still. No one would publish it today. I'm working on the Robert Penn Warren lecture, which means thinking about my recent death and resurrection.

July 1

This morning I went to Sterling and *wrote*. About the vanity, dignity, and cruelty of the very sick and those who tend them. It *may* be coming back, the writing. Don't know yet.

I loved your motel memoir. The surge and roar of traffic, all of that. Let us pray to the household gods of Pollock-Krasner that they will gaze upon you with favor. I've done my level best.[9]

July 2

The *Newsday* piece was just fine.[10] Everyone should have such a grand press, Janet and I both agree on that. Let's hope it attracts a lot of attention. The photographs are wonderful, though I would have liked a close-up of Kevin Larkin, as I have no idea what he looks like. I'm *very* excited about you these days. There is—yes, I catch it!—the whiff of success in the air. I'll light a candle in church for you . . . tho' that might queer the deal.

Joe Caldwell, friend and novelist, wrote from Yaddo—he is the greeter this summer. Great guy—very poor. Once I gave him the sport jacket off my back. It looked a lot better on him.[11]

My latest x-ray (Tuesday), just so you'll know, shows improvement on the (L), worsening on the (R). Altogether, a report I can gladly accept. I shall perdure (look it up).

July 4

This morning spent retyping the last two pages of *Troy*. It is one huge mess. In any case, off it goes to Harvey Ginsberg and I await the howl of outrage. I shall tell him that I've been ordered back to bed by the doctors and am unable to work on it. Not too far from the truth, as my former colleagues want to do a bronchoscopy on my beautiful white body. The very idea of someone thrusting a tube ever again into one of my penetralia lifts my gorge. But I am strung high with fever at eventide, no question, and spent from lunchtime on.

The apricots ripened, all thousand of them at once. This morning I picked those within reach. A neighbor climbed the ladder and did the rest. In return I have to go next door and read the Declaration of Independence aloud with him and his wife. Janet heard about it and fled to the beach with two or three mystery novels.

I have high hopes for the Pollock-Krasner grant. Let them be speedy and come through right after the holiday weekend. How many problems that would solve for you right now! If you get it, you must live frugally to stretch it out. My last stepfather, George Allan, who was a hobo during the Depression, boasted to me that he could live for a week on a ten-penny nail. Do you likewise, hear?

JULY 10, 1991

Dear Peter,

Well, well, well! And Bravissimo! I am truly thrilled over this piece of good luck. You surely do deserve it—not to have to worry—for a while—about money. But you must be notoriously frugal—a penny-pincher—no playing Lord Bountiful among the populace. Enough cool advice from me. Go ahead and enjoy your foothold in the Middle Class. Janet was delighted too.

Emmy (Germany grandchild) had laser surgery today on her eyes. I pray that it is a success. Two blind grandchildren would be excessive even for Fate. If I could, I'd have my own eyes scooped out and send one to each child. I've seen as much as I want to. The rest would be superfluous. I *have* been writing in my notebook every morning, but rereading it in the afternoon is a disappointment. It is nowhere near my former level. Once *Saints* is hung, I'll take a morning ferry from Bridgeport and meet you in Port Jefferson. It is high time I saw your work again.

Word came yesterday that *Imagine a Woman* was sold to a Japanese publisher—same one as before, same translator. I hope it is liked over there, but I would never think of going there now. If I go anywhere abroad it will be to Germany. I do specialize in our WWII enemies.

Continued good luck.

                                                                       Love

                                                                        R

JULY 17, 1991

San Pietro, Caro,

The Conversion of St. Mary Magdalene is terrific. Really—strange and evocative and . . . I love it. Bravo! Or rather—Brando![12] Now I'm ever more eager to see the rest of the exhibit. Plus I'm still glowing over the Pollock-Krasner coup. One oughtn't to be made happy by money, but in this case I can't help it. Me? I'm a discard. The fever came back three nights ago, just enough to remind me that Hades is still licking His chops. I won't deny that a bit of my bravado is gone and I am rather less charming and adorable at 100.6 than at 98.6. I am to have another x-ray tomorrow to appease the dragon. Meanwhile I try to meditate upon my illness and the stack of paper grows higher. The prose, however, remains earthbound and leaden-footed.

Kenneth Cavander phoned. He had reread *Swan* and is still interested in directing it. He made many important suggestions—none of which I can carry out. "Needs another short scene here . . ." "Have to keep it moving at a brisk pace . . ." He is meeting with Alyssa McGuiness next Wednesday.

Getting sick ain't half bad. I have now had my twenty-fifth letter from the Sundance crew of 1990, each one swearing undying affection, unlimited sex and hilarity if only I will get well. The future editor of my correspondence will peruse them with gorge rising, but *I* rather like it. You will tell me all your plans when you are able. I think of you and Kevin hauling, nailing, and hanging night and day, transforming Mills Pond House into a Louvre.

Love

R

August 20, 1991

Dear Peter, Kevin

Many, many thanks for a grand experience. The boat rides themselves were restorative—the fresh air, sea-breeze, all of that. I was by far the best-looking passenger, so you can imagine the general ugliness that prevailed. Mills Pond House itself is a work of art—a perfect setting for the paintings. The way it gleams in the afternoon—it does seem filled with light and air.

The *Lives of the Saints* is a revelation—marvelous, a unique body of work, full of color and texture and mischief. I do hope the opportunity arrives to spread the word. I'd like to describe it in terms of alchemy, the process of transforming lead into gold, junk into art. It certainly confirms the law of nature that matter can be neither created nor destroyed. How acutely the two of you recognize the life that exists in inanimate opaque objects! I should also mention the spontaneity of the work—its sparky, improvisational character. It has a playfulness, but also a touching innocence and bravery—the two of you playing soldier? Also a touch of madness there. But surely these paintings are no more mad than the saints who inspired them—Simeon Stylites, Anthony and the rest. No reviewer, marching past, can be expected to do you justice. Don't worry about that. These pieces require leisurely perusal and even the guidance of the artists such as I was privileged to have.

I must return to the vision I have of you guys exhuming from the void the half-buried rejectimenta of the human race—torn postcards, shards of green glass, coathangers, bits of caning unwoven from a chair and regrouped as a burst of light. The *two*-ness of creation flies in the face of the tradition of the artist as solitary figure, plumbing his own depths. But here is a tribe of two, speaking the same language, expressing the same culture.

Art, like literature, doesn't really exist without someone to look at it, feel it, palpate it. The application of the viewer's sensory organs to the painting is 50% of the worth of the piece. That's what *changes* it each time, keeps it fresh and lively. I'm grateful for the chance to have seen these grand and powerful pieces. They will be hard to forget.

Love to you all
Richard

AUGUST 22, 1991

Dear Peter,

The more I think about it, the more horrified I am that I asked you to put my Lazarus in shape.[13] It is, I see, an enormous job—so you can honorably withdraw—really, I mean it. I keep adding fragments to it in my usual disorderly fashion. Organization! I was born without the gene for it, and must flop around endlessly while the rest of the world marches by in close-order drill. Presently, I am torn between a separate book, and inserting it just before the ending of *Troy*. It *might* go there. The *New York Times Magazine* asked me for an article on assisted death—very timely, what with that book all over the place. I sent them the part of *Troy* that deals with my brief sojourn in that area. They'll get it tomorrow and if they like it, I shall have to clear it with the survivor.

I'm still dreaming about your paintings. While each component is identifiable and realistic, the total effect is often one of *abstraction*. It seems to me that it is abstraction used as a means of neutralizing the painful and personal. Pain is thereby reduced to a few vaguely evocative shapes. That applies to the reality as well—the use of known materials. It's a way of easing pain by objectifying it. And there is plenty of pain in these paintings. Yours, Kevin's, and the saints'. In some ways it is a celebration of martyrdom. Perhaps it is fitting that a surgeon be called upon to examine this work. Any reviewer must be prepared to carry out a vivisection on these paintings—to dissect them down to nerve, artery, bone—in order to see how they work. No small burden in these times of deadlines, first impressions, and the lust for derision as shown by the *Times* art critic. Forget all of that. I dismissed that stuff years ago. Personally, I love the idea of your searching for God (through his saints) in every heap of rubbish on Long Island. Looking for God where He is most apt to be found. Such are my late afternoon thoughts on the *Lives of the Saints*.

Love
R

August 25, 1991

Dear Peter,

Thanks more than the word can ever mean for dealing with Lazarus. Never was writer more in need of harness, reins, bit, and whip. So, ride!

I *am* (kind of) looking forward to my Thursday in New York City with all those professionals. Doubtless I shall shrink down to a leak and only drip once or twice an hour. But I do know *The Black Swan* needs a lot of doing and I want to do my share. Ellen Burstyn would prefer a larger theatre, so I suppose we shall all have to see about renting Madison Square Garden.

Love
R

August 25, 1991

Dear Peter,

Thanks for your warning about theatre in general. I shall keep all you said *in pectore* as the pope says (look it up). In fact, I haven't any illusions about this experience and very little sense of anticipation. I *am* grateful that my one and only play is being regarded. It would be swinish not to be. But as you know, I do not give a fig for fame, riches, etc. Only to do my work. *Like you.* Which won't keep me from trying to get La Burstyn to fall in love with me. That couldn't hurt. I shall keep you intimately informed.

Today I had lunch with Peter—you know. He's quite a bit more cautious about the *Times* piece but hasn't said no, so I will go ahead, I think. He told me many things I did not know. He is a very strange (to me) religious ideologue—there's no talking to those guys, but even being an atheist I think I am more "religious" than he. Something fake about it all. We discussed the Resurrection of the Flesh. He tells me that yes we will be resurrected, but "utterly changed." I don't buy it. Either the flesh rises as it was or it don't. Anyway, he just spent a week at Fire Island and has had a lover post-Luis in California. He is disgracefully handsome. I fear I shall have all his friends for enemies when the article comes out.

Harvey Ginsberg called—he loves the manuscript, especially the first 150 pages, says he has some suggestions about the rest. The problem is the title. He insists it have something to do with *doctor* or *surgery*, otherwise we have another money-loser. I said go ahead and name it then. Here's what he came up with: *The Boy Became a Surgeon*. Ugh. How about *Doctor's Boy: A Memoir?* I don't know *what* to call it. But I'm on the defensive—like Gorbachev.[14]

Love

R

August 27, 1991

Dear Peter,

And now comes the survivor of my assisted death episode objecting all over the place to publication of the piece in the *New York Times*. I can smell the hysteria, he being egged on by his friends—one the very poet who suggested he contact me in the first place. So now I suppose I shall appeal to the newspaper to return it. Wouldn't be worth the acrimony. What would *you* do?[15]

The meeting with Ellen Burstyn, Kenneth Cavander, and Alyssa went quite well. Ellen Burstyn is very beautiful—in her late fifties I'd guess—a presence, and very smart. She had done her homework by reading the Thomas Mann novella; I, by watching her in an otherwise dreadful movie called *Alice Doesn't Live Here Anymore*. For an hour or so she tested the water with her big toe, asking about Kenneth, Alyssa, and me. Then she said she had wanted to do it from the minute she read it. Her conditions: (1) Alyssa must raise the money, $500,000, for a "full-scale" production; (2) It has to open in a large Off Broadway or small Broadway theatre—she won't agree to the theatre on 21st Street. I have no idea where Alyssa plans to get that money, but she seems hopeful about it. Ellen Burstyn's name won't hurt, I guess. I have no more misgivings about her. She is right for Rosalie. She wants to be present at the other casting, which is good too. She won't be free to start til November. It will be eight weeks of development and rehearsal. All of a sudden my life is too busy. It is disquieting. I am best when not being noticed—the real reason for my elusive ways. It interferes with my sleep, my writing.

Love

R

SEPTEMBER 18, 1991

Dear Peter,

I handed Ken Warren *Said* and he thought it was the manuscript of the book they are trying to extract from me. I explained, and urged him to read it and pass it on to Robert Stewart at Scribners. Today I'll pick up another segment of Lazarus from the typist. Never engage a Jewish typist, as she won't work on Rosh Hashanah or Yom Kippur, and now I won't have all the manuscript to work on during the train ride to Virginia tomorrow. I am very eager to see my son, grandson, and daughter-in-law. This life is strange and surreal, taken up with the trivialities of a writer's life. The *real* real gets only the occasional glance and hug.

       Love

       R

SEPTEMBER 29, 1991

Dear Peter,

So, I am once again the toast of New Haven. Well, make that Yale. Make that the Medical School. Make that about 1/1000 of the Medical School. And now I am a little bug again. It's what I like.

Ken Warren called at 8:30 next morning in great excitement. His neighbor, one Jeffrey Webber, a cable TV station owner and producer with whom Ken sometimes rides the train into Manhattan (this is an endless sentence, going off the cliff—I can't stop it) . . . when he heard that Ken had attended my lecture (he had just read the *New York Times*), he said that he'd been meaning all along to contact me—he's read my stories, he says—with the idea of adapting some of them for TV (because of their *spirituality*). So Ken the mover and shaker called Jeffrey Webber, Webber called me, and now we are in business. Meanwhile, on October 7, I must meet Kenneth Cavander and *discuss The Black Swan*. Changes, new scenes to be written, others to be deleted. I told him to go ahead and *do it himself*, but for some reason he insists that *I* do it. For God's sake, what's the point of having a director if he won't rewrite your play?

       Love

       R

OCTOBER 1, 1991

Dear Peter,

Every day, it seems, some vague new rumor draws near, disturbs, then drifts away never to be heard from again. I've had no word from Alyssa in two weeks, so I begin to wonder and to doubt, as you so wisely advised. And today Bob Putz, the finest man alive in the universe, my son's boss—in Virginia—a superb environmentalist and a bona fide genius—called to say that he had lent my books to a publisher from the Soviet Union who is also a filmmaker making a movie of Bob's work in fish hatcheries (is this sentence still growing?), and the man wants to publish my books in Russia. I don't get paid—just rubles, which aren't worth anything, especially as I don't plan a trip to that country, but I don't mind. It will be just fine to be published in the land of my forefathers.

The trip to Troy was awful. Such lethargic, passive students in an overheated room and no help from the three teachers. I was driven wild by two boys who talked and giggled while I perspired. I was supposed to stay overnight but left for New Haven right after class and got home at 9 p.m. happy to have escaped. I'm too old and crotchety for all that youthful rudeness and the carelessness of a mediocre faculty. I do need to be pampered, I guess. The ride up was lovely—pastel shades on the mountains, hawks, Troy, but I'm pretty sour on it today. You are just leaving for Austerlitz, I gather. I surely do hope it proves to be a good stay. I have heard how *quiet* it is. If you get crazy, go to Troy. I'm still of a mind to fly up (automobile) to distract you from serious business.

Ken Warren hasn't called in a few days—he's in England for a week. Send him the streamlined *Said*, altho' I do wonder if he really will read it. The man is besotted. Tell me what do you make of it? I shan't deliver on the book he wants. What else?

Love
R

P.S. I've picked the title of the Troy book. *Down from Troy: A Doctor Comes of Age*, and that's that.

October 6, 1991

Dear Peter,

I do hope all is cozy at Millay [Colony for the Arts]. Settle in and enjoy it. Next week the foliage will be gorgeous and you'll be too dazzled to work. Janet left for Germany an hour ago. I do hope she has a grand time with our newest baby, that Jon remembers to meet her at the station, that she doesn't get hijacked. She was terribly hesitant at the last minute, and I got lost on the way to the limousine.

I read in the *New York Times* that Ellen Burstyn is opening in a play in April. It is not *my play*! The first of any number of betrayals? Kenneth too is baffled but is used to such shenanigans.

I am thoroughly enjoying your last gift to me, *The Pleasures of Diaries*. It is just a delight, and of course it has done two things: started me writing my own again, and introduced me to a dozen diarists whose works will keep me entertained for months to come. I had slides made of the Casserius anatomical drawings and I think I'll present them as one of the talks to demonstrate how the diagnostic, clinical gaze can be carried over into art and language. On Thursday night I have the privilege of attending a reception in honor of Kurt Vonnegut. How could the same people have invited us *both*? It shows the callowness and opportunism of academia, which is why I turned down a job at Washington University in St. Louis as Distinguished Professor, etc. Howard Nemerov's place—he died. I'm only half so. Ergo, let's get Selzer. I say: take Vonnegut.

Love

R

OCTOBER 8, 1991

Dear Peter,

Here's news: Borchardt phoned a moment ago to say that American Playhouse wants to option my *New York Times* piece for an hour-long play—David Rabe to write—me to have no say. Since I've never watched American Playhouse, nor seen any of David Rabe's plays, I am leery. But Borchardt said I must do it, so I said yes. I can only hope that they are people of taste, tact, and integrity. But I must say that I am dazzled by so much recent attention, and me such an ancient pile of dry sticks—and coughing again, and dog-tired at 9 a.m. I am keeping my diary every day, so ink gets spilled and paper covered. I'm planning to spend all day tomorrow in bed to save up for Indiana. Better not forget my cane this time.

I love having the old house to myself for these few days. So silent and whispery. I wouldn't mind a bit if a mouse appeared to keep me company. About the heartache in Virginia (Hank), we shall be sucking at that acid teat from now on. The hands one is dealt!

Love

R

OCTOBER 12, 1991

Dear Peter,

It is 8 p.m. and I am waiting for some Japanese chemists to visit. There are to be three, not two, as they have cloned en route. This is going to be a circus until Janet returns to help me hosting them. Doubtless they will have names like Hayakashi and you know I'm not going to get them straight.

The trip to Indianapolis was good and bad. Good because Chuck Schuster was there and we bummed around. Good because my two presentations were well received. At the Medical School I read *Lazarus* again to the same wild acclaim. To the university crowd I showed my brand new Casserius slides, talked about Leonardo da Vinci, and then read from *Troy*. Bad is that the place is rather unedifying. The air is so polluted you can smell it. The countryside is utterly flat and there are no rivers or lakes. But everyone was kind to a fault. Kurt Vonnegut was there and gave the keynote address after a fancy dinner in a ballroom that is the *nth* degree of kitsch: a night sky ceiling with moons (lots), stars that twinkle, clouds that actually drift, crystal chandeliers, a balcony done in Spanish so as to resemble a village near Barcelona, and a stage hung with pink satin caught into heavy folds by satin ropes. On the stage two inaudible musicians: a blind mulatto pianist and a flutist in a white suit. To the *crème de la crème* of Indiana who dined at $75 per head, Kurt V was the adored Hoosier returning in triumph. In fact he satirized the place viciously, but it was either ignored or went over their heads. The night prior to my two talks I came down with diarrhea and vomiting and was up all night, but I soldiered on and nobody knew.

Love

R

October 15, 1991

Dear Peter,

The three Japanese chemistry professors are now two, one having departed or been distilled in some laboratory accident. They and I are *best friends*. My Japanese lingo has returned and they are in stitches over it day and night. I do *not* laugh at their English, which speaks volumes about the levels of civilization among the two cultures. Anyway, this morning *they* made and served *my* breakfast, which I accepted as a kind of war reparation—delayed from 1945. They are absolutely charming guys—both about thirty, I'd say. Nonome-San is bulky and shy, kept referring to the holiday as KORRUMBUSDA-I. Ichegami-San is tiny and inexplicably optimistic. I have turned over the house to them entirely and they stride from room to room like conquerors. Next thing I shall be ordered from the premises.

Love

R

OCTOBER 18, 1991

Dear Peter,

Thanks for your cautionary letter. No I won't count on anybody for anything. It all has to be done by *me*. I know that. Ellen Burstyn really *does* want to do this play. Alyssa is off to California tomorrow for five weeks, where I believe she is trying to raise the money.

I had a terrible letter from a woman I don't know—no return address given—accusing me of betraying Peter and Luis, and "asking" (telling) me to remove that piece from my forthcoming book and promise never to see it published again! Presumptuous and arrogant. I can't imagine what could ever cause *me* to write to *her* in an effort to interfere with her life and work. Whoever she is, I must ignore such intrusions, although it isn't easy to do so.

Harvey Ginsberg doesn't want *Legionnaire* in the memoir, so the book is again pitifully short. "You will never be accused of writing *War and Peace*," he said. The manuscript is being retyped now at another $1000 and then I'm through. Let Borchardt, Ginsberg, and God decide.

       Love

       R

OCTOBER 22, 1991

Dear Pyotr,

Janet got home last night, so I don't have to make breakfast for my Japanese friends anymore. I offered them a choice of eggs: scrambled, fried, or raw. If anyone had asked for poached, I'd have had to dial 911. The Japanese chemistry professors all read *Mortal Lessons* in Japanese and insisted thereafter on making *my* breakfast. Our Japanese guests were joined Sunday morning at eight by a photographer—one Nancy Crampton—come up from New York City to take my picture for a Harcourt Brace anthology. I had to make her eggs too! I must confess to purposely breaking the Japanese' eggs so I could shrug quite charmingly and say *o-punk-oo* (flat tire).

As for the *Swan*, James Spader will play the young man, did I tell you? No money yet, but Rocco Landesman, of Broadway Alliance, is gung-ho and, considering what is being produced on Broadway this year, *Swan* is a shoo-in. Incidentally, I expect all this will redound to your benefit if TV, movies, and theatres latch on, as I insist they do.

Such a firestorm about the *New York Times* piece. Good thing I keep to myself. 95% of the letters have been positive, but the surviving lover and his wicked witch advisors are angry. Oh so glad that I showed him the article first and offered to kill it. Now he's mad, but can't do a thing about it. Or can he?

It is exceedingly difficult to deal with grieving men (or women). I throw reason out the window. One continues to feel compassion.

Love

R

OCTOBER 27, 1991

Dear Peter,

How you can say that I write you seldom, I don't know. I seem to be jotting *Dear Peter* all day and night.

The biography of Chekhov is all read and I am in mourning over his death. What a noble, brave, and lovable man. I adore him, I want to become *like* him. It is a clear case of infatuation and hero worship. The book is titled *Chekhov: Observer Without Illusion* by Daniel Gillès. It is the very best biography of my life. When you are in New Haven I shall borrow it for you.

You will be interested to learn that all the month of October, every single day, I have been writing in my diary. I plan to keep on with it until I am involved in a major project again. The play should not prevent me from keeping the journal. Today's entry was about Chinese burial customs. I must have, over the years, a thousand pages like this. It is strewn about my study and elsewhere. If you behave I'll let you read October '91. Tomorrow morning I pick up *Troy* from the typist for the last time. I much want to include the anatomy drawings of Casserius in the book, plus "The Execution of Lady Jane Grey." Otherwise, it won't make sense. I now believe that omitting *Legionnaire* was a mistake, but I have already agreed to that and won't insist.

R

YALE CLUB
FIFTY VANDERBILT AVENUE AT FORTY-FOURTH STREET
NEW YORK, N.Y. 10017

OCTOBER 30, 1991

Dear Peter,

I am sitting in the vast ornamental throne room of this place. I don't belong to it—only use their toilet when I leave Grand Central. I can pass for one of them—easy. I checked in at the Women's Republican Club on 51st Street—our austere, not to say dreary, caravansary. A portrait of George Bush dominates the entry. It makes me sad to think that people actually have to *live* there. But then,

I suppose it is a step up from your condition—homelessness. From there I drifted up to Rockefeller Plaza—had coffee *al fresco* and watched the crowd. Then to Harvey Ginsberg with the freshly typed manuscript. He has agreed to use four of the Casserius etchings, for which I am grateful. He then handed me five assignments. One, I am to write an 800-word impression of the book to be used for the dust jacket. I did really think that the editor performed that chore. Next, I am to fill out a long form asking for many inconsequentia. Some people have a genius for giving out tasks, then tapping a foot to let you know they are *waiting*. From there to Georges Borchardt, then in search of one of those souvlaki trucks, but there weren't any, so I went to the Oyster Bar at Grand Central. When I finish writing in the diary, I'll mosey back to the Women's Republican Club and take a Woman's Republican nap. I do hope I do not have to perform tonight. Don't I deserve to get out of one little thing? It's at a rehearsal hall at Lincoln Center. Peter Martins is the "host." The *corps de ballet* will dance. Perhaps I will too.

Love

R

November 4, 1991

Dear Peter,

I send this to St. James in the hope that you have not yet turned your back on the church. But where *have* you set down your satchel? Are you at the Brooklyn Shelter for the Homeless? Or slowly fermenting in a bog on Long Island, a la "Lindow Man" [in *Imagine a Woman*]? As for me, I have ceased to be productive entirely. My sole *product* for forty days has been a daily entry in my diary. If ever I get the zip, I'll type it up just to see. But I plan to go on with it indefinitely as I have become addicted to the keeping.

Saturday, [composer] Tom Whitman arrives to talk about opera. Swans are mute until the moment of death and then only do they sing. I have no intention of inviting trouble by raising my voice prematurely. My main caveat is that Tom seems to me lacking in passion—fire—a sense of melodramatic thunder without which opera ain't opera.

Tomorrow another of the Sundancers, Rick Gould—playwright—arrives. He is applying to Yale Drama School. This is his second (annual) try. A lapsed Mormon from Salt Lake City. Half Japanese, half Caucasian. Writes the most savage scenes— one in which a mother and father calmly cook and eat their baby. Now I ask you!

Love

R

NOVEMBER 10, 1991

Dear Peter,

Home! (I should not express rapture to the homeless, I realize.) It was a pretty harrowing (mentally) trip from which I have returned with a heavy cold and deaf. My host in Albuquerque, a surgeon and would-be writer, insisted that I stay with him in his mountain retreat. His wife and child were banished to the city-house in Albuquerque so that he and I could talk "writing." Part of my job, in addition to (1) addressing the local society of surgeons and spouses; (2) a two-hour session including lunch with fifty medical students (the *only* good part of this trip); and (3) a reading to the State Medical Society—in addition, I say, to those three, I had to go over his two manuscripts line by line and give instruction for the future. It is beyond prostitution, it is total buggery, but I did it anyway. New Mexico, despite all those claims for the *Land of Enchantment*, seems to me an arid, uninteresting landscape, the Mexican influence not congenial to me, and the mentality strictly gun ownership. Still, I was catered to, held aloft, fêted. Three days of that and off to Chicago, where I spoke to a group of rheumatologists, one-quarter of whom walked out early, but I think I made some friends.

Tom Whitman is keen to compose the opera and *will do it no matter what*. He played a few pages of music and we talked for several hours before I expelled him. He is ecstatic to do it, but let me know that I am not to intrude. *Very severe*, I think, so I suggested he write the libretto himself based on the play and count me out. No way! I must take part. I haven't any doubt it'll be written—give him three years. A rather unappetizing prospect for me. How do I get into these situations? I have forty of them at any given time.

Love

R

NOVEMBER 13, 1991

Dear Peter,

Of course you were right all along. About the play there appear to be complications. Alyssa, out there in Happy Land, can't admit to the movie people that she doesn't have the rights to *The Black Swan*, but she needs them to put up the money for the play. If she proposes it and says that she has no rights, the movie people can then bypass *us* and just write their own screenplay. Who'd even have thought? I'm in favor of ditching La Burstyn, withdrawing to Alyssa's tiny theatre, and doing the production right there on a budget. No stars, no Broadway, no nothing—just a good job. I told her so. Also, there seems to be a problem in acceptance of a first-time producer, first-time director, and first-time playwright. We *are* all amateurs. Frankly, my dear, I don't give a damn. I've had a sodden, thick, viscous cold for eight days, so I haven't done anything but read and keep my diary. I have a ton of material in that diary and would like to see it materialize as a manuscript. I hope I can just sit down and type it. Ken Warren, I fear, has become a bit weary of my hesitations. I'm weary of his pushiness, so we're even. I can't believe that Scribners is serious anyway. Come up and see me soon. I miss you.

Love

R

November 15, 1991

Dear Peter,

You're right. These daily long entries in my diary have piled up into many thousands of words. Whatever should be done? I can't seem to stop. And no, unlike Boswell or Cheever, I'm telling nuthin'. My follies and sins are *my own*. Let the curious and the lubricious wonder. Suffice it to say I'm rather *too* human in the regards that excite interest. But, private as a diary may intend itself to be, it not infrequently insists on publication. So it may yet one day fall to your lot to transcribe, ruin your vision, grow constipated and insomniac in trying to bring this mass of gibberish to light. If the thought of it appalls you, why you must right away plunge a dagger in your breast. It would be the only thing could save ye.

Robert Brustein phoned, inviting me to take part in a panel discussion of the American Repertory Theatre's production of *The Seagull* in March. I said yes and *then* found out that the essay would be due no later than December 2!! So it's drop everything and run once again. But I *think* it might be fun, especially if I have a play in the works. Chekhov</>Selzer, don't you know. Yesterday, Kenneth Cavander called to see how far I'd got with the changes in the *Swan*.

"Not too far."

"Why not?"

"Been sick."

"Montaigne wrote with bladder stones pronging his innards."

"*I'm* a sissy."

Seems we must meet in New York City, but with the Mann rights in question and Alyssa fainting all over California, I'm not exactly inclined to write witty dialogue for the Doctor and Rosalie. Borchardt says I *must not* sign a contract with Alyssa until she raises the money. Meanwhile, the report from my upper respiratory tract is not good. I am two weeks into this cold, still deaf, coughing, a

Dubrovnik of a human being. I am reading the Henry James/Edith Wharton letters which you gave me. I actively dislike both of them—him especially, her by the company she kept.

To work. Do you the same.

R

November 28, 1991

Dear Peter,

Ah, so there you are! I am glad of it, but your stay will be so short. Can't you arrange an extension? I've been struggling to write the essay on Chekhov. Mostly, I cough and spit, which is also Chekhovian. The more I learn about the man, the more I love him. The other day at the library I went to look at the large illuminated globe of the earth, gave it a little spin, braked with my hand when I had the Crimea in view, found the city of Taganrov, where Chekhov was born and raised. Then I found Odessa where my family lived for generations and where my father was born. They are a mere 300 miles apart, an overnight steamship ride around the Crimean peninsula. Yalta, where Chekhov spent so much of his adult life, is 150 miles from Odessa. Ever since I saw that map I've had the notion that Chekhov and I are related. Here's how it doubtless happened:

A man and a woman are standing side by side at the railing of the deck of the steamboat. She is holding a tiny white dog in one arm, he is wearing a straw hat and a pince-nez on a long black ribbon. They do not know each other. One is a Chekhov, the other a Selzer (or whatever we were called then). Slowly they become aware of each other, a look is exchanged. They begin to talk, to laugh. Within three hours they have fallen in love. Then the deck steward announces that there will be a four-hour stopover at, say, Balaclava for repairs. Along with the other passengers, the man and woman disembark arm in arm. She is still holding the small dog. At the hotel (it all looks exactly like the wharf at Port Jefferson) she waits on the veranda while he arranges for a room. "What name did you use?" she asks between passionate kisses.

"Gomov. Dmitri Dmitrich Gomov. Do you like it?"

"Do I. It could be the hero of a romantic novel."

"No," he replied with a touch of melancholy. "Not a novel. Only a short story."

What happened then? Well, they parted. She was met at Yalta by her husband—a doctor in a top hat and carrying a cane. He watched her debark. She never once looked back. Nine months later the woman, Anna, delivered a baby boy with gray eyes and chestnut-colored hair.

"He'll grow up to be a surgeon," said the proud 'father.'

"Nonsense. He'll be a poet. Already his eyes have that yonderly look."

So, Chekhov: I might have known! No wonder I love you. How I would kiss your hands, your eyes, stroke the thin racked body to rub away the cough, as though I were smoothing a wrinkle in a piece of cloth. And then we would talk:

Chekhov: "How beautiful life could have been."
Me: "I too let it slip by, let it slip by."
Chekhov: "It is already too late to dream."
Me: "It's all the same."
Chekhov: "Goodnight now."
Me: "Tovarich, Cousin Anton."
End of Daydream.

By the way, Gomov and Anna are the characters in Chekhov's lovely short story "The Lady with a Small Dog." It is about a brief love affair at Yalta. But none of this is getting my essay written. What shall I do? And you not here to get me out of this jam.

Your eleven-hour gallop [to Sweet Briar] was Herculean. The very idea makes me weak in the knees. I love your washing your face in the river at Manassas. You'd do anything for sentiment, wouldn't you? Cows on the grounds? Lovely. Meanwhile, I went to my doctor yesterday. It's not in my chest: the x-ray is okay, but you could have fooled me. Gretchen says it is from my brain. Brain drain?

Love
R

DECEMBER 1

The copy editor of *Down from Troy* is Amy Edelman, the same editor I had at Random House for *Imagine a Woman*. She also does freelance, heard about *Down from Troy*, phoned Morrow, and begged to do it, so I *am* lucky and blessed to have so expert and caring an editor. She is a national treasure and in my next life I am going to marry her. The fact is, I *need* to be married to a copy editor. She has written me a wonderful laudatory letter. I have the manuscript back but have only looked to see that *every page* is heavily marked with red pencil, so there will be much to do, and Harvey Ginsberg says he *must* have it back by December 9. I have never had so many deadlines as now in my wizened dotage.

DECEMBER 4

I read and read and read. It is quite mad—how much I read. The seasons come and go and still I read. People marry, divorce, die, and I go on *reading*. It would take a direct *nukular* hit to make me stop.

DECEMBER 7

I, just an hour ago, finished going over the manuscript of *Troy* edited by that angel from on high, Amy Edelman, a brilliant, expert, affectionate treatment of my feeble manuscript. I adore her without having met her. Is that possible? I am also in love with Anton Chekhov, so you can call me any names you wish. I love the dead and the unknown. It is the living and the known that give me trouble.

What with the collapse of the Maxwell empire, I fear our friend Ken Warren will soon be out of a job and *hors de combat*. Surely I'm not unhappy, as I never thought really that Robert Stewart (Scribners) was fully interested in me. I am not really interested in *him*, either.

DECEMBER 11

Robert Brustein phoned to say that he "adores" me, and incidentally my piece on Chekhov. In fact, as I think of it, he *is* one of my kissing friends—he and Harold Bloom. You wouldn't know, but it is a burden to be so adorable.

DECEMBER 16

Ran into Howard Lamar today on the street. He reassured me (without my asking) that he had written for you, said also that you were very impressive on paper, that he'd like to meet you next time you're in New Haven. So that's a terrific chance to get a smashing blurb for *The Wounded River* and to make an important new contact. Also—he said that he thought you had a *very good* shot at the Beinecke fellowship.

It is twenty minutes to 2 a.m. I am in the kitchen reading the letters of Lamb. Damb! Dambit! Goddambitall! You shouldn't have sent them to me, as I am re-hooked, like any lapsed addict. Ah but they are wondrous constructions. And last night (you'd have loved it) I, together with Janet, went to the Ezra Stiles Christmas party, hobnobbed with your mann Vann [Woodward] and numerous other luminosities. I got home at 10 quite tipsy. As for work, I have been getting ready for Yaddo, sorting out all the notebook pages and stacks of paper into two piles: those that might be included in the diary, and those that won't be. Now all I'll have to do is sink into a chair and begin. Trouble is, I keep writing in the diary every day, so there is no end to it.

Ken Warren phoned. His job is hanging by a thread now that Robert Maxwell is ensconced on the Mount of Olives in Jerusalem with all the other pious men. I finished off all possibility of writing a book for Scribners. It wasn't hard to do, as the editor instructed by Ken to call me never did. While I am mostly relieved, I appeared to take umbrage and quite sanctimoniously eased myself out. I pray that Ken will (A) forget it, and (B) stay friends. I think I'm okay with B.

Swan is at the typists. Have I told you that the theatre rights *are* available, and Borchardt will make an offer to the Mann estate that will doubtless put me in debtor's prison? The movie rights have been optioned by a foreign film company. Who could that be? How dare they?

Virginia must be one of the glories of North America. You say nothing of colleagues. Are they congenial? Brilliant? Available? Tell me. And finish that lousy introduction to *The Wounded River*.

DECEMBER 19, 1991

Dear Peter,

The library, which had turned into a pest-house with a thousand Yalies—the Hope of the World—coughing, sneezing, spitting, and sniffling—has returned to its original silence. It is a silence as if Jesus had just been born. Or has the building died? And all of us in it? Anyhow, it is quiet and I am trying to work.

I read the galleys of Lewis Thomas's new collection of essays, sent by Ken Warren for me to write a blurb. It is shockingly bad. A careless job of editing, or, more likely, non-editing by Robert Stewart. I always thought Lewis Thomas overrated and now he'll be disgraced. Having said all that, I lavished praise on the book for the dust jacket, merely to stand in front of the old essayist to hide his nakedness with my broad carcass. I did, however, tell Ken Warren precisely what I thought of it all, that he had done only harm to Thomas, whose old-age vanity is too foolish. Scribners is just latching on to the name. Pfui!

I've decided (I think) to expand *Lazarus* and make it into a short volume. I'll work on it at Yaddo. As for *Swan*, it is too confusing. I *do* have verbal permission from the Mann estate to explore possibilities, raise money, obtain a theatre. *Then* and not before will they sign a contract with me. But how to raise money, obtain a theatre *until* I have a written contract with Mann? Borchardt says they wouldn't grant the rights to do it in Alyssa's theatre—too small—no profit for them. She is going to be upset, but I will try to remain above the fray. Which did not keep me from making the revisions in the script, for which the typist charged me $230 even though there were only fifteen pages of new material. I shall have to ask about that. And get a new typist. Altogether a dim view of the world? Not at all. I remain strangely cheerful, reasonably peppy, and looking forward to Yaddo and Troy. What next in the itinerancy of Monsieur Jo Zeephe? Such a nomad.

                                        Love

                                          R

December 23, 1991

Dear Peter,

Just watched an hour-long interview of Jan Peerce by Isaac Stern interspersed with the great tenor singing. It wouldn't have meant doodly-shit to you, but the tears fairly streamed down *my* face. It is a day gone by and never to be retrieved. So beautiful!

The entire *Swan* thing is silly. Tomorrow I'll call Borchardt and say that I want to do the damn thing at the tiny little theatre on 21st Street. Now I must obtain *written* rights from Thomas Mann's spermatozoa which have been freeze-dried in a test tube in Berchtesgarden.

Today I walked down to the library minus my cane, which had hidden in a corner somewhere. Well may he hang his head, Monsieur Cane. More about that later: a teeny little kiddy story about a man and his cane. But not til after I've done *Lazarus* and Volume I of the diary. Anyone so mentally unbalanced as to dip into my diary will see at once that (a) I do not live in service to a noble cause and am therefore a toad and a poltroon; and (b) I make no effort to subdue my personality. But I had hoped the diary would contain something other than my own borborygmi. At Yaddo I have decided to eschew all social blandishments in

Richard Selzer's study or "scriptorium" at St. Ronan Terrace.

the interests of work. I'm reading the autobiography of Thackeray—written by some Englishwoman as *he would have* written it. Poor Thackeray—eclipsed by Dickens, and in terrible love with the wife of his friend. It's all a mess—rather like everyone else's life.

Love
R

December 30, 1991

Dear Peter,

I have spent three days cleaning my study in accordance with a resolution I made several years ago. There are now neat cartons of letters and assorted papers instead of the carefree strew by which the little scriptorium was known. Another day or two should have it shipshape, so that should I die at Yaddo you will have only to tape everything shut and haul it away. Janet and Gretchen are staring at me suspiciously. Have I gone mad?

I keep my pair of Lambs in my bed and every night I have to turn on the light and read a page or two. A lovely present that I love now and always will. Thank you. I have decided to stop berating you for your spendthriftiness, as I see that it is hopeless. You *will* impoverish yourself.

It is Sunday afternoon and raining. I had meant to pick up *The Black Swan* at the typist's, but there's no one at home. Why do people insist on leading their private lives when I want my manuscript? So! The world does not revolve around me. Could it be true?

Love
R

driving the quill

1992

JANUARY 3, 1992

Dear Peter,

A call from an associate of the cable TV man who, after a long look at "the work," has chosen "Whither Thou Goest" and just may produce it. On February 5, I go to New York City to be interviewed on their cable station, then I shall try to firm down the idea. I can't go earlier, as I leave on Tuesday for Eldorado—Yaddo. How I long to get away to that heavenly place! The world is too much with me.

I worked at the Medical Library today. Well, not *worked* so much as browsed and wept for the passing of a better day. Picked up an Atlas of the Brain in Cross-Section and fell into a state of rapture. I'll tell you all about it, the way the brain of the newly dead is retrieved, preserved, hung on a string (so as to prevent deformity), then sliced and stained and photographed. It is obvious that in each slice there is a beautiful creature that undergoes metamorphosis from one part of the brain to another. Now it is an exotic moth, now a delicate raccoon or a fawn. Whatever the neuroanatomists say, *I* say it is the very imagination itself that dwells at the bottom of the brain, flutters its wings, preens, grooms its fox fur, and clucks along the calcific streets in search of metaphors.

I have been reading *Journeys in Dream and Imagination*, Artur Lundkvist's account of his two-month coma after a heart attack. I am willing to believe, but cannot quite. My own account is rooted in reality; his is afloat in poetry, but so interesting.

Your *apartment*!!! I am bowled over. You have digs—you have *dug* your own grave! You abide *somewhere*. You *dwell*! It is amazing. Please make sure your landlady falls in love with you so that when you can no longer pay the rent she won't evict you. Overlooking the Sound? You're *posh*.[1]

Love

R

January 5, 1992

So, Pietro!

Yaddo—day after tomorrow! Three weeks. I hope I can finish *Lazarus* while there. It has taken a number of more interesting turns already, and I'm grateful to everyone who told me not to include it in *Down from Troy*. I believe it will be a small book unto itself outside the diary. Otherwise it would capsize the little rowboat. All my friends from Troy, Albany, Schenectady, and Saratoga have phoned. Yaddo begins to resemble Versailles, so I have decided to refrain from all society. I have spent a busy few days trying to reassure my beloved lunatics that I will definitely come back in three weeks. What time? I don't know. In the morning? Afternoon? I can't say. Is it *exactly* three weeks? That would be the 28th of January. Well, I might stay another three days. They are so polite, wouldn't object out loud, but the terror of being abandoned is clear in their eyes, hands, the tilt of their heads. Oh my ministry, my poor lunatics! But they know where I'm going and I can only hope that no one is so desperate as to *show up*. What would I do then?

Love

R

January 9, 1992

Dear Peter,

I am empalaced at Southwoods, the ancestral home of the presidents of Yaddo. It is large and lonely. My duties are not onerous. I greet one or two newcomers every few days, show them the system, and that is that. John Nelson [the president] comes for a drink @ 5 p.m. The painters seem more substantial than the writers this time. One poet told me that he writes *ten* poems per day, so you can imagine the calibre. Three weeks seems now a long time to stay, and I may up and quit before that—it depends on how the work goes. I plan to put Fanny d'Arblay just ahead of *Lazarus* and use John Donne's "Devotions Upon Emergent Occasions" as well. That will make a small book either suitable for Whittle, or to be included in the diary— I have not yet decided what to do. But I'm surely uncertain over the quality of *Lazarus* in a way I never was about my other work. It is a huge risk. I'll just hold my nose and jump in. I found a lovely bit by Paul Éluard for the epigraph:

> *In laying myself down like ash after the flame*
> *Have I surrendered?*
> *No, I am sleeping and despite night's power*
> *Learning like a child that I shall awake.*[2]

Now that's gorgeous, right?

I have with me eight filled notebooks, plus 1000 pages to be used in the diary. Just to start typing and keep at it all day is my task. I'm reading a dozen books at once, none of which captivates entirely. Mostly travel stories—*The Slaves of Timbuctoo, Tobogganing in the Alps, The Cathedrals of Provence*, that sort of thing. It gives me the appearance of sophistication but it is the appearance only.

Take care of yourself

R

JANUARY 12, 1992

Dear Peter,

Thanks for the call. And of course I'm delighted over the show of your work at the Lutheran Church in New York City.[3] And to make an Altar Piece—shades of the Flemish Masters and Giotto! I do hope there will be flashes of gold, the suggestion of starlight and wings. Will you use candles and shadows? I am all worked up over this project of yours. You must drop everything and begin. It is doubtless the only way you will ever secure the Keys of the Kingdom. I am also delighted that you might do *Little Saint Hugh* in the sanctuary. I shall be there, I promise. Sanctuaries, unless miked, are notoriously unacoustic. No one more than twenty feet away ever gets to hear anything. You must watch out for that. Also, I hope the play will take place at some elevation. If it is done at the same level it won't be seen, either. Take heed from the Old Bastard Son of Medicine & Literature.[4]

Yaddo is, well, Yaddo. I always swear never to return and here I am. The house is convenient, large, with many flat surfaces upon which to pile and strew

Dining room in the mansion of the artists' colony Yaddo, in Saratoga Springs, New York.

papers and books and otherwise to write upon. I have not taken part in the general conviviality—out of sheer inertia, I guess. Also, I am twenty years older than anyone else and I am shy. Old age makes one bashful: the dewlaps and wrinkles, the aluminum hair. At meals I try to sit with one of the painters or one of the composers with whom I share an interest in birds, nature, books. There is a good deal of attempted one-upmanship among the youth. My timidity and deferential nature would cause me to step aside with a bow and a sweep of my plumed hat.

The thing about Mme. Eglantine [the Prioress] in "Little Saint Hugh": she is the ideal heroine (courtly) found in medieval romances such as *Roman de la Rose*, but overdone just enough to suggest that she might *not* be the aristocrat she pretends to be. I wish I had time to write her for you. By the way, Eglantine is another name for the briar rose, one of the three crowns of thorns worn by Jesus when He was brought before Caiaphus. So consider yourself told all about it, Buster.

Love
R

JANUARY 13

I'm still agog over the *Saints'* future (by definition, should be immortal). Will it be in spring or fall? I'll be there. Your apartment is an adventure. For how many hours each day are you literally awash? Sounds rather like "Poe's Light-house." Yaddo is not amusing this time around, not at all. Meals are dominated by a clique of guys trying to one-up each other, very showoff-y. I eat and leave immediately for my quarters. But I am getting work done and, if I can stick it out, I will return to New Haven with a manuscript of heft. Heft, however, is only heft, as we all know. Today I walked around the lakes for the first time. Beautiful in the snow. I heard the Great Horned Owl but did not sight him.

JANUARY 14

For Gosh sakes, MD magazine phoned *this very house* and got through. How? Truth to tell, I was glad to talk to *anyone*. It is very isolated for me here. No news as to the rights for *Swan*. We are all ready. Where are *you*, Thomas Mann?

Lovely rain all night, propped up on pillows and read the memoirs of E. F. Benson, about the 1890s at Cambridge. Useless but so much fun. John Nelson leant me a Whittle book called *The Doctor Watchers*, one of those truly awful, soulless, conservative diatribes against government interference in medicine, just what the doctors want to read. What they wouldn't want to read is my Lazarus. It is absurd to think that they would publish it, and I myself grow cool to the idea. I may end up putting it in the diary after all, then accept my destiny at the podium for all time. I've had the grandest respite from all that and it doesn't resume til mid-February when I address the Yale medical students. I dare not peek at the calendar any further—too daunting. I simply *must* be told to shut up about it and stop whining. Anyone would die to take my place. Yep, I know, so I'll behave.

After weeks of no trouble, the craving for tobacco came back. I had to have a gin at *noon*. That relieved it. I did not have to drive to Saratoga and to disaster. It has been nine and a half months. Ye Gods! What an ordeal.

JANUARY 15

Solitary confinement. The temperature is below 0 degrees. One opens the door at his own risk. And that is not the only freeze on hereabouts. One of the writers has quite stupidly misinterpreted an effort on my part to be jocular, and taken permanent offense. He has agitated among the young painters and writers and I am now excommunicated—for the first time in my life. I did inform him that he had misinterpreted, but I refuse to apologize. So now I remain entirely by myself. Ah, it don't matter. I've less than two weeks to stay. By then I'll have transcribed and typed most of the diary.

MD calls again. Alyssa calls. Kenneth calls. I might as well be in New Haven. Denise calls. Ken Warren calls. Everybody calls. John Nelson comes for a drink every day at 5. Today I greeted and toured a composer named—Lazarus. Rembrandt would not have used him as the model for the Resurrection. He is large, soft, beefy.

January 16

If I worked for the duration, I would not come to the end of this garrulous diary. Who could believe I wrote down such a lot of airy persiflage? Meanwhile my outside keeps trying to get inside. My lunatics have all phoned up. They are awaiting the 28th of January like chickens waiting to be fed. O my beloved lunatics! One of them, unable to live up to his promise, phoned saying that it was an emergency, so of course he got through and of course it was not an emergency. He just had to hear my voice, poor boy. I had to scold him. Poor New Haven, getting crazier and crazier without RS there to listen to its shenanigans.

Ah well, Ah well, Peter. I've just read the galleys of a novel written by one of the artists here—I was a captive—and wrote a wonderful blurb for the dust jacket. The book is a flop, but who am I to throw cold water on an enterprise? And the author, an Englishman, is quite a nice man. Meanwhile, I've sold to MD magazine an excerpt from *Troy*. But it is the play I *want* to do. I never *want* to do anything, but I *want* to do *this*, so doubtless I shall not be permitted to.

January 17

February 5, I go to New York City to appear on a religious TV program sponsored by Trinity Church, there to talk about "Whither Thou Goest," but I seem to think they only do half-hour plays and that is not enough time for this story. I am getting eager to get back home—Gretchen's baby comes on February 3 and Janet and I have every right to be nervous. One reason I came here was to keep busy this month.

January 18

I spoke to Janet this morning. She is thriving in my absence. I could live anywhere, I believe. Suspended from a raincloud by the toes. I had lunch with Howard Keith of the Lyrical Ballad bookstore, then an intimate tour of the place. It burrows underground, room after room full of treasures. One could die there happily. They would simply label and sell your bones:

Femur of Richard Selzer: $16.00.
12th rib of Richard Selzer (with a fracture): $4.25 + tax.

JANUARY 20

I've been thinking over Ken Warren's reaction to the *Said* book and spoke to him about it. I guess what I'd do at this point is shelve it for the time being. Its worth, if any, would be related to the future esteem in which my works may be held, so this is not the time for it to be published. All this explained to me, and I must say it sounds reasonable. Spare yourself the hurt and nuisance of future rejections. Maybe after my death? I'm serious.

JANUARY 25

Sounds as if you are enjoying your new apartment. Too much? One can get overused to solitude, and one is known by the company he keeps, so I'd ask someone over if I were you just to have a cup of hot water or a spritz of tahini. Nothing heavy, hear? Last night I had a "date," I'd call it, with the beauteous Carol Bullard (the name doesn't go, does it?).[5] First she came over for "an aperitif"—red sweet vermouth sipped in the intimacy of the "second" parlor of Southwoods. I thought I'd save the best parlor for later? Then we went to a restaurant in Saratoga where we were the only customers. Had she rented it for the evening? She generously allowed me to pay the bill, which means that there is nothing left to give Yaddo for the rest of the year. Hours later, I was dropped off at my door with one of those warmly tossed off see you's! Tonight Bill McQuiston and a lady friend come at 5:30, then we'll go out to dinner. I'm already in my pajamas, though. Wonder if they'd mind if I went like that?

Good thing I'm leaving on Tuesday. Really, I should go tomorrow. My working hours at Yaddo are over and I am reading my way through the shelves at West House. It is what you call compulsive reading. The fact is that I am exceedingly nervous about Gretchen. The Caesarian section is scheduled for February 3. With the obstetrical ill-fortune we have known lately, I am having nightmares. So is Janet, but we don't mention it.

JANUARY 26

So I have thrown out (don't I wish for it) my L. sacroiliac joint and am in the vise of the devil, as opposed to the devil's vice to which *you* are in thrall. Can't sit at all, only stand up or lie down—the latter achieved by flinging myself on the bed while screaming. Hits Orful. Serves me right for sliding on the ice like a lil boy. I'm driving home Tuesday, so I will be *sitting* at the wheel by then no matter what. I'd leave today, but John Nelson has invited me to dinner Monday night along with two old acquaintances from New Haven, so I cannot go early, altho' I have been known to do so and leave dinner to the survivors. This place begins to pall. I have written a farewell note to be read after my departure: "So long—

it's been nice knowing most of you." I've always wanted to say that. In any case, I am through writing here. Am only reading, walking, drinking (fermented potatos: v---a), and dreaming of cigarettes.

Dinner with Bill Mc Quiston and his lady friend. She gives support seminars to anxiety-ridden vice-presidents of Disney Corporation. Advice to the mice, I suppose—altho' Mickey & Minnie would *eschew* such *crumby* psychologies. I have been plagued with dreams—mostly about Gretchen and the forthcoming Caesarian. And about Hank and . . . everybody.

I have (I think) made a decision about Whittle. *No*. And will spend the next ten years paying back the advance. I just *can't* write that book. I'd much rather go to jail for eighteen months with time off f. g. b. h. Do they add time for bad behavior? And just what *does* that consist of? Don't! I don't want to know. Keep it to yourself, hear?

January 27

No doubt about it: one should always leave Yaddo a day earlier. There comes that moment when no more work is forthcoming, the car is packed, one has said goodbye—and then suddenly you have to wait overnight to be allowed to leave. Yesterday I flopped from bed to divan to gold velvet ottoman scarcely able to raise my heart to a drooping syllable, as, I think, Emily Dickinson put it. And today—well Jesus doesn't love me today. I can't think why, as the only thing I ever did to Him was to crucify Him, and that was before I was born.

I have found another guest whom I dislike—a militant feminist who lectured on the subject at breakfast. So I am planning to leave that note after all—to be read after my departure: "So long! It has been a pleasure knowing one or two of you."[6] It's all part of the Selzeryssey, I suppose. You will hear next from the Manorial House on St. Ronan Terrace.

February 6, 1992

Dear Peter,

Yes, well I surely am glad to hear of your ant-like progress on the introduction to *River*. My goodness! After all! Gloryosky! 'Bout time! Gretchen gave birth to Lucy on February 3, so I have been in hospital myself these days. And each time hugged and kissed by a score of my darling black nurses, greeted so warmly by my buddies of that race—those who do the real work of the work—orderlies, guards, technicians.

I went into New York City yesterday, had a visit with Ken Warren and the editors of Scribners. Then by Macmillan-paid limo (!) I was taken to Trinity

Church and I saw the Brooklyn Bridge for the first time. It *is* beautiful—all those intersecting cables—graceful—no wonder Whitman, Hart Crane, Joseph Stella, and others. The driver gave me a mini-tour of the area. Trinity Church was founded 300 years ago and the lower half of Manhattan was given to it by Queen Anne. That church owns Wall Street. Every month the wheelbarrow full of money drives up and they have an inexhaustible store of funds. Their TV, radio, publishing building is at 74 Trinity Place—connected by a causeway with the church. I taped an interview for their cable TV station—"Vision"—with 10,000,000 subscribers and growing. We (three of them, all terrific, and me) had lunch at an Irish pub called Branigan's, then we talked about "Whither Thou Goest," which they hope to do as a half-hour film. Bad is that the agent for Thomas Mann demands 40% of any earned income (by me) for *The Black Swan*. So I said yes, and we will now actually do the darn thing at the Column Theatre. I am outraged that *Little Saint Hugh* will cost *anything*. You should have it for free. What, tell me, can I do?

Love
R

February 12, 1992

Dear Peter,

Thanks for your congratulatory call. We are hugely relieved after all that has befallen our family in the departments of obstetrics and pediatrics. As for any news, I am more befuddled than ever, spending hours each day looking for something I've lost. The same back that I sprained at Yaddo throbs on, but I am resolved to tough this one out. As for "Whither Thou Goest," Vision Cable at Trinity Church will do it as a half-hour play. Kenneth Cavander to write the screenplay, I get to kibbitz. Kenneth will use this tape to try to interest someone in a larger film. Then there is the *Swan*. Kenneth insists that I be present at auditions (so strict!), so the whole thing is put off til mid-March, much to the disgust of everyone, but I won't budge on that one. What! Go to New York with my family in New Haven? It would be to laugh, as they say in Russia. I asked Kenneth about a friend attending the auditions. He returned to me a glare that I only saw once before on the face of Jehovah in stained glass. So, I guess not. I see right off the bat just who is the boss in this venture. Once again I am the *mujik* (Russian peasant) bowing before the Tsar. You have enough to do without mucking around in *Swan*shit, anyway.

Down from Troy is with Ginsberg (in God'sburg). I cannot alter so much as a comma. Ken Warren pronounced hisself enchanted, except for the inclusion of that assisted death piece from the *New York Times*. He is right, of course. I called

Harvey to ask about deleting it. He said *No*! I'll have to live with it. Morrow invited me to meet a few hundred book critics at a cocktail party in New York, but I am speaking at Benedictine Hospital in Kingston that night. It is both too bad and very lucky. So now you know everything. Tell it not in Gath (City of the Philistines).

Love

R

Who Knows the Day

Today I read the letters of Chekhov. A dozen times I literally burst into tears. Such a beautiful character in such a *concentrate* of sensitivity. And doomed. It is not fair. Anyway, my hope is to resuscitate him on the stage of the American Repertory Theatre in Cambridge. I owe it to my cousin Anton.

February 12

Just read "A Dreary Story" by Chekhov. It is marvelous. He is my great love. I kiss his sleeve, his buttons, I hold his palm against my neck, I do all sorts of Russian acts of endearment and worship. I drink a glass of tea from the samovar with him, we roar with laughter—he coughs and coughs, I stroke the cough from his chest as though it were a wrinkle. *I love Chekhov*, and that's final. How odd, you say, to lay one's heart at the feet of a writer, a man yet, dead almost 100 years. It is perverse. Well, odd and perverse it may be, but he is *my* human being. And the knowledge of that is all in all—I need no other fulfillment.

February 18

I suppose I *should* be upset, but I'm not. I'm enjoying the "situation." Here's what happened: Unbeknownst to anyone else in the world, Alyssa hired a casting director, sent out a call, and listed the role of Anna as cast—with *herself* in the role. Kenneth was shocked, called me and said he would withdraw if that were allowed to stand. He could *not* direct the person who has the right to fire him, and also it was just not professional. Now it turns out that what Alyssa really wanted all along was the role of Anna. She will, she says, relinquish her producer's role to a sidekick named Bonnie whom I haven't met, nor shall I. So Kenneth won't stay. And I'm taking flight. Bye-bye to Column Theatre. Now I plan to begin again and get a *theatrical agent* to present this play and Ellen Burstyn to other producers and see what happens. So I am in show business after all. No thanks!

I am now at the Medical School in the same room where you heard Lazarus, waiting for the students to arrive. They are all eating, and I am informed that at precisely five to 1 p.m. they will get up and leave, as they all have a class at 1 o'clock. Is this any way to treat an old resurrectee? Ah well, poor things, I am sure they have much stress. I vaguely remember it.

LATER

The talk went well despite the mass exodus. There were two Nobel laureates in the audience sitting side by side—like a pair of extinct dodo birds.

I mailed *The Black Swan* to Gil Parker at the William Morris Agency. We'll see if he likes it. Calls from the distraught Alyssa reminding me of all her labor, the money she has spent, her faith in my word—all the plaints of the abandoned woman. My heart is a stone.

MARCH 9, 1992

Dear Peter,

The Boston trek was delightful because Cambridge is delightful. I loved walking and browsing and gaping. Ken Warren drove me up and came to *The Seagull* one night and the symposium the next. I was incredibly stupid and knew it, in contrast to the others who were incredibly stupid and did not know it. Self-knowledge rather deflates life, after all. The production was interesting if somewhat misguided. Bob Brustein—most affectionate and warm. It appears that we are to be friends for life. He is a huge success there, with an excellent company that does five plays in repertory. The theatre is always sold out—a full house even for the symposium.

The Alma College gig was one you'd have enjoyed. It's a small, very fine liberal arts school in the middle of cornfields in central Michigan. There are no ugly human beings out there. As there is nothing whatsoever to do there, I was the whole show for five days, all classes canceled and vast audiences for my presentations. I dissected a human cadaver before 800 people. I used the Casserius drawings to good effect. Altogether seven "performances" plus innumberable meetings, meals, interviews, etc., so I am rather thinly nerved—topped off by a terrible trip home, trapped on a plane becalmed on the Detroit runway for three hours. We all died and had to be Lazarated one by one. I got home at 3 a.m. But there is now wherewithal in the bank accont to last a month or two.

I so look forward to seeing *Hugh* performed. Yes, I suppose theatre *is* exciting. Me, I'd rather have a cup of hot chocolate laced with vodka. I just sent off *The Black Swan* to my friend Pirkko, whose son-in-law runs the Finnish Nat'l Theatre. If they do it, I told her, I'll be in Helsinki to rehearse and escort her to opening night. Item in the *Helsinki Times*: "During the single intermission, the lady was seen calming the playwright behind the folds of a curtain. We must all be indebted to her for dealing *humanely* and *sensibly* with the overwrought American Selzer. God bless the brave women of Finland!"

Love

R

MARCH 18, 1992

Mon Cher,

The pace quickens even as I rapidly senesce. Yesterday I addressed the medical staff of Benedictine Hospital in Kingston after a lovely two and a half hour ride (driver provided; I sat in the back seat like an emir). The agent at William Morris turned down *The Black Swan*. "While I admire . . . I cannot bring enthusiasm. . . ." So I remain up for grabs. And unconcerned. Every dog will have its day—woof! I am on the 8:04 train to Grand Central heading for Trinity Playhouse. The contract is there waiting to be signed, so I guess this *is* going forward. Kenneth sees the play in a Christian light (to accommodate the church sponsor). Hannah, a fundamental Christian, is born again, not by faith in God but by the epiphany of flesh and blood at the end. I like that, and I'm dying to see how he pulls it off. Tomorrow I go up to Middletown for lunch with Annie Dillard. I'll keep you posted.

Love

R

EASTER SUNDAY, 1992

Dear Peter,

I've been struggling with sinking spirits as I dictate Lazarus on tapes. It seems to me absolute BUNK and worthless. What at first I thought a daring experiment in prose appears to me as a self-indulgent and poorly realized chronicle. I don't know what to do save finish dictating it and get it typed. It badly needs a wise, kindly (yet severe) editor who has the vision to know what I tried to do and keeps that in mind even as he/she wields the knife. To top that, I dipped into the pages of my diary and found it perfectly *awful*. A lot of unpublishable rejectimenta. So there I am—and thinking I ought to stop writing and start doing some good in this Godforsaken town. There's so much that could be done, I swear I'm going to quit scribbling and pitch in, you'll see.

Kenneth Cavander sent the second draft of *Whither Thou Goest*. It looks okay to me. Not, by any means, what I had hoped for, but . . . The rewrite is due at Trinity May 15. Then we have to find actors, a director, and get on with it. I am now only looking to have *done* with the project. KC strangely relying on *me*. For what?! Meanwhile, the spring migration of birds is on and I haven't gone to the park more than once. And then there is Birmingham, Alabama this week. Then I will come as promised on Friday, damnit, so shut up. At least Ken Warren has been away for eighteen days—steamboat trip on the Mississippi with his wife on a jazz history voyage all the way to New Orleans, then back. Luxury—you and I will not achieve it. He had wanted to take *me* but I said NYET, so he took his dear wife instead.

I read *Othello* all afternoon. It is just plain gorgeous, every word. How can we ever thank that man? And why read anyone else?

Love

R

P.S. The introduction to *The Wounded River* is simply *wonderful*. I mean it. A great job. I hope to tell the world.

MARCH 29, 1992

Dear Peter,

I hope this finds you asymptomatic. Keep me up on things, will you? If not, go straight to Hades, hear?

Yesterday, after three worthless days, I went to New York City. At 10 a.m. I was interviewed for BBC TV. I tried manfully to answer questions that ought only to be asked by the Recording Angel on Judgment Day. Then I brought Ken Warren the whole of the diary and, with a break for lunch, we spent hours at the copying machine. The deal is for me to submit the *Newsday* article on writing about illness, Fanny Burney and Lazarus to Whittle or to Harvey Ginsberg. Ken Warren will keep the rest, only now I have much to write, as he has located many gaps. Also, reworking Lazarus, I have decided it is utter rubbish and I'm quite deflated over it. I went Wednesday night to the Fellows meeting at Ezra Stiles. Richard Sewall spoke about "Old Yale"—rambled on for two hours—very sad—but I'm not that much better—the holes are getting bigger every day. I'm tired and lazy, what Lady MacBeth called MacB, "infirm of purpose." Should I kill the king or not? Not, I think. All around me at Yale there are Japanese chemistry professors and Russian theoretical physicists. In every building, the stairs and hallways go pittypat as they pace back and forth solving problems. Why can't I solve problems? Why can't you?

Love

R

P.S. I am appalled over the rights to Little Saint Hugh. As soon as I get the check—if I do get a check—I'll make it over to you. That is money I don't want.

P.P.S. Trinity is amazing. They are downplaying any religious angle, even want to change the title to avoid the biblical suggestion. I've given up on Swan.

MARCH 30, 1992

Dear Peter

It is exactly one day shy of one year since I smoked. There is not much to be said for abstinence. I am not an iota happier. I have exactly, if not more, the same quantity of self-loathing, and I have grown out of my wits by half. I have the sensation that grass is growing inside my head. It could all be cured by one pack of Lucky Strikes.

Clara and Ferenc Gyorgyey call hourly in an effort to persuade me toward Long Island and the Lam Qua Grotesques, but I so far have resisted all blandishments. My God! You dedicated the exhibition to me? But I contributed nothing! Ah, I see. I am a *living* grotesque who might have stepped out of one of the canvasses to walk among humankind. Well, thanks anyway.

Love
R

P.S. The packet just came. The Peter Parker/Lam Qua essay is wonderful, just right. The Cheever bit ["The John Cheever Story," from *Said*] as always made me squirm and wish I were dead.

APRIL 2, 1992

Dear Peter,

Last evening Harvey Ginsberg phoned to tell me he's resigning from William Morrow as of June 1. *Troy* comes out in July. Once again I shall be minus a shepherd. It happened once before with *Letters to a Young Doctor* at Simon & Schuster—with unfortunate results, and again at Random House, where Becky Saletan decamped before the ink was dry on *Imagine a Woman*. It is a measure of the sorry intellectual health of publishing, a corrupt and hollow business at best. Borchardt will now scurry to see me attached, however unenthusiastically, to another editor at Morrow.

I visited Trinity College Tuesday, taught a class in which "Imelda" and "Impostor" had been read, then I had supper with the students. I stayed overnight and drove to New Haven in time to talk to an inner city high school audience—all black and Hispanic save for one scrawny undersized brilliant Jew—the runt of the litter. If it had been a pet shop instead of a high school, I'd have bought him

and brought him home. He even looks like me—the same skull shape, myopia—
it was like beholding my reincarnation, thinking *Well! Here I go again!* Meanwhile, Janet has guests visiting here, peeking around to get a look at me. A wolf
would urinate on the banister and mantelpiece to warn them off his territory. I
simply hide in my room.

Your foolish

R

APRIL 27, 1992

Dear Peter,

So! I have drawn a bead on you. What? A soldier and afeard? Fie! my Lord, fie!
All of which means that now that success (in the form of an *MD* assignment and
a teaching gig at Alma College) has dropped into your lap, you wish you were back
amongst the rejected and despised whose work never see the light of day, right?[7]
You're only happy as the underdog, the outcast, so that you can rally your ragged
regiment and attack the Philistines. Well, forget it. Get busy writing the article for
MD and start preparing for Alma, Buster. I'm watching you, Little Brother.

I was delighted with the Chinese Grotesques and I long for a report on the
symposium, I've finished dictating Laz. It is a wretched piece of clumsiness. I am
desolate. It goes to the typist tomorrow. Problem is, I've overworked it and lost
my way in the thicket. And now, losing zest—so it all seems bleak. Meanwhile I
am reading *Othello*, *Lear*, and *Richard III* all at the same time. I am so glad not to
have died, if only so as to reread these plays. I plan to read them all.

I so much want to write in favor of your grand book. Again, thanks for doing
it. I am in your debt for a lot. Then there is *Hugh*, about which I jot in my diary,
so it's none of your business, but I do look forward to November. The problem:
how to wait til then? Very exciting.

Love

R

N.B. Janet and I are going to a "Tea Dance" at the Lawn Club in one and a half
hours. I hate to dance—I don't know how!

MAY 2, 1992

Dear Peter,

My brain hurts. I've been speaking to French guests. They're from Paris. So
this letter will be even stupider than usual. I had no sooner gotten to the library

than my poet friend arrived and corralled me into going to his apartment to say some sentences into the tape recorder. "Soon you will have sex with a female." "From now on you will be lucky." Sounds easy? Forget it! I must labor over each minuscule accent and repeat until I get it right. Trouble is, there are pigeons roosting on the window ledge of his room and their cooing disturbs him, so that he must go and pound on the wall until they are quiet. But they won't be, so in the end he turns on the air conditioner to drown them out. Meanwhile, I am disconsolate—it is all too depressing for words. Then another one phones—he's won two tickets to a concert in New London, can't understand *why* Janet and I say no thanks. He's cut to the bone. And so the ministry goes on.

Kenneth Cavander called and we together rewrote the script for *Whither*. It couldn't be better, but you never know what the Trinitarians will say. If they don't like it, screw 'em, I say. I've been typing material for my California visit every day, but what with the warblers in, I'm not sticking to it very well. I imagine I'll have enough for the four lectures. They're all big deals and I mustn't repeat. Try that on for size, I dare ye! But the pay is good, and my goodness we have got poor again behind my back.

SUNDAY.

Ecstatic morning in the park. So many beauties—especially *two* Blackburnian Warblers in the same field of my glasses—a never-to-be-forgotten sighting. Birding is just this side of paradise, I tell you. As a result, nothing done in the way of work. This afternoon I attended a rally of Korean-Americans. Very moving, as the students beat their native drums and cymbals for peace. I'm definitely going to quit writing as soon as Lazarus is published. Oh I'll jot down in my diary, but nothing else. I want to (a) be useful, and (b) have fun. The taxes on the house just doubled, so I guess I must stagger up to the podium until the last chapter.

Love

R

MAY 10, 1992

Dear Peter,

They have been five Edenish days with Larry, Rossi, and Hank. The last has quite enslaved us—we are to do his bidding. It is *so* thrilling to see evidence that his brain is functioning well, that he can see a great deal. And his nature is incredibly sweet. He is a parcel of pure innocence (and they name the *popes* Innocent!). He is as fat as a sumo wrestler, though, and not easy to heft by a grandpa and grandma who are not exactly with Herculean sinews strung. But we oofed and aarghed and gritted our teeth and managed quite well. All this to say nothing of the mornings of birdwatching in the park with Larry. Four hours of Heaven. Every father should have a son like that one. He is strong, tender, witty, solicitous, wise, and a shrewd and alert birdwatcher. We saw *everything* there was to see. My eyes are still flitty with birds. Am I not lucky to have Larry on one hand and Hank on the other? Just think: out of the immensity of sorrow has come an equal-sized joy and, I think, we are *all* wiser for having passed through the flames of Hell. But no use to go on about the birds with so pavement-oriented a Philistine as *you*.

I have to leave for Sacramento on Tuesday. It is Faust handing over his soul all over again. I'll be there for six days. But I must *not* whine, says Janet. "It is the way you take care of us." I need to prepare and deliver *four* major addresses. (1) A university-wide lecture called the Nelson Lecture. (I doubt it is the same Lord you and I know about from the English Admiralty.) (2) Medical Grand Rounds. (3) Surgical Grand Rounds. (4) The Alpha Omega Alpha (Honorary Society of Medicine) Induction Address. Four—count 'em. 4. IV. Quatre. Fier. Quattro. So stop *your* whining and pay homage to a sixty-three-year-old sufferer.

The cover of *Troy* arrived. It is inoffensive. Lazarus is now renamed. It will be called *Raising the Dead*. Do you like it? The script for *Whither* has now undergone its third revision and will be submitted tomorrow to the Trinitarians. Please Jesus

The rock face of East Rock Park in New Haven, Connecticut.

they will like it. The *Times* review of Lam Qua is just wonderful, an unqualified success. It should go from gallery to gallery around the U.S.A., with *you* lecturing in each foyer and earning a living.

Love

R

MAY 20, 1992

Dear Peter,

I was delighted to read the casting call for *Little Saint Hugh*. So, it is really happening! I spent overnight in Poughkeepsie. From my hotel room, a splendid view of the Hudson River. Later I walked down to its bank, found a twig, and wrote my name in the water. I addressed the Mid-Hudson Surgical Society after dinner at a restaurant, fighting the music box all the way. Met no one to remember, only a number of surgeons each desirous of writing his memoirs and wanting to know how to go about getting it published. This, without a single sentence having been written. Vodka enables one to remain congenial long after one's tolerance for arrogance, stupidity, and boredom has been exceeded. I drove home through a glory of countryside this morning.

My goodness but life is *busy*. It shall be carved on my tombstone: *He kept busy*. I went birding this morning at 6 a.m. and met a graduate student of physics in the park—most congenial. He knew all the bird calls and has the eye of a falcon himself. Took me in hand, he did, and showed the old codger a thang or two.

Kenneth Cavander called. The Trinitarians are satisfied with his script. A director named Tony Giordano may be hired on Tuesday. I hope that if we all do a good job, *you* might check in and rein your horse at that post too. As for *The Black Swan*, nothing, so forget it. When are you coming to New Haven? I plan to write the paragraph you wanted under your very nose, not before.[8] I have just heard that *Confessions of a Knife* is to be published in Portuguese. Brazil, Portugal, Angola—wow. And it was published in 1979 unless I'm mistaken. So I'm here to stay. So be you.

Love

R

MAY 24

All day overhead army helicopters in ones, twos, and threes flying low over the house. I think it is because Gorbachev is in town to receive an honorary degree

Bust of Shakespeare in the garden of the Yale Elizabethan Club.

tomorrow. Yale never lets on who is getting one until the very moment, and the honorands are sworn to secrecy.

JUNE 10

I'm waiting to hear about the first rehearsal of *Hugh*. Leave no detail out. As for *Swan*, I fear it is a dead bird—no one shows the least interest. I must say my own has dropped off too. I'm waiting for the summons to New York City for the casting of *Whither*. The script has now been worked over to death and beyond. I liked it better the first time.

JUNE 15

I mightily enjoyed all the vicissitudes of the first rehearsal of *Hugh*. So many situations, each one delicious. Do solve them all and put everyone in a good working mood. I *know* you can. The initial John de Lexinton sounds a bad lot. I'm glad he's out. I'm just back from New York City, where I delivered *Raising the Dead* to the beauteous Denise Shannon, who did *not* invite me into her office, as I had not made an appointment. I worshipped anyway. *Raising the Dead* has officially been accepted as my Whittle book. Thank God. Growth hormone costs $18,000 per year. I am free of all podia for the foreseeable future. O bliss! I just want to stay here and wallow. To hell with writing. To hell with my diary. Eight books, that's enough.

June 17

You! Midlander! Yes you! I am writing to you—don't look at me with that WHO ME? face either. What I want to know is how you are using your time in Paradise. It is fleeting—Hermes-heeled—so get cracking at that Index [for *The Wounded River*]. What's this about new short stories? My, my! And new paintings? Another *my*! Well at least you can't direct a play out there—or can you? Hereabouts, I've been overcome with my old enemy—lassitude. I awake at 2:30 a.m., get up at 5 a.m. and am exhausted by 9 a.m. So everything is becalmed with no land in sight. I *am* reading—ten books at once. Most fun is Angela Carter, English novelist. Then I'm on a Shakespeare kick and reading *Antony and Cleopatra*—after *Troilus and Cressida*, *All's Well*, and *Merchant of Venice*. What dopey characters they all were, but ennobled, *deified* by his language.

I learned that Recorded Books has optioned audio rights for *Troy*, *Repairs*, and *Confessions of a Knife*. That *Confessions of a Knife*—it's just coming into its own after thirteen years.

I have taken to eating lunch al fresco at the hospital—so many ethnic stands. I like lo mein with veggies best. I ran into Ferenc, but couldn't visit more than to praise the Lam Qua exhibition at Mills Pond House. He was pleased that I went. As for *Whither*, it's turning out to be less rather than more. The director is busy running roughshod over the story. It is quite eviscerated already. There is to be no suggestion of the erotic, which I insist is necessary to highlight the spiritual. And many other outrages. They'll all be in "deep doo-doo" (as George Bush says) on Judgment Day, unless, of course, the latter is a misnomer.

June 18

Long walk with one of my poor loonies. On and on he raves, although quietly. This ministry is weighty some days.

The director continues to misconceive *Whither Thou Goest*. Kenneth has argued the case for me but I think it is no use. The film will *not* be good.

June 19

Phone call (three at once—but then what can you expect from a Trinity?) to browbeat me into letting Henry Pope (recipient of the heart) be in his mid-fifties; in other words, fatherly rather than a possible sexual partner. Quite ruins the story, but I yielded—out of fatigue. The *New York Times* requested old photos; I sent 'em, they asked for more! "Why so many?" I asked. The photographer let slip something about "extensive coverage"—needs "one for outside, one for inside." Could that mean a front-page review? Too incredible, unless of course someone like Bill Kennedy wrote the review.[9] We'll know all on July 12. It is a bit distracting I confess. I have to give myself a slap in the brains and get on with my verbiage.

JUNE 20

Troy is in the local bookstores and I've signed all the copies. It does look nice, and I have to say, with all its faults, I do like that book. Let us hope the *New York Times* likes it too, it would make life so much easier. If it does get attention, I will use that clout to get *Repairs* and *Imagine* into paperback.

Kenneth and I are fed up with the Holy Trinity. What *is* wrong with these producers? Everyone insists on expressing himself or herself and it never, never redounds to the benefit of Art. It's all a kind of stupid kindergarten handraising. I can't deal with it. The alternative is to put your trust in posterity. But then again, what has posterity ever done for *me*? So, you are used and it isn't fun. Arrogance and pretension rule at Trinity Television, all masked by the broadest Christian grins in the history of the church. Would Jesus Christ be proud to have them on his team? I ask you.

JUNE 23

Tomorrow I am sixty-four. How did you let this happen? Only last week I reached puberty and now—this! What next? It's the last time I leave you in charge of my life.

Georges Borchardt phoned to say that, in his opinion, *Raising the Dead* is the best thing I have written. So there. Also, Holt has made a small paperback bid for *Troy*. Too small to count, but a least I know there will be a paperback. And Tuesday I'll give a reading from the book at the Yale Co-op Bookstore. I hope this sort of thing happens to you and *River*. You deserve it.

I've forgotten when you are due back East, but I'm telling you outright that I am *not* writing to you every day. May I suggest that you embark on a sexual relationship with one of the other scholars? Then you won't need me to provide an envelope of nonsense every twenty-four hours. Be sensible! Besides, what is it? Six to ten minutes of pumping. Think of it as push-ups at a gym.

JUNE 24

Sixty-four! And for the occasion, Morpheus gifted me with a solid night in his arms. It is already noon and I am not tired. Ssh! I feel I've gotten away with murder after last April. The rest is gravy, right?

The *Times* review has been bumped from the July 12 issue and also from the front page. So, I am once again a member of the proletariat. I had so hoped to stir the jealousy of . . . of whom? I have neither rival nor enemy, so who would there be to gnash his teeth and green up? Just as well. Better to keep company with Modesty. She's less likely to give you the clap.

JULY 2

Well, I seem to have arrived but exactly where I don't know. A lady from *Publishers Weekly*, Sybil Steinberg, is going to interview me, said she's been waiting years for my "breakthrough book" and here it is. First I ever heard that a tiny memoir of Troy is a "b-t-b." Incidentally, BTB in birdwatching parlance stands for the Black-throated Blue Warbler, my favorite, so I guess it's only right. Somehow or other I'm more excited this time around. Maybe because I already died and the joy is greater thereafter?

On the 20th I go to New York for the first read-through of *Whither*. I do want to address the cast, the director, and the Holy Trinity to let them know that I am let down. The director turns out to be bossy in a schoolmarmish way, opinionated and not easily persuaded otherwise. Also very glib, so I can't get a word in edgewise. It's all a crying shame, as it was my one chance to have a film done properly. Still, I am on the good side of the Trinity and I *think* (don't know for sure) they'll be interested in another, so get ready. Also, I want to invite them to see *Little Saint Hugh* and to meet you in November, so I've got to be nice.

JULY 3

Nothing new, except a phone call from Roseanna, the girl next door as of fifty years ago. She had just finished reading *Troy*, called to say it was amazing how much alike we were, are, and shall ever be. I was gentlemanly enough not to reminisce over long summer afternoons of secret delight.

Richard Sewall is going to let me swim in the stream this summer, so I may drown after all. If so, you have to put the diary together and ship it to Harvey Ginsberg. Nobody else. Just you. For your peccadillos. Annie Dillard is savaged by Bruce Bower in the June *New Criterion*. She's hurt, but it's just a vicious working over, I tell her. Not to mope. If they do it to Annie, nobody's safe.

JULY 7

I'm newsless today but that's no excuse for not writing. My days are taken up with the diary, which, if I say so myself, begins to look promising. But as what? I fear it will be like dispensing free ham to orthodox Jews: it may smell delicious but they can't eat it. But I take some perverse pleasure in writing down whatever pops in, then elaborating on it—rather like those jazz musicians who can take the simplest tune and erect a complex architecture of chords about it. Only *you* would die laughing at some of my criminal perpetrations.

The *Times* wants to interview me—the *Book Review*—so it will be one of those short boxed things. I guess I'll be well-covered even if there isn't a cover review. They certainly must be running low on good books if they're down to me. I haven't had this much fuss over a new book since *Mortal Lessons*. The secret of success is longevity. You just have to endure long enough for them to finally take notice. Remember that, Mister. Tomorrow is the daily *Times* review. The *Boston Globe* will review it too, and I am to be interviewed by the *Troy Record*, the *Albany Times Union*, and Connecticut Public Radio. It's enough to turn a boy's head, and me only sixty-four, a mere pickle of a tiny chap.

Guess what? I'm the oldest person at the Yale gym. People gather to watch me strain and perspire. I am the cynosure of all eyes. And our fellow has decided that I must *lift weights*. So now I shall be instructed in the arcane mysteries of body building. Next thing you know—the *Playgirl* centerfold, then on to Muscle Beach, porno flix, anatomy atlases. I knew it: I *am* the Apollo Belvedere, just as I thought back in 8th grade.

JULY 9

Well now, Peter, I said I would *not* go to any casting of *Whither*, right? So what am I doing on the train to New York City? Last night, an urgent conference call from the Holy Trinity. Very important that I be present, they say. I can't think why, but as usual I caved in. It ain't over til 5 p.m. so only the Holy Ghost knows what time the corpse will return home. And then Ms. Publicity from William Morrow phoned to say that the review would be in today's *Times*. It wasn't, but there was a review of a book about garbage disposal called *Rubbish*. I surely do hope there is no connection, but I am inclined to put a good deal of stock in such subliminal events. They are usually prophetic.

Now comes the news that Clinton has picked Al Gore for his Vice President. My man, a true environmentalist. Now I know for whom to vote, so that's settled. I had briefly thought to toss it away on Perot.

JULY 10

It's barbaric is what it is—casting. Never again will I sit in the chair of power while some poor soul perspires to show himself/herself in the best light. My shame was acute; I could have died of it. There were twenty "callbacks" and the Trinity, the director and I were to vote or veto. First of all the three men who read for Henry Pope were all twenty years too old. Once again I remonstrated and got nowhere. These people are fucking up the story. I can only hope it will survive *despite*. Four gals read for Hannah—mine didn't win. They picked a hard-looking woman who has won a Tony on Broadway. Ivy Love will be a better choice, a fat auntie type but with lots of pizzazz. For Sam there were four or five sinfully handsome men in their thirties. Who in real life looks like that? Again mine didn't win, as he was the one who found subtleties and nuance in the soliloquy. With Kenneth in California it's all up to me, but I can't deal with these theatre people.

The *Sunday Times* review (sshh! I'm not allowed to tell) will be July 26. A big spread, I think. They're using three photographs: Father, Mother, Billy. What with five interviews next week, I can't work at all, just hanging around all day long getting crabby and run-down.

July 11, 1992

Dear Peter,

It's no use. I can't work. Too much going on around here. And all because of that damned *Troy*. Today I spent getting ready to be interviewed by the *Times Book Review*—by telephone at 6 p.m. What should I say? And you *not* here to tell me, but off in some ridiculous place called anonymously Midland. What's its real name? You can tell me. No place is called MIDLAND. Maybe its real name is NOPLACE. Anyway, I must be witty, not to say charming. The interviewer is a woman—perhaps she's susceptible to a certain hemiquaver of the voice, especially in the baritone range? We'll try. But don't ever show this letter to a soul or you know I'll be called a macho pig. And while *we* know I'm not, it would be hard to convince anyone else.

Since I am awake ALL night now, and sleep not at all, I am exhausted by 9 a.m. and have to nap before lunch. Nap after lunch. Nap at the gym. The mat upon which I lie is the only one not slick with sweat: I'm napping while all around me ferocious youth is perspiring mightily. I lie there and catch the breeze of their push-ups and sit-ups. Very soothing. Pretty soon it's time to be hauled up by a kind Yalie and go home for a vodka.

I hope you are enjoying yourself in that meshuganeh state. Perhaps you have found a playmate? And perhaps you have gotten some work done? I've told everyone I know about *Hugh*. I do hope they'll come and see it. *Maybe* my new fame will be of some use after all? I'll surely use it whenever I get the chance. Williamstown just rejected my *Swan*. "We cannot find a *slot* for it." Imagine! It's not a subway token. Really!

              Love
              Dr. Samuel Johnson, Esq.

July 17, 1992

Caro,

Giambattista della Porta was born in 1535 and died in 1615. He was a man after your own heart—with twelve thousand interests, including human physiognomy, meteorology, cosmetics, architecture, optics, astronomy, astrology, botany, and pneumatics. He wrote his great book *Natural Magick* when still a young man, although not, as he claimed, at the age of fifteen. *Magic* is not sorcery but the Persian word for wisdom. So: *Wisdom of Nature*. He also wrote something called *Ars Reminiscendi* or *How to Improve Your Memory*. Then there were fourteen prose comedies, two tragedies, and a number of plays. He was a child prodigy but was full of vanity and he also told many lies. He founded a club called Otiosi—Men of Leisure—which met at his house in Naples. Because these guys dabbled in the occult, Porta was made to go see Pope Paul V and "explain himself." Next he established the Academy of the Lynxes (of which Galileo was a member)—dedicated to the pursuit of science and the erasure of ignorance. A very entertaining fellow. *Natural Magick* is a marvel, a masterpiece, this despite the fact that practically none of it makes any sense today. You have to remember that he wrote it as Elizabeth I was ascending the throne of England and before Shakespeare was even born. Do read it when you return from Mars.

Today the interview was with the *Troy Record*. People are not asking good questions. The Long Island *Newsday* review was laudatory, only the guy complained about the malpractice chapter, said it was self-pitying. Never mind, it was a good review with quotes. Meanwhile I'm tired and feel some congestion in my chest. What I need is someone to make me a tisane of lemon blossoms and feed it to me spoon by spoon. She should be naked, preferably . . . or wearing, at the most, a string of beads. Around her neck.

My physical reconstruction at the gym staggers on. It is no cinch to discollapse a sixty-four-year-old frame, unstoop, and raise the head that droopeth like a snowdrop. Yesterday at the gym I was snidely referred to as The Velocipede. Really! And here's a letter from Emily Jane, signed "Longingly." Wouldn't you know, about fifty years too late. And another from "Aida" who is living at a different intensity than the rest of us. I have to keep it in a special container as it is highly flammable. "I shall go to bed repeating: don't be overwhelmed; he's just a man. But I am and you're not. Goodnight, Richard. Te adora para siempre—Aida."

Yours,

Notaman

JULY 18, 1992

Dear Peter,

Well, if I haven't arrived, who has? Now it's *People* magazine doing a review and asking for a different photo other than the one on the dust jacket. So I rummaged in the desk and found one taken by Carol Bullard, although why a magazine of photography can't come up and take its own, I don't know. So I am to be all over—like the measles. Janet says that if I flub this one she's going to kill me. When *Mortal Lessons* came out I just didn't want to cooperate. And here's David Rabe calling to say that he has finished a play for television of *Mercy*, says it's very powerful, "maybe too powerful for American Playhouse. It's not politically correct." So what? Neither am I. He is thinking it ought to be a stage play first. I'll read it Wednesday, then I may just ask him to read *The Black Swan*. He seems very decent on the phone. Such a lot of distractions. This fatigue is a chronic pain in the ass. It makes no sense bellyaching about a pain in the ass, either socially *or* anatomically, except I'm supposed to behave like a mature adult, not a horse with the staggers.

The only writing I do gets mailed to you. I am glad that you called and that you have a conduit of tahini to keep you going. And you have accomplished so much. *Epic*, your perspiration. I think this is going to be *your* year. Just a hunch.

July 22, 1992

Dear Peter,

Mr. Lehmann-Haupt did not like my book. In fact he despised it for four columns in the *Times*. But then here comes the *Sunday Times* to snatch victory from the jaws of defeat. I hope you will see it and help me rejoice. All the dear faces—there for all to see after all these many decades! You can imagine my delight at the photographs. All the other reviews have been extremely positive—the *Chicago Tribune* used up a whole page to heap praise (too much).

I'm just returned from the Shaker Museum, which is in a beautiful town twenty miles south of Troy. The large room was crowded, everyone attentive, laughing, crying, including fifteen of my high school classmates who all came together as a surprise. A grand lot of hugs and kisses. I was put up all by myself in a huge creaky old farmhouse in the country. I have never seen so amiable a place, and that includes the likes of Bellagio and Yaddo.

David Rabe sent his teleplay of *Mercy*. It is powerful. Too powerful. I cannot imagine that American Playhouse will do it. Gives you the willies just *reading it*. If they do not accept it he will try to find another "venue"—stage play, film, I don't know. I'll show it to you when you deign to return East. The read-through of *Whither* went well. I got a chance to speak to the actors privately and told them what I had in mind. They seemed to agree. Best is that they all love the story and are bound to do it well. Tony Giordano has turned out to be much better than I believed. He is doing a splendid job of "blocking," etc. He is attentive to every detail. I watched him rehearse the last scene between Henry Pope and Hannah. It's going to be *amazing*! Trinity is presently reading *Troy* to see if there might be something therein to use for another program. David Rabe said yes—to send him *The Black Swan*, so I did. Tony Giordano will also read it. I shall have two opinions. But there is, I am told, very little hope.

Love
R

July 24, 1992

Dear Peter,

I am entirely out-of-news, newsless, do you understand? I would make some up but you would find out and think ill of me. Oh, here's something. On the way to the library today I fell in with one of those gloomy academic professors who suffers from chronic nameless dread: "Some unborn sorrow, ripe in fortune's womb/Is coming towards me, and my inward soul/With nothing trembles" (*Richard II*, Act II, Scene II). That sort of thing. I could not help but notice that this morning the man was quite perky. He skipped along, pointing a toe, humming a tune. I remarked that he looked unusually cheerful, at which he confided in me that after weeks of constipation he had taken an enema. "With the most excellent results." Such is what used to pass for conversation in my former life, but which now renders me *touché* and unable to thrust back. So there's your bit of news.

The daily *Times* review of *Troy*, I fear, will damage my chances at paperback, foreign, subsidiary, and other rights. And I thought that writing was all about ART. Phooey. As for *Swan*, "my inch of taper will be burnt and done" before that bird alights on any stage. (I don't know why I keep quoting Shakespeare today. It's part of my own nameless dread.)

Really now, you're too silly staying out there in Michigan when all the activity is here. Come home. And get cracking on *Hugh*. I've told everyone I know about it, so there will be *someone* in the pews. Do you know there is a word that rhymes with tahini? Wahini—the Hawaiian word for wife or woman. Couldn't you write a rock song? Something like: MAH WAHINI EAT TAHINI? You do it.

Love
R

July 29

Now that I know how contented you are out there, I see no reason to write all these stupid letters in an effort to cheer you up. You are actually happy! What next?

Any number of people I once knew but have long since forgotten call up in either commiseration or congratulation. All I know is that Morrow printed another 2000 copies ordered by the "wholesaler," whatever that is. And one of the Holy Trinity called to say that he went to the bookstore near Wall Street and they were sold out. He also talked me into changing the name of the play from *Whither Thou Goest* to *Harvest*. They are afraid the religion angle will turn off viewers. So I said okay, sheep that I am. They are presently "cutting." I should have the "product" in September.

You'll be amused to learn that another professor is attending to my work in his Ph.D. He sent the last chapter, which deals with the influence of Walt Whitman on my writing, especially "A Wound Dresser's Diary," "Imelda" [in *Letters to a Young Doctor*], "Raccoon" [in *Confessions of a Knife*], and two or three others. His subject is Whitman. I'm just tacked on, I imagine. But it is quite interesting to find out what I was really doing when I *thought* I was writing some stories.

Numerous letters on *Troy*, one squawk of anguish from "Aida" of El Paso recoiling from my admission on p. 216 that I'd had "a few crepuscular urges of my own." Which she took either as a lapse of taste, or a hint that I am a pederast! Best thing is I don't have to answer—no address given.

Troy, New York

AUGUST 3

I just realized that the Olympics are on. I haven't watched a minute of it, to my shame. I seem to care more about the famine in Somalia and the siege of Sarajevo. Just can't get up for sports.

AUGUST 4

Hour-long "call-in" radio show—only nobody called in! So I blabbed on. I came home to find two dozen messages pertaining, and a phone call from a woman in Westport—her friend is a producer. Can we meet and talk about a project related to *Troy*? "Why yes," I said, "we can."

"Can we entice you to Westport?"

"Why yes, but only if I know the producer has *read Down from Troy*. We have to talk about *something*."

So now we'll see. But she did sound a bit crazy, rather too rich-crazy, and so I don't know. But then, Trinity was hatched on a commuter train and look what happened, so I'll follow it up. After my reading today a truly gorgeous woman came up, said: "We *have* to get married. I love you." I told her yes. Only I can't remember her name now. Such are the vicissitudes of old age.

AUGUST 7

There's this woman—Aida—(no last name, address, or phone number given) who has been writing long passionate letters to me for some years. Some I read, some not, and for a long while I just threw them away. For some reason I've read and kept the last four. *And* she has phoned me twice—briefly, impulsively. The fact is I've begun to think about her—that obsession that is like being possessed. It is *fierce*. I'm her hallucination, the inhabitant of her fantasies—called upon wherever she has the urge to nourish her pleasure. I have no idea of her age, beauty, etc. Only that she is literate and cultivated. Her voice and speech tell me so. Again and again in her letters she relives the birth of her love. It has become the protocol of her obsession. There is something *virile* in her passion; something *feminine* in the roles she has assigned to me. In one sense, it's perfect: we are both utterly safe, there is no conflict. I am her invention, her figment. I have no chance to respond. The power is all hers and it is absolute. I can only resort to discarding the letters unread. But I don't anymore. I have the feeling that she has a doll that is my effigy into which she is sticking pins. It's voodoo. Twice now she has broken the silence by phoning. Both were outbursts rather than prepared talks. But now she has heard my voice, which has become yet another erotic avenue! It was risky of her to call, to break the silence that is absolutely necessary for the obsession to endure. Perhaps, if she breaks it a third time, the obsession will die. And along with it—Aida. It is a strange thing to be the bodiless, adored one—sterile, mute—until it is her need to speak to me. I am safe, anesthetized; *she* is enchanted. In a way it is a form of molestation, isn't it? *But*: now I've begun to write about *her* in my diary. The voodoo is working. I am coming under the spell of her fixation. Kindly remember that this is a sixty-four-year-old man to whom this is happening. The only thing I know is that the letters are postmarked El Paso, Texas. And that she is fluent in Spanish, writes poems in that language, but has no accent. Her letters are worthy of Eloise's to Abelard. And there isn't a damn thing I *can* do about it.

August 12, 1992

Dear Peter,

Welcome home! Such a long long drive, but you have inner resources. Plus you have to learn your lines. Plus you can listen to a book on tape. Plus every now and then you must stop and swallow a dollop of tahini. So time passeth and you arrive. As for food, I have just made a large pot of beef borsht. You wouldn't touch it with a hose, but Jon and Regine will love it.

I'm blaming my inertia on the *Troy* book, but I fear it's deeper than that. We'll talk about it anon. A small but favorable review in the *New Yorker*, an interview in *Publishers Weekly*. People tell me it is a best-seller, but Morrow has only 12,000 total in print and they are timid about more. Anyway, I've already been paid by having my parents' pictures in the *Book Review*. You just couldn't buy that. The rest is all extra.

Here's the latest on *Whither Thou Goest*. Kenneth C and Tony G are at daggers drawn. K hates T's direction and his meddling with the script. They are to battle it out in NYC next week. In fact the film is *not* what I had hoped for. Fault is both TG's and Trinity's, and KC's, who went off to California for three weeks at the critical period. *I* couldn't cope because I simply know nothing about theatre. It gets worse. TG said to me: "You should write a play." I said to TG: "I did." He read *Swan*, called to say that he loves it and would kill to direct it, wants to use all of his connections but insists that I sign an exclusive agreement with *him*. Now KC has been in on this from when it was first developed for Williamstown, and my tacit understanding is for *him* to direct. Kenneth is a gentleman and would say—*by all means*. Still, I don't want to hurt him or exclude him. I just want to get it *done*.[10] Meanwhile, I write nothing, am horribly tired and a bit depressed. I think I must go away for a bit. Maybe I'll rent a house in Schuylerville for a month and sit by the Hudson.

                                                                    Love

                                                                     R

AUGUST 14, 1992

Dear Peter,

Today I got two letters from my boyhood friends Leon and Larry. Both said *Troy* was okay but I forgot to write about *this* and *this* and *that*, so I wrote back for *them* to each write their own version of what happened. But it is gratifying to hear from people I knew when I was ten years old, guys who haven't read a book in years and have read this one. Nice—all these letters from people who are sparked to remember their own childhood.

Now, do you know your lines by heart? If not, prepare for a whipping. I am very good at administering them. Ask Jon and Gretch. So be forewarned. Tell me what I can do to raise an audience. I really should be lying on a verandah somewhere in the mountains—taking the cure. Doubt I'll ever write another sentence. It's going to be up to you to put the diary together.

Love

R

AUGUST 18, 1992

Dear Peter,

You are such a fine, fine writer, as the Lam Qua piece proves. It reads beautifully and is well crafted. Really! I had better look to my laurels, I fear. The paintings look *sensational* in MD. Imagine what you have done—dug them out of the library basement and held them up to the light. Bravo! I am extremely proud of you. They made far too much of my tiny contribution, dammit. Sorry. Nothing to do.

Yesterday I pulled myself together and went to New York City for a radio talk show at WNYC on the twenty-fifth floor of the Municipal Building, way down. I stank. Then I had lunch with Ken Warren, who is looking for a job. He is planning to move to England so that will have been that. (What is that verb form called? *Will have been.* I'll have to look it up and teach it to you.) While in New York I dropped in at the *Book Review* and gave back the book I had agreed to review: Jessica Mitford's *The American Way of Birth*. Just didn't want to. That is the second book I've turned back in one month. The editor was friendly. I heaped thanks for the front page on *Troy*. She said that I was the only person to her knowledge who turned down the chance to write for them. "Are you difficult, by any chance?" I had to admit that I was. "Very," I told her. "It's the only way to be." I was home by 5:10 p.m. and heard the good news that *Troy* has "gone back" for a third printing. Here's the score: first—8000; second—2000; third—1500. So 11,500 copies, which is not much but enough for me. I don't do well with scads and scads. I like little steps better, one scad at a time. Best is that I have *three* reasons to go to Troy:

(1) A Victorian Ball benefit for the Troy Public Library. Bill Kennedy is Exhibit A, I'm Exhibit B.

(2) A reading at RPI.

(3) Commencement at Russell Sage College, where I'm to receive a *Doctor of Fine Arts* (incredible), and this without lifting a paintbrush or a chisel. Best of all is that I don't have to deliver the commencement address, so I said yes and I'll invite brother Billy and his lady friend—they'll love it.

I'm glad to report that my depression (yes that's what it was—the fatigue) is lifting and today I felt quite perky—even wrote in my notebook—a few pages. So I think I'll be okay, not to fret.

> Love
>
> R

August 20, 1992

Dear Peter,

Such a nasty trip home, all but that grandiose and pathetic attempt to match Niagara by urinating nearby. Pshaw! And Bravo for the sale of a painting. I *am* both impressed and delighted. That carries you safely through *Hugh*.

More reviews of *Troy*. One deplores my "straining for effect" as in "a chasm across which swings only the frayed rope bridge of memory." These boobs don't know that diamonds owe their sparkle to the unbearable heat and pressure they have endured. All of which goes to show that the other side of celebrity is contempt.

So many phone calls and letters from my women. It's no cinch being adorable. Be glad you're ugly and obnoxious. Another letter from Aida—ten pages single-spaced. You have to read it to believe. In it I learn that she has a tight vagina, has chosen a life of celibacy, conquers her sexual desire with transcendental meditation. But she would, she swears, emerge from chastity for *me*. She wonders if I have handsome buttocks. Let her wonder, I say.

The film of *Whither Thou Goest* [called *Harvest*] is extremely mediocre (oxymoronic.) It is entirely miscast and has an amateurish look; also, the director changed any number of lines so as not to make sense. Kenneth Cavander wrote so bluntly about this to Trinity that they have not invited him to the editing. In fact I think he has cooked our goose there.

My sister-in-law (schizophrenic) has been called for jury duty. I have had a hilarious correspondence (ten letters) with the bureaucrats in the Department of Justice. If she doesn't show up, they say, an officer will come and lead her thru the streets of New Haven in manacles. I want to be there for *that*. They are not amused by my attitude, which borders on Contempt of Court.

Love
R

August 23, 1992

Dear Peter,

I am basically a friendly man, or rather a solitary man who feels he *ought* to make friends, and so I find myself again and again interlaced with the oddest outscourings of the human race. I set up, or agreed to, two lunches this week. One turned out to be yet another fake writer and champion blowhard who first demolished my spirit and then gave me his short story to read. He went on and on about the two books he is writing

The Troy Public Library.

(nothing down on paper yet, mind you), and his intention to *teach writing* (!) at the University of Western Australia in Perth. The Australians do not need this person and I would like to head him off at the pass just for the sake of international relations. Altho', is it true that that continent was first settled by such as he? Maybe they're accustomed? No!

The second lunch was with a nice young man with the name McPhee. Now, you know my weakness for the Irish. But this one is vagueness personified. He arrived carrying a can of paint which actually held a camera, his wallet, and a number of odd objects he'd picked up on the way. He uses a paint can for a briefcase because who would steal it? I liked that. But then he told me his favorite writer was D. H. Lawrence. So I began—but no, he hadn't read *any* of DHL's fiction or poetry, only his nonfiction. I didn't know he'd written any. A lovely guy really (he smokes with incredible grace), and next I must go to his "place" to see his photographs. Janet curls her lip at my shenanigans. Doubtless she is right. But actually I am one of them, so I am among my people, right?

All Troy has now written to me, each one giving his/her version of HOW IT WAS, taking issue, shedding tears, slobbering, tee-heeing. It's quite a wallow for me. I love it. The whole town is reading the book and laying for me, I think. I'll find out in October when I read at RPI. The event is open to the public, so expect 10,000 Trojans armed with tomatoes. The next day I read at the Albany College of Pharmacy, then I carouse with the Troy High School class of '45—who are all agog, the old bats and farts (I'm one of *them* too). I really can't wait to get there. Next I go on for a "Victorian Ball" benefit at the Public Library. H'ain't we I-falutin? I go back in May—for an Honorary Degree at Russell Sage. My mother would absolutely radiate if she knew. Maybe she does. She was Troy's worst snobbess and Sage-o-phile. My last stepfather, George, is the French Canuck roofer who put new roofs on all the Sage buildings. You *must* plan to come up for at least one of these things, then I'll turn you over to La Bullard for an hour or two of lascivious carriage. O do not disparage lascivious carriage/It beats the bejeez outta registered marriage. But then I don't know, I don't know, *I'm* the one who's adorable, maybe *I* should do it.

Love
R

August 24, 1992

All right you Peter,

Let's get cracking on *Hugh*—right? I want to be stunned—atom-bombed when I get to the altar. But your schedule of events sounds like Henry Kissinger's or the pope's. However will you even attend all of these? But I know you will—such a good driver. Use High Test. The *MD* "Lam Qua" is gorgeous. Very, very. The *Imaginary Invalid? Uríne;* or, *You're in.* I'll do it—the translation—*but only* if you swear by your grotésticles—(grow-testicles)—I can't spell it—that you will commit yourself to a production. I like the idea of music, *but*: it must be *melody*, ariose—not intellectual, discordant, or complexly dissonant. I hate all that stuff. So shall we? It's a stupendous idea and just *could*, if we all perspire, be good.[11]

Such a nice review today from the *Houston Chronicle*. Rather peps me up. *And* sitting over an iced tea on Chapel Street—scribbling—no fewer than three people came up: Aren't you Richard Selzer? That sort of thing. So I am going to have to buy a blue velvet dinner jacket and lederhosen so as to look the part.

The Scribners thing is over. Borchardt scotched it. He said that I am committed to William Morrow for the next book and no fooling around or it's handcuffs and the clink. I'm just as glad. But I don't seem able to get going on organizing this diary. Paralysis has set in. You tell me what to do.

Love
R

AUGUST 26, 1992

Dear Hotspur,

I hope this letter is in time to head you off at the pass. It would be *most impolitic*, not to say downright *self-destructive* to confront MD over their, yes, unconscionable tampering. It is a marvelous avenue for your future work and I don't want you to close it off. Think ahead, not back. Also, every writer has suffered the same outrageous insult—me especially. I still get heavily edited by pipsqueaks. Don't, I implore you. Let it go. *Onward*! Besides, I loved seeing the Lam Quas, and *you* did that. Tell you what, I'll buy you a can of tahini (it comes in a can?) if you behave. *Don't*, I'm telling you.

More letters from Trojans who have settled in California, Montana, wherever—all lapping up the past as I have dished it out, each one adding some additional detail. I *am*—yes it has happened!—I *am* the Bard of Troy. As Samuel Johnson said to Fanny Burney on the day her novel *Evalina* was published: "Miss Burney, die tonight." And so I should too.

Now don't sulk. Come on, smile. Whassa difference! Want some tahini? There, I knew you'd see it my way.

Love
R

AUGUST 28, 1992

Dear Peter,

David Rabe phoned to say that he thinks American Playhouse *will* proceed with *A Question of Mercy*. They want him to do a rewrite, so I guess he'll fight them off. He is also keen on making it into a stage play and is sending it to Yale Rep, but it's a mess there. The new guy is inaccessible and "never" reads plays, so his assistant reads them and he is presently "swamped." That's why I'm not showing *Swan* there. Rabe read *Swan* and said two things. (1) It would have to have a "surreal" production. (2) It would be best done at a university theatre that would do it in repertory for four to six weeks and not have to make money. That would be fine with me. He also had his publisher send me a first novel he's just written, for a blurb. It is a book called *Recital of the Dog*. And Kenneth Cavander now wants to meet to discuss another project. It's all the fault of that damned front-page review. I get zillions of suggestions these days. I feel like one of those Judy Garland/Donald O'Connor movies where someone says: "Let's put on a show!"

I went thru *Raising the Dead* and put in all my new inserts. It is a boringly interesting book, if you want the oxymoronic truth from the horse's mouth. I'm going to read from it at RPI.

"Smoking a Picasso"? You are beyond the limits of civilization—adrift in chaos. You have become the busiest person I know. All my other friends are languishing, sagging against pillars, toeing dirt, but you are hanging paintings, learning roles, writing stories, and I guess giving lectures. *An Enema of the People*—really! Act your age.

Nice review from Vermont today. I knew I liked that state.

Yer `zawstid mystwo

R

SEPTEMBER 5

Was interviewed on Connecticut Public Radio. Aside from my unfortunate vocal equipment as we say in opera, and my regrettable manner of speech (not human), I was excessively stupid. Felt sickish afterwards. Why do I do this? I was as ingratiating as an old whore trying to sell her wrinkles.

The book review editor of the *Boston Globe* called to say that he'd edited a review I wrote of Tom Starzl's memoirs (transplant surgeon). Not being Peter Josyph, I said be my guest.

SEPTEMBER 6

All right, then, I have recommended you to Hawthornden Castle. Just what you need: the forsaken wing of a palace—tapestries, torches in sconces, a unicorn in the garden—where you can loiter and mope, appear at midnight in the Great Hall, pen in hand, wearing a cape and an otherworldly expression. Only remember—one's best work will remain unwritten. It is the Fate of the Author. Now were I to go to Hawthornden, I'd request the dungeon. There I would write Keatsish odes with the wing of a nightingale dipped in lemon juice. The poems would only grow visible when breathed upon by my ardent readers. But no, I'd better not go to Scotland. I detest bagpipes—not the sound so much as the fact that they look like the bag and udders of a nannygoat. Then too there is the danger of the kilt. And everyone with the wrong-colored hair.

About *Le Malade Imaginaire*, you are far too piece-of-cake-ish. It would be the height of folly to translate Moliere after Richard Wilbur's *Tartuffe*. All the comparisons would be odious—to *me*. Besides, I can't imagine the enema-music. Is it something like the *Liebestod*, or the Fate theme in *Carmen*, only peristaltic, I think, with antiphonal borborygmi?

A while ago I awakened on the floor of the Cross Campus Library and staggered to the Men's looking like something torn up by the roots and *flung*. Returning to my table, I noticed that the students too were all asleep, strewn charmingly about the place—doubtless bewitched. The thought occurs: could this be Lethe? I begin to wonder.

Made a killing at a tag sale, where the Forestry students were selling pots, pans, books, etc. There on the grass was an electric typewriter *exactly* like mine which has broken down. I bought it + 6 cartridges for $15. Wow! Best is that I saved $2000 by once again not buying a word processor.

SEPTEMBER 10

Forgive the hoofprints on the page. The devil stomped on it—doubtless to rejoice in the fact that I've begun translating *Le Malade Imaginaire*. It's rather fun, I admit, but quite insane. I'm not a rhymester, can't write singable lines, etc. But I'll just get it all in English and then we'll see. Meanwhile I keep wondering and thinking—poor *Hugh*! with no one to act but Chaucer himself. Why don't you just take *all* the roles and do it yourself? Might have to hop around a bit, but it's a way of making sure that the entire cast will actually show up.

Took Endo-San, a Japanese friend, to the Yale Art Gallery to see the Ivory Crucifixion—but it wasn't there.[12] Damn fools keep taking it down, I keep making them put it back up. Endo goes back to Tokyo Saturday. I shall miss him. I have commanded him to return or else the 1945 peace treaty is off.

SEPTEMBER 13

There's only one way to do *Malade* and that's the way Mozart did *The Marriage of Figaro* or Rossini did *The Barber of Seville*—preferably the latter—buffo, bombastic, sly, fetching, perhaps even using Rossini's music (good idea!) and fitting the prose to *it*. Could be good.

Façade of the Yale Art Gallery.

My big achievement this week: to put brand new shoelaces in my shoes. I have never felt more *secure*. Also, I was sitting in the garden when a sudden gust of wind came and turned every page of *Troy* lickety-split, then whooshed away, doubtless to tell its fellow blowhards what it had read. I am at *one* with Nature. I was actually going to go for a swim at Richard Sewall's pond and had enlisted young Guy Madden to come too, as I have been made to swear I won't do it alone ever again. But Guy is utterly daft and can't get it straight, so I didn't go. You must meet *this* one. His insanity is of enormous size. On the other hand, he is extremely sweet and gentle and kind. Being with him is like standing in front of a beautiful waterfall. After a while, you just want to walk away.

September 14

I'm only writing today to keep your spirits up. Maybe they're already up and you don't need me to lift them? In that case, I am superfluous. Also exhausted. Little, Brown (I always want to add Jug) has beat out its rivals for the privilege of being the paperback publisher of *Troy*. But I won't unless they bring out *Repairs* and *Imagine*, which I will give them free. In case you wonder how it works: Little, Brown pays $25,000. Half goes to Morrow. The other half goes to Morrow—to count against the advance. The advance was $26,000. So, I still owe Morrow $14,500 (or so) before I get a dime. That ain't bad pay—three years of work at 25,000 = $8,333.33. So you and I earn approximately the same. And *you* are a pauper. Meanwhile, I'm signing up to *do* every library in Connecticut and upper New York State. No pay, but it is for the good of the printed word.

September 16

The publishers, the agents, all, all are duplicitous bastards. Everyone *knew* that I wanted *Imagine* and *Repairs* back in print and that I would accept any paperback offer that agreed to do that along with *Troy*. Denise Shannon and Morrow failed to communicate. I was not informed. Little, Brown knew nothing about these books, and now I am digging in my heels and Morrow is pissed—and so there we are. I *won't* agree to it. I don't know whose fault it is—they all blame each other—but I am threatening to leave them all unless it is ironed out. Boy O boy—to say that I am upset is an understatement. If ever I write another book I'll keep it to myself, let Hank deal with the nonsense of publishing. Except that he'll just plant slobbering kisses on them and try to make nice. That's his way. Mine is to challenge someone to a duel. No pretending. Take the buttons off the foils. En garde! Touché! You're all dead. Hah! Midst of it all the editor from Whittle called about *Raising the Dead*. There will be no editing other than what *I* do. Good Lord, is this a publisher? She told me a long story about her horse needing a tooth pulled. These people are all fakes. No different from theatre, I assure you.

SEPTEMBER 17

I've decided to lie low, don't return calls, don't answer the phone. Agent and publishers can all wait til I've finished sulking. Angry, today I go to Richard Sewall's for a skinnydip and a sandwich. Before that I must take a walk with T—he is way past Mars and heading for Pluto.

SEPTEMBER 24

So *proud* of you. Hanging the paintings at the altar. I should think the angels in the stained glass windows would fly down to take a close peek. So you are poor again? Well! I'm not surprised. But you have had a splendid time and will again—only keep the tahini flowing.

I was in New York City with Kenneth Cavander yesterday. After lunch, we sat in Bryant Park. It's gorgeous. Very French. I loved it there. We discussed his writing a film based on *Troy*. He told me that a friend of his—who is, yes, *Ellen Burstyn's intimate friend*—I can't find a way to finish this sentence. Anyway, Burstyn asked her about *The Black Swan*. Seems that Burstyn is on the board of directors of a new theatre in Stamford, Connecticut. Maybe she'd like to do it there? No recent news from David Rabe and American Playhouse. I read *Mercy* again and decided it was overwritten.

I've landed at Little, Brown with the paperback. The guy is reading *Repairs* and *Imagine* and will condescend or not to publish them. I race to prepare for Troy. Despite 1000 years at the podium, I am scared to death of my Trojans.

SEPTEMBER 28

Have you perished yet? Well, then, write from Purgatory. I assume your soul will not have gone straight to Heaven without a holdover of a few days anyway.

Bill Coffin (the Reverend William Sloan) came to preach at one of the churches on the Green. He stayed overnight with Richard Sewall. Bill Coffin phoned me to say that a friend had praised this book *Down from Troy* to the skies and showed it to him, whereupon Bill shouted: "I know him!" Bill phoned to tell me all this and to ensure that I go to church on Sunday. His friend would be there—up from New York City—and wanted to meet me. Standing outside the church—okay?—this man @ sixty—white beard and beautiful wife—walks up. "Are you Rich'd Selzer?" I had to admit it. Well! "*Troy* has changed my life. It is marvelous." Come to find out he is Robert Benton, screenwriter of *Bonnie and Clyde*, director of *Kramer vs. Kramer* and all the rest. I told him that Kenneth and I were in the process of writing a script for *Troy*. He said *yes* it ought to be done (he didn't say *he'd* do it) and he gave me his phone number in New York City, said if there were *any* way he could help with the script or see it into production, he'd consider it an honor.

October 4, 1992

Dear Peter,

My sojourn in Troy was a semester in Paradise. There was the lovely old town, more beautiful than ever—it reminds me of Florence. I stayed with Tom Phelan, ate good food, toured about, visited my two old loves: the library, the river. Went to St. Paul's Church and saw the great Tiffany windows. Went to the Music Hall, stood on the stage, and sang to a few workmen who were getting the place set up for a concert. They applauded politely. My two presentations, one at RPI, the other at Albany College of Pharmacy, were *events*—my picture in store windows all over town, the audiences great. And then there were my beloved high school classmates. We had a riotous senile party. Emily Jane drove up from Virginia with her husband. She's still a dish, told me she'd always loved me—now that it's too late. Altogether the time of my life. Oh how lucky I was to be born there and to be able to go back so often. I made many new friends and saw all the old ones, including (why weren't you there?) Pat Quinn and the architects. You'd have liked it all—that being Eye-rish at each other.

But now it is Down with a Thud from Troy. Wednesday I drive to Dartmouth, and on Thursday I give a class (Grace Paley's) and a reading. I am writing nothing. I hope *you* are being more productive. Of course I wonder about *Hugh*—but if it doesn't happen now, it will later, so not to worry. It's like *Swan*. It tries to fly but can't yet. Meanwhile I have an *in* at Capitol Rep and will follow up all other leads. Isn't that what the agent is for? Maybe I should call *her*.

Love

R

October 21, 1992

Peter!!!

Hugh arrived just now. He is beautiful—as a martyr should be. Congratulations. You've outdone yourself. The musicality, the steadily heightening tension, the lovely antiphony of the voices—it's all there. I do love the way you handled the nun. Very clever. So—I'm racing but had to say Bravo! And thank you!

Love

R

OCTOBER 26, 1992

Dear Peter,

Welcome to Yaddo. I am so pleased that you are there and I hope you will be able to arrange to stay on and on and on. Now, listen: on November 17 I'll be reading at the Yale Club in New York City (evening), I'll be staying overnight and would like to see the cathedral the next a.m. Would that be possible—before I fling my poor old carcass back to New Haven? If you can arrange to stay at Yaddo longer, never mind, I'll go there myself, just give me the directions.

Little Saint Hugh is gorgeous. Oh, I want you to produce it everywhere and I will call Denise tomorrow and *merge*, whatever that is. No money to be paid in this direction at all. Hear? Just go ahead and do it.

I don't know Cormac McCarthy at all, but I'll make it my business to. This morning I heard readings by William Gass and John Edgar Weidman—sensational. Why am *I* bothering to write when there are such people alive and working?

Gosh, everything's happening. I read in Albany this week. Large crowd of Albanians and Trojans. My old sweetheart, Mary Aileen Sapone, of thirty-five years ago showed up—still beautiful and just as sweet. Oh, I love her all over again.

Love to you

R

OCTOBER 29, 1992

Dear Yaddisher,

I hope this locates you near the summit of Mt. Parnassus but one piton away from a masterpiece. Another masterpiece. Little *Hugh*ey is one too.

Today at 4 p.m. I shall attend a lecture by a physician at the Medical School. It is about religion in medicine, I gather. Rumor hath it that he will attack my "Brute" [in *Letters to a Young Doctor*] as a "Missed opportunity for Grace." I can't miss the opportunity to hoot and holler. Yet another manipulator of my texts to suit the purposes of the ideologues. Down with Political Correctness!

LATER.

Sat among a throng of Medics and Divines to hear myself held up as an example of a writer closed to Grace, in contrast to Flannery O'Connor, Graham Greene, and John Steinbeck. The speaker committed nothing short of literary molestation. No mention of "Brute" as a letter to a young doctor in which the narrator confesses his ancient misdeed in order to *teach*. No suggestion that the act of writing the account was an act of penitence itself. No mention of the sense of atonement and guilt, the redemption at the end—only a few of the violent passages lifted out of context and hurled from the pulpit. Also, in these few instances, he misquoted twice. He called the sutures *wire* when they were *silk* (but wire is crueler, don't you know, so change it by all means). And he has the doctor say "Now you fucker hold still," instead of "Now *you* fuckin hold still," thus weakening the artistic force by robbing it of the power of reiteration and incantation (the patient had previously said "You fucking hold still"). These are *not* minor matters, but all important to the writer striving to make art. The audience was heavily weighted with his worshippers. I had no chance to rebut. This morning I wrote him a letter, but can't decide to mail it.[13]

All of which confirms me in my private, solitary round. *Mio piccolo mondo antico*. Outside is a nest of vipers. If I mail the letter, he will, of course, show it all over the Medical School and Divinity School and to those in the faculty who despise me for the *New York Times* piece. Also he will try to weasel out, and I should have to defend myself even more vigorously. And everything done in the name of Christianity! Could Jesus really *want* these guys on his team?

                                         Love

                                         R

OCTOBER 31, 1992

Peter, Thou,

The broadside announcing your forthcoming podiac appearance landed in my mailbox. I wish you deafening applause, an ovation, cries of *bravissimo*, and I confess to a bit of ignoble pleasure in the thought of *you* striving to occupy, then depart from, a lectern without disgrace. Such is *my* Monday/Wednesday/Friday challenge—and curse.

Along with that comes the news that I am handsome. No less than three seemingly sane adults have so said this week. Two charming women and our mutual friend Bill Palmer from Alma College, who described me thus in an article. What could it mean? Have the standards of physical beauty reversed themselves behind my back? It is no easy adjustment from sixty-four and a half years of ugliness to the sudden burst of comeliness. Such a transformation takes time to grow accustomed. You who have always been gorgeous—from birth—can have no idea what an added burden beauty can be among the elderly. For instance.... Oh well, never mind—I was almost indiscreet.

After sleeping on my letter of challenge to a duel to [the speaker who misrepresented "Brute"], I have decided against it. Wrote a much quieter riposte which gives the varmint a chance to slither back under his stone. Meanwhile, I am reading some of H. P. Lovecraft's letters. Despite his bigotry and craziness, I am enjoying them. Yesterday I opened the Lizzy vault for the first time. It took me six tries. This morning I will go over and *practice*. It *was* thrilling to show visitors the First Folio Shakespeare, the Quartos, the lock of Byron's hair. I like being a librarian. It is rather like being guardian of a cave of treasures and asking people in.

Love

R

November 4, 1992

Dear Peter,

I strove, root and branch, to stay awake for the election returns, but Morpheus had other plans and drew me inexorably into his arms. I learned the happy news of dethronement from the morning papers. Whatever be Clinton, George Bush is a false, cynical, and puerile man. Good riddance, I say.

Today I must go to Wallingford to give a benefit reading for a hospital there. It is to be a dreaded "luncheon." However did that *eon* become the ornamental tassel of plain old *lunch*? Unless to suggest that such an affair seems to last an eon. I must sit at the "head" table next to the chairperson of the Women's Auxiliary who will perspire to engage me in small talk. I am not allowed to begin until everyone has been served dessert and coffee. To top it off, the Medical Director, who invited me ages ago, won't be there, so I am destined to be *handled*. Oh well, it's for the good and I should stop whining, except that whining does me the world of good—especially when I have to do the same thing tomorrow night at Gretchen's old high school.

It is possible that I may be in New York City the night of November 17. If so, I shall stay overnight and go to see the church Altar next morning. Send the particulars.

Love

R

November 13, 1992

Dear Peter,

Joe Caldwell is a dream, isn't he? I do love him so much. Such a sweet, kind, witty man. And talented too. *The Uncle from Rome* is wonderful. He keeps getting better and better. By the way, ask him about the Academy in Rome. *You* might like to go there.

I've about had it. One of my old "flames" from the Stone Age—still gorgeous—would like to have "a fling." I met her good, kind, fine husband. No chance, I told her. He's a nice man. "Why don't you have a fling with *HIM*, then?" comes the retort. So there you are. I keep to myself now. It's so much better. But she *is* gorgeous. You haven't seen gorgeous until you've seen this woman.

Love
R

November 21

Thanks to you and Kevin, my New York visit was interesting and pleasant. The highlight was our adventure at and around the church and your magnificent Altar Piece, which I truly love. It *belongs* where it is and I hope there'll be a way to leave it there. The pastor was the second revelation. He is, in a word, *wondrous*. In another word, *noble*. His soul is visible—I love him. He represents all that is good in the Church, no question about it. I feel honored to have met that man. It was very nice and generous of Ken Warren to take us to breakfast at the Harvard Club, but to tell the truth I thought the Harvard Club a big come-down from the Lutheran Church of the Advent on 93rd Street and Broadway. For all its dark polished wood, red-coated waiters and Sargent portraits, give *me* that lovely, simple, poverty-stricken church and its radiant pastor. But I'm glad you both got to see the Harvard Club. Anyway, I'm home and jotting down in my diary is all I can do. I am enjoying your gift of Sir Walter Scott's journal. He is a lovable character. But the print is very small and I can only read a few pages before it all turns swimmy on me.

I'm through with Yaddo. The one I would keep is Joe Caldwell. It is no accident that his initials are the same as you know *Who's*.

November 23

I am so very *much* enjoying your gift: the *Journal of Sir Walter Scott*. It is just my cup of tea. You *do* know exactly what I will like. No one else does. Scott was a dear man, so decent and honorable. Laboring under a burden of debt, he set out to pay back his creditors by the works of his pen. And what a job it was. *But* he did it. His instincts are all so fine, and his descriptions of Scotland, the landscape and the people. His favorite writer was Byron, whom he thought a rare genius. Like everyone else, he knew about Byron's homosexuality but preferred to ignore it. It is curious that so much of Scott's writing is unreadable today (save for a brilliant paragraph or a page here and there). The poetry is still lovely: *Lochinvar* and *The Lady of the Lake*. My boyhood ecstasies erupted from them. Whenever his muse lay down on the job, he'd spur her on: "Spin, you jade, spin!" Don't you love that?

Still gloating over having seen your altarpiece. It's terrific. I pray you won't have to take it down. Wasn't *that* an adventure? And the *PASTOR!*—one of the noblemen of our time.

December 7

Happy Pearl Harbor Day. Which is an inappropenation if ever there were one. Oh, I remember the terror, the solemnity of that time that "will live in infamy." Roosevelt's voice!

Your last letters—they are Homeric in their cataloguing of woes. What's to be done? Let a grant come through, Heavenly Father! Or a residency with all expenses paid for three years. Still, I see that you are giving readings and spreading the word, so I take some encouragement from that. To the barricades!

The tape from Trinity Playhouse came. It is just *awful*. An amateurish job. *And* they spelled my name *Seltzer*. Don't I have any recourse?

December 12

Did you read the article about a poor artist living in a cold-water walk-up, no place to store his paintings, no gallery, etc.? It was in the *New York Times* this week. I could have wept. How many of you *are* there? I thought you and Kevin were the only ones. You simply *must* be taken into one of the colonies for an extended period. I wish Yaddo would give you Joe's position if he decides to leave. Then you'd be safe and secure and have plenty of time to do your work and three meals a day and hot water and Rosemary and Carol. Now that is Paradise. I've been kept hearthside by the storm. All the trees are quite hysterical and the gusts of rain have slapped the house silly.

The diary has been more fun lately. Such a lot of froth and no school to keep. There's a word in Italian: *spazzature*. It means sweepings. It was what was left of the precious metals in the tray of the goldsmiths or silversmiths after the sculpture or whatever had been made. These sweepings were of small value compared to the crafted piece, but they *were* worth something. Such are the effusions, or sparks, or shavings—*spazzature*—of my diary.[14]

I am three-quarters through the *Journal of Sir Walter Scott*. A masterpiece it is *not*, but I'm enjoying it hugely. I *love* him. Such a grand man of principle and honor and chivalry. I would love to make a pilgrimage to Abbotsford to see where he lived.

December 17

I pretend to work on the diary, fool around translating Ovid, visit with cronies, and generally fritter. But it is much better than poor Walter Scott's lot. Deeply in debt, he was forced to turn out pages of drivel each day, worry over his reputation, fight depression, etc. And now what? He has almost no readers—certainly not for the novels. I did read *Ivanhoe* in high school, and "The stag at eve has drunk his fill" [*The Lady of the Lake*] a number of times since. And he, the most famous, most adored writer of his day and a century after his death. It is also true of Henry Wadsworth Longfellow. Something strange in all that. I've finished reading the journal which you gave me. While I found it entertaining (mildly), I doubt that anyone else will read it. I enjoyed the old Scotsman—a loveable character. Now I read the autobiography of Benvenuto Cellini, another kettle of fish altogether. Feisty, pugilistic, hot-tempered, rich. He was part of the Florentine and Roman art scene which included Michel Agnolo (*his* spelling), Pietro Torrigiano, and all the rest. Then there is Shakespeare—my daily fix. I've finished *Romeo and Juliet* and will go on to *Love's Labor's Lost*. Romeo was a wimp, sobbing about his sentence of exile when by rights he should have been executed for killing Tybalt. Juliet's soliloquy to Night is the most beautiful love poetry of all time. Well, I'm off to the gym for my afternoon flagellations.

December 24

Merry Christmas, Happy New Year. May benevolence befall you in 1993. God knows you need it. I shudder at the thought of that cliff-that-was. And now, open to the least wave and gust. Get out of there! I'm all for sustaining life and limb. I'd have made it off the *Titanic*. You would have *not*.

December 28

Well that were good news all right. First the promise of three thousand to do *Hugh*. And your idea of the conversation to open it is splendissimus. This is a project well worth working toward. And Hawthornden Castle to boot. You must have a kilt made, a long ankle-length one so your weenie won't show. I hope it will be like the Castle of Glaws or Cawdor in *Macbeth*, with torches on the walls and tapestries; a dungeon with shackles and chains embedded in a wall and a shaft at the bottom with a river far underground for disposing of the corpses. And a tower in which, on certain moonlit nights, a young woman, white as a lily and thin as a wand, can be seen floating. You must look on the map to see *where* it is, how far from Abbotsford, Walter Scott's house, and from Ben Nevis Mountain. I wish I were going too. Not till November? Good! Gives you time to worry about your air fare. Besides, good things come in threes and you get one more. A grant would be nice.

Richard Selzer

Did you know all along and didn't tell me that George Washington sold the horse that had carried him through so many battles? Where's the greatness in that?

Living alone is just my cup of tea. But one tends to let down standards, grow scurfy, unzipped. Sometimes I can hear my own shadow laughing at the sight of me. When I turn around guiltily to see, he stops.

I found two bits of catterel (unworthy to be called doggerel) written in the early 1970s. It was my last secret, so now you know the worst.

December 30, 1992

Dear Peter,

Buried my mother-in-law Mollie today, and with Janet in Germany. Picture a tiny, postage stamp-size cemetery with the fog and rain and Gretchen hanging on my arm, nobody else. The mound of raw earth, the trench, the workmen shoveling. It is a pain in the ass not to believe in God. You are so lucky to even *suspect* a hereafter. But you will have a foretaste of it in Scotland. Can one *work* with bagpipes skirling in the next room? Bring ear plugs.

Meanwhile, I translate Ovid's *Metamorphosis* with immense delight. Such stories—and the language! And I read the letters of Keats (again) and some half dozen other books. And every ten minutes I am invited to come give a talk in Cleveland or Allentown. Speaking of the latter, a professor of freshman composition assigned *Letters to a Young Doctor* to her class, then assigned them to write to me. So I have just read forty critiques of the book. I'm very touched—and conceited. What I liked best is that a few liked "Impostor" and knew what it was about.

Have you slid into the sea yet? And do you wear seaweed and algae in your hair? What is to become of you? As for me, tomorrow I must drive my quill like mad to get ready for my appearances and articles. (All, all is vanity.) But I must have lunch with a young poet and shower blessings from on high. And no gym yet in which to perspire, so I grow into an accordion, fat and wheezy. Don't you do the same.

                    Love

                    R

Notes

YOU WILL BELIEVE IN CIVILIZATION
1988

1. Richard discusses urination and his once-favorite urinal, located in Troy, New York, in "The Grand Urinal of the Elks," in *Letters to a Young Doctor*. There is also this undated entry in his diary:

> Strange and marvelous are the ways of our construction. Take urination. After some sixty years of visiting public toilets in airports, train stations, and a hundred away-from-home situations, I have observed that a great many men will spit into the urinal prior to relieving themselves. These are men who, by and large, do not spit elsewhere or otherwise. Spitting, for them, is a ceremonial act that is somehow necessary in order for the upper bladder to contract while the outlet relaxes, allowing for the expression and passage of urine. Without spitting, such men would have to stand there for who knows how long, and with only so-so results. Still other men, fewer in number, whistle or make soft whispery noises in order to initiate the flow. Could there be, somewhere in the automatic nervous system, an auriculo-vesical pathway (ear to bladder) that transmits the sound of expectoration to the complex mechanism of urination?

See also Sleepwalking and Daydreaming, 1989, n.12.

2. In a letter of 10.26.88, Richard wrote: "The *New York Times* man comes tomorrow to riffle my studio for more pieces, but I plan to be difficult. It is not a good idea to appear there too often, and three times in two months is too much."

3. On a short trip he had taken during the time we were at the artists' colony Yaddo together, Richard met an attractive and engaging couple from San Francisco, Art and Agnieszka Winkler, who were on their way to New England to look at the foliage and to scout for artwork. "There's no foliage *there*," Richard told them (it was fall), "and the best art in the world's at Yaddo now. The painter's name is Peter Josyph. You must go see his work." When Richard returned to tell the story, the community of artists appreciated his advocacy, but none of us expected the couple to come. Shortly after his stay at Yaddo had ended, the Winklers called to tell me they were arriving on a chartered plane. After I took them to every studio and showed them slides of every artist's work, they bought several of my paintings. Richard beamed over his part in this success for many years.

4. Richard's essay about the Gardner Earl Memorial Chapel and Crematorium in Troy, New York, was published as chapter 12 of *Down from Troy: A Doctor Comes of Age*. It is one of his most uniquely Selzerean pieces. In *What One Man Said to Another*, chapter 12, "Beyond the Horrific," is a conversational treatment of the subject.

5. Richard's play *The Black Swan*, about a woman who believes that her love for a younger man is bringing back her youth when in fact she is dying of cancer, is an adaptation of his own short story "'The Black Swan' Revisited," itself an adaptation of a Thomas Mann novella. After analyzing a version of the play that was read at the Williamstown Theatre Festival, I told Richard that, even taking into account deletions and suggestions by his friend Kenneth Cavander, the play—the project itself—was unsuitable for the stage. At one point, as a way of suggesting how he might make the best of his commitment, I constructed a one-act reduction that entailed a major shift of dramatic focus. Although I once saw a reading that was an unsuccessful hybrid of this and longer versions of the play, I have never seen *The Black Swan* performed.

In a letter of 6.27.89, Richard wrote: "About *Swan*, I know you are right, and doubtless I am throwing good effort after bad. I suppose I'm going to Utah [Sundance Theatre Festival] just to convince myself that it is time to discard this adventure once and for all." But Richard's belief in *Swan*, and his enthusiasm to see it produced, constitute one of the most enduring threads of his correspondence. In nearly twenty years, neither of our opinions have changed about it. In the fall of 1994, *The Black Swan*, directed by Henry I. Schvey, premiered in St. Louis at Washington University's Edison Theatre as part of their Stage Left series. Richard attended rehearsals and has written about the event in his diary and in his letters to me.

In March 1991, Richard gave a talk to commemorate the Limited Editions Club's edition of Thomas Mann's *The Black Swan*. The novella was printed on fine paper with illustrations by Richard's friend John Hejduk. The talk was privately printed as a pamphlet called *Afterlife of The Black Swan*, Lecture Series: Number Two, New York: The Limited Editions Club, 1991. Richard's story "'The Black Swan' Revisited" appears in *Taking the World in for Repairs*. The composer Tom Whitman, whom Richard and I met at Yaddo, used Richard's story and Mann's novella as the basis for a chamber opera in two acts that, with a libretto by Nathalie Anderson, premiered September 11, 1998, at the Lang Performing Arts Center of Swarthmore College.

SLEEPWALKING AND DAYDREAMING
1989

1. Georges Borchardt, Inc., is Richard's literary agency throughout this correspondence and it continues to represent him.

2. Robert Brustein, theatre critic and former director of Yale Rep, had lived two doors from Richard on St. Ronan Terrace. At the time of this letter, Brustein was artistic director of the American Repertory Theatre in Boston. The literary biographer Richard Ellmann lived on the same block. Both Brustein and Ellmann encouraged Richard in his writing. For more details see *Said*, chapter 3, "This Little Street."

3. Thanks to a professional partnership with Norma Cohen, then executive director of the Smithtown Township Arts Council, which is located in the historic landmark Mills Pond House (c. 1838) in St. James, Long Island, I received a grant from the New York State Commission on the Bicentennial of the U.S. Constitution that sponsored a series of paintings that would first exhibit in three of the gallery rooms, then tour to public spaces. I used one of these rooms as a studio until the pictures were ready to hang. Then I became the artist-in-residence and painted in that room for many years.

4. When, in September 1992, I sent him a quill pen and bottles of ink, Richard wrote: "My next to you will be thrillingly scratched. What next? Papyrus? A tablet of baked clay? How far back are you sending me?"

To say that Richard wrote these letters in *long*hand carries the implication that a keyboard is faster, but the few typed sheets he has sent me over the years bear the unmistakable signs of an awkward event—with one exception, the long letter of 1.12.90, which is nearly perfect and which contains a paragraph (omitted in this volume) in which he says: "Aren't you bowled over by my typing? I have writer's cramp and can't wield the Mont Blanc today. It won't happen again." His even rarer printouts showed that, until recently, computers too had resisted his authority. In June 1992, he wrote: "Spent a day at the typewriter which, in the middle of the word *revenge*, gave a sputter, then a gasp, and perished. So I must look to buy another. No one *repairs* a typewriter anymore. You just throw it away and buy a word processor. But my stand on the WP is by now well known, so I shall either find a typewriter or go to the hardware store for a chisel and mallet to make hieroglyphs." In an undated entry in the diary, he writes:

> Above all other writing implements, I prefer the pen. Using it is a spiritual act. A feeling of Zen prevails. There is your hand, at the ready. There is the pen with its nibful of ink, waiting too. All their impulse is toward union—like lovers who long to lose themselves in each other—a blend of surrender and mastery. The pen is the writer's taproot with which he reaches down to the underground stream of the past. At the same time, all around the rhizome, bubbles of myth rise to the surface. I don't believe literature is possible without the incorporation of the past and of mythology.

In an interview with Lynn McGee (*Columbia*, #40, 2004), Allen Ginsberg, in discussing the use of computers, said: "old hand is always the best," a preference with which Richard would agree, but not only with respect to the art of writing. Although he appreciated advances in technology, for Dr. Selzer the practice of medicine was grounded in the hands. They dissected the cadaver in order to teach the student the "mortal lessons" of his profession; they palpated the patient, feeling a way—sometimes groping—toward a viable diagnosis; and, of course, they held the scalpel, cut, drew blood—sawed bones. That he should have chosen the pen, which he has called "a distant cousin of the knife," as the means by which he expresses himself has made poetic sense to him. "Blood and ink," he has told me, "at least in my hands, have a certain similarity. When you use a scalpel, blood is shed; when you use a pen, ink is spilled. Something is *let* in each of these acts." About retreating to his kitchen in the middle of the night, between the hours of one and three, during the years the Yale surgeon was teaching himself to write, he has said: "From somewhere in my mind it would register that the flat of my hand—the hypothenar eminence—was moving across the page in quick little hisses, each one telling me work was getting done."

5. The occasion of Richard's second talk at the Columbia College of Physicians and Surgeons in upper Manhattan enabled us to begin the conversations that became *What One Man Said to Another: Talks with Richard Selzer*. Our meetings there and at the Terminal Bar in Grand Central Station, referred to later in this letter, are recounted in the preface to that book.

6. See chapter 7 of *Said*, "A Day at the Races," for an animated discussion of this incident.

7. Richard and Janet Selzer have three children: Jonathan (Jon), born in 1958 and married to Regine (they now have two children, Emily and Daniel); Lawrence (Larry, or Doon), born in 1960 and married to Rossi (they now have three children, Hank, Ned, and Eleanor); and Gretchen, born in 1962 and married to Eric (now divorced). The confinement of which Richard is speaking is for his first grandchild, Gretchen and Eric's daughter Rebecca (Gretchen later gave birth to another daughter, Lucy). During the time of these letters, Jon and Regine were living in Germany; Larry and Rossi were in Virginia; and Gretchen and Eric were nearby in Connecticut. Richard Selzer was born in 1928. His brother William (Bill or Billy) was born in 1927.

8. Richard is referring to a break-in burglary of my car while I sat with him in Grand Central.

9. From Lt. Gen. Dave Palmer at West Point: "On behalf of the United States Core of Cadets, I am very happy to invite you to deliver the annual Sol Feinstone Lecture on the Meaning of Freedom. . . . The general subject for the lecture . . . has remained fixed, but the lecture has provided a forum for diverse points of view. Speakers have included Barbara Tuchman, Alistair Cooke, Isaac Singer, Carl Sagan, George Will . . . Tom Wolfe, Elie Wiesel, and A. Bartlett Giamatti." For more on the West Point affair, see *Said*, chapter 23, "Eve of the Battle," and chapter 24, "West Point."

10. The *Down from Troy* to be published in Japan was not the book *Down from Troy: A Doctor Comes of Age*, which was not yet written, but the *Down from Troy* section of *Mortal Lessons*. In "From the Diaries 2" in *The Whistlers' Room*, Richard writes about working with a Japanese profes-

sor, Koju Fujieda, while Fugieda-san was teaching *Letters to a Young Doctor* in English to students at Fukui Medical College.

11. In *Journeys in Divers Places*, a memoir by the sixteenth-century surgeon Ambroise Paré, Paré helps a man to sleep by simulating the sound of rain under his bedroom window. When I sent the piece to Richard, suggesting that he write a novel about it, his response was: "*You* write the novel. Let me wallow in peace." A few years later, Richard wrote a scene in which his father recounts the Paré incident to him. It appears in chapter 2 of *Down from Troy*, a book formed out of much of the nonfiction discussed in the early letters. In "Writer's Block," which appears in the anthology *The Exact Location of the Soul*, Richard prescribes Paré's contraption for artificial rain (along with a train whistle and church bells) for writers who live in lands with little rain.

12. From Richard's diary of June 1991:

Tea-time at the Elizabethan Club at Yale (the Lizzie). It is an old white-frame house with a vault containing a large number of priceless literary editions. Every Friday the vault is opened by one of five faculty members, of whom I am blessed to be one. Hack the flesh from our bones and we shall not reveal the combination of the lock! But this is Tuesday. The clubhouse is dense with Professors of Polite Learning, despite that the sandwiches on Tuesday are only cucumber. It is widely accepted that Wednesday and Friday are the best days: chicken salad and tuna salad respectively. You would be amazed at how important these distinctions are in Academe.

Richard loves swinging open the vault's huge heavy doors to show guests First Folio Shakespeares and a lock of Byron's hair. Upstairs, he once showed me something else: an old-fashioned WC that he encouraged me to flush with great enthusiasm. "Tell me this is not beautiful," he said. "A carved, ornate porcelain loo. It has festoons of floral around it. We are all very proud of it. And here is Shakespeare to watch you pee." I have made it a rule not to ask him for medical advice—he suffers enough of that wherever he goes—but once, in the quiet garden behind the Elizabethan Club, with a stone bust of Shakespeare presiding over the premises, Richard tested me for a complaint that had me worried. His diagnosis was correct (there was nothing wrong), and never before or since have I had such a civilized exam.

13. The Civil War letters of John Vance Lauderdale, a physician from Geneseo, New York, were shown to Richard by curator Archie Hanna when they first arrived in the Western Americana Collection at Yale's Beinecke Rare Book and Manuscripts Library. They inspired Richard's story "Pages from a Wound Dresser's Diary," published in his third collection, *Confessions of a Knife*. After Richard showed the letters to me, I edited them into a book, *The Wounded River: The Civil War Letters of John Vance Lauderdale, M.D.*, published in 1993 by Michigan State University Press, which also published *Said*. Historian Geoffrey C. Ward writes about his role in getting the letters to Hanna, and about *The Wounded River*, in "Dr. Lauderdale Goes to War," *American Heritage*, December 1993.

14. This paragraph represents two typical instances of Richard's approach to self-evaluation in these letters. The slip in the phrase "I worry that you are not wasting good time on me"—Richard's inadvertent inclusion of the word *not*—demonstrates a fundamental awareness of self-worth. Similarly, the notion that his letters "are to be read once and filed" is contradicted by his offer, the following week, to gather his letters should I wish to edit a volume of them after the book of talks. The phrase "All this having been said" is Richard's tribute to Latin, for the phrase exemplifies the ablative absolute, a form more common in Latin than in English. Richard has enjoyed reading Latin throughout his adult life.

15. At the Beinecke, where he wanted to show me the Civil War letters, Richard couldn't remember the name of John Vance Lauderdale. After bemoaning the fact that Archie Hanna, the curator who had showed him the letters, was dead, he was delighted when a librarian put him on the phone to Hanna. Speaking to his old friend, Richard said: "This is just like calling Heaven!"

16. Nan Talese, an old friend of Richard's and a senior editor at Doubleday to whom I brought an excerpt of *Said*. Although she received me graciously, Nan never responded to either of us about the project.

17. Richard's sketch about his desk appears in chapter 11 of *Down from Troy*. There is also a section beginning "A word about my desk" in his introduction to the anthology *The Doctor Stories*.

18. Pat Quinn appears with Richard in Part One of *America's First River: Bill Moyers on the Hudson*, which aired on PBS in April 2002.

19. Richard Sewall, whom Richard brought me to meet during the making of *Said*, is best known for his two-volume biography of Emily Dickinson, which won a National Book Award. Short, thin, somewhere in his seventies, Sewall exuded immense vitality, warmth, good humor, a deep affection for Richard, and an abiding enthusiasm for his subject—of whom there was one confirmed photograph and one not.

SELZER: Now that other picture isn't her.

JOSYPH: We decided it wasn't her because we didn't want it to be.

SEWALL: When it came up in the last stages of that book, I got a note from a fellow down on Long Island, a book dealer, and he said: "I have a little carte de visite"—a visiting card, they used to have little pictures on them in those days—very handy, I should think—"and it has E"—Emily Dickinson—"on it, and 1865 on the back of it. Is it genuine?" I sent it to six or eight of the leading Dickinson people and they were about divided. Some were absolutely sure that it *was* she, some were absolutely sure that it wasn't. Then Jay Leyda [author of *The Years and Hours of Emily Dickinson*], who was the best of them all, said: "Why don't you just put it someplace in the book with a note explaining where it came from, and the uncertainty, and see what happens? Somebody will write in and say: 'That isn't Emily Dickinson, that's my Aunt Minnie, who died at the age of ninety-seven just a few years ago.'"

SELZER: So what happened? You put it in—

SEWALL: I put it in, and I've had he most *interesting* set of communications about it. Some are mad about it. "O, it couldn't be *anybody* else." And then others say: "No, it couldn't *possibly* be Emily Dickinson!"

A pond by Sewall's house was Richard's favorite swimming hole, to which he disappears during some of these letters.

20. From a letter of 5.8.89: "On Saturday, Alistair Reid came and we spent the day in the garden chatting. He is vastly amusing, at the same time emitting an aura of strength. We talked about writing—he is excited over my 'Crematorium,' says it is *exactly* my subject. He is writing about the negative effect of tourism on a Spanish village where he and Robert Graves lived for many years. Also about the rise of Scottish nationalism. A learned man."

21. Richard's letters to me were never used for *Said* except in prefatory material or endnotes.

22. A version of this article, which was published as "Trial and Tribulation" in the *New York Times Magazine* (9.23.90), became chapter 5 of *Down from Troy*. The trial is discussed in chapter 16 of *Said*, "Taking the Surgeon in for Repairs."

23. From a letter of 6.27.89: "As for INTERPLAST, I've decided not to go. For one thing, I'm coolish about a *New Yorker* profile—especially one oriented toward an activity that plays so small a part in my life now. I told the writer *she* should go and do a story on the children themselves, or on INTERPLAST. She is plenty sore about it, but I have spoken. Besides, I will be deep in my new story by then and would be unwilling to leave it."

24. Ted Solataroff had been an editor at *Esquire* when Richard was published there. During our meeting in his office at Harper & Row about *Said*, which he had not yet seen, Solataroff displayed such a callous attitude that I recalled something Richard had once told me, and which I now understood: "Once a year I put on my suit, I get on the train and I go to New York and I meet with my publisher, and that's *it*."

25. From a letter of 6.20.89: "I am millimetering along in the new story, which is taking on mythic proportions. All about the light of angels, garbage and other cosmic themes." On June 27: "The story is trying hard to get itself written, but I am having labor pains. Many false starts, but here and there a phrase to keep."

26. My companion Barbara Mann, who converted the bulk of this correspondence from handwritten text to computer file, initially assisted in the typing of *Said*.

27. This notion is discussed in chapter 26 of *Said*, "The Selzer Theories of Creativity, Family Fat, His Majesty Queen Elizabeth, Miltongate, Premonitory Dreams, and the Boomerang."

28. The Yale Medical Historical Library, of which Richard's friend Ferenc (Frank) Gyorgyey was the director, owns an extraordinary series of paintings by the nineteenth-century Chinese portraitist Lam Qua. Never properly exhibited, not even at Yale, they depict the most extreme surgical patients of Peter Parker, an influential medical missionary from Yale, and they easily justify Richard's shorthand for them: "The Grotesques." With Ferenc's cooperation, Norma Cohen and I showed the work at the Mills Pond House Gallery (March 28–May 10, 1992) with a related conference at Stony Brook University. I wrote a monograph for the occasion, *From Yale to Canton*, and when I wrote about the pictures for the now defunct journal *MD* in August 1992, Richard preceded the article with a note called "The Grotesques of Lam Qua":

> The year was 1955. In a Quonset hut dispensary I was holding sickcall for what seemed like an endless line of Korean peasants and refugees. From the doorway I scanned the line of patients. All at once, my arrested gaze returned to focus on an elderly man dressed in white pantaloons, short white jacket, and white rubber shoes turned up at the tip—the costume of rural Korea where I had been stationed. He was some 200 feet from where I stood. What captured my attention and caused my heart to thump was the appearance of two heads on the same man. One held up and somewhat to the right, the other lolling on his left shoulder. At last it was his turn, and I saw that the second head was none such but a head-sized sebaceous cyst of long standing attached to the man's cheek by a thin pedicle. This man too wore an enigmatic mask of tranquility. Later that day under local anesthesia I removed the cyst and closed the skin at the base. I recall how, watching the huge cyst carried away from his face, the man's expression did not change. Looking at these grotesques of Lam Qua, described by Peter Josyph in the following pages, I see not only a depiction of medical exotica but the strange inextinguishable beauty of the wound.

Richard discusses the work of Lam Qua in chapters 18 and 19 of *Said*, both called "Return of the Native." Fictionalized versions of his time in Korea are recounted in the short story "Korea" in *Rituals of Surgery*; in "Lessons from the Art" in *Mortal Lessons*; and in his novel *Knife Song Korea*. See Into the Cave of Aeolus, 1990, n.7.

29. See n.33.

30. Richard is forgetting that he saw my work at Yaddo, including two portraits of him, one of which he had sat for. As it was among the pictures purchased by the Winklers, the couple he sent to my studio, one could say that for my sake he sold himself to the Winklers.

31. The anatomical drawings of Casserius are discussed in chapter 11 of *Down from Troy*, in which the publisher, William Morrow, used four of the drawings for endpapers—but with no credit to Casserius. Ten of them illustrate Richard's "On Casserius" in the May 1984 *Art & Antiques*.

32. The youngest daughter of Barbara Mann had received a written threat of rape at her school.

33. I had suggested that Richard's multinarrative story "Little Saint Hugh," in *Rituals of Surgery*, would make a fine voice play, especially if he added a fourth character, the Prioress. He never did, but I adapted it into a piece that I directed for Victory Rep in 1992 at a small Manhattan theatre, Inner Space, along with *Answering Chaucer*, a curtainraiser based on an unpublished talk we had recorded during the making of *Said*. "Hugh" deconstructs the anti-Semitic blood libel that inspired Chaucer's "The Prioress's Tale," in which a young Christian boy is allegedly murdered

by Jews in Lincoln, England. "Hugh" is told from three first-person perspectives: John de Lexinton, sheriff of Lincoln; Hugh himself; and Geoffrey Chaucer. In the Victory Rep production of *Hugh*, I played John de Lexinton, and in *Answering Chaucer* I played Selzer and Raymond Todd played Josyph, an assignment of roles we repeated when we recorded *What One Man Said to Another* for Blackstone Audiobooks in 2002.

34. An undated fragment in the diary speaks to this issue of smoking: "Though I myself have abstained for five years, my aura remains tobacco-colored. When I think with what a flair I used to smoke! The artistry of it. Oh, I have come down, no question about it." See also "Smoking" in *Mortal Lessons*, and for a discussion of that essay, see *Said*, n.30, pp. 260–261.

35. In the diary of 1992 there is this memorable love-at-first-sight: "Once at the post office I fell in love at the sight of a woman licking a stamp. Even now, thirty years later, I have only to close my eyes to see again the pink tip of her organelle."

36. Richard had told me that Bill Ober, a pathologist who wrote the popular books *Boswell's Clap* and *Bottoms Up*, sent him letters filled with sex and scatology.

37. For more about Richard's visits with Ron, see *Said*, chapter 23, "Eve of the Battle."

38. The friend here is the dearest of what Richard has called, affectionately, "my beloved lunatics" or "my loonies," a collection of characters around and about Yale who have become a part of Richard's "ministry," the volunteer time he has allotted to attending the psychologically desperate. In this context, Richard's use of the word *lunatic* is unique in my experience, as it carries not a trace of derision, irritation, or revulsion. "I'm not their doctor, don't know anything about psychiatry, just consider them cut on the slant," he has told me; but I have always viewed this ministry as another kind of practice, with a new breed of patient that is "seen" not in the consulting room but on the streets of New Haven or among the vending machines in the Cross-Campus Library (what Richard calls Machine City). In fact he once said, about one of these troubled (and troublesome) cases: "He was *terribly* abusive, but what could I do? I was his 'doctor,'" by which I was sure that he meant that there was no one else *attending*. Schizophrenia, Obsessive-Compulsive Disorder, and practically every other manifestation of psychosis has fallen under his gift. He generally has half a dozen loonies at any time, most of whom are bound by unbreakable rules about approaching him in public, and about when and how frequently they may call him. Of course the rules are broken, but, for his own survival, he is forced to establish the principle that failure to comply could result in cancellation. My own observation of four such characters showed me that these were not charmingly neurotic Richard Selzer fans, or down-on-their-luck vagrants, but some of the neediest cases in town.

One could add to the number of official lunatics the madwomen who, while they might not be clinically diagnosed, exhibit psychotic behavior in convincing themselves that they are in love with Richard and are destined to steal him away from his wife. Recently, within a six-month period, two such madwomen were stalking him at work. One of them lied her way into the Beinecke Library and waited for him there while Richard was forced to bide his time, out of sight, until the coast was clear. On a subsequent occasion the library guards assisted his getaway through a staff-only exit.

The case of the poet-friend with OCD is exceptional in that Richard developed a genuine comradery with him, and in several letters he is referred to as "my friend" with no indication that he is part of the ministry—and perhaps it is fair to say that he was not. The fact that Richard regarded him as brilliant—not as a poet, but as man who was fiercely engaged with literature—separated him from most of Richard's other charges. But Richard has spoken to me about the calls he would get to come to his friend's apartment and tape record the sentences necessary to placate his OCD. "When I read these sentences into the tape recorder," he has told me, "he put bits of rolled up paper in the cracks of the windows so that none of the sounds from outside would be heard on the tape. I would have to say these sentences over and over again, twenty and thirty times, or else he would hear certain words and he would have to *atone* for them—unless he could play the tapes I had made. When I had finally read them to his satisfaction, I would race out of there, vowing never to do it again, but he would come to the landing and call down the stairs to thank me and tell me that I had saved his life. But then, of course, when it had worn off and he had to atone again, he would come to me in the library and beg me to do it again. All his defenses were down, he'd say, and I was his only hope."

39. In collaboration with the painter Kevin Larkin, I had undertaken to fill the entire Mills Pond House with portraits of people who had resided or worked in Smithtown. Called *Portrait of an American Town: A Duet for Two Brushes*, the exhibition included canvases, works on paper, assemblages, photography, and texts. I wrote a monograph for the occasion.

40. Myra Sklarew, writer, poet, professor at American University, was president of Yaddo during some of our visits there. Her small book *Travels of the Itinerant Freda Aharon* (New York: Water Mark, 1985) is a poetic gem. From letters of 8.22.06 and 10.10.06: "In the mail today, a letter from Myra Sklarew—a dear friend, superb poet, and recorder of the Holocaust. She is one of those marvelous women I have met. I have been lucky in having known them. I carry them in the chambers of my heart. Myra is doing a major work on the slain Jewish community of Lithuania, including her family. She has a book of poems entitled *Lithuania*. A sterling character. She will love hearing from you."

41. About the voodoo art, Richard has told me: "That painting has got it in for me—I *know* it does." From a letter of 10.20.89: "There it goes again! The voodoo priestess gritting her teeth. There is malevolence in her. One day she will descend from the top of the bookcase. I shall feel her long arms squeezing the life out of me. Now and then I put down my pen and hold up my palmar stigmata to drive her back. It is the vampire and the cross all over again—religious warfare on St. Ronan Terrace. If the worst happens, it will be yours to report to the world." In Richard's diary there is an undated entry about a different sort of painting at St. Ronan, one that projects, for him, another kind of supernaturality. Painted by the Czech-born artist Jan Matulka, it hangs in the livingroom, where Richard has spoken to me about it with fondness and even a kind of awe.

> It has been there for almost forty years. Perhaps—I don't know—it is not what some would call a great painting. It did not seem so to me when I first saw it. A village scene is depicted, East European, I suspect, as the painter, Jan Matulka, was from Czechoslovakia. It is nighttime and the village is bathed in bluish moonlight. The walls, trees, even the two cows that have been left to spend the night outdoors are flaked with this light. A path winds through the shadows, alternately bright and dark. Over the years this picture has become the repository of my dreams. I have discovered its secret of narrative richness, its legendary life. Within a few minutes of contemplation I find myself walking along the path that winds through the village up to an orchard. There is nothing surreal or abstract about it. One looks and sees what is meant to be seen—a cow, a tree, a house—all neatly arranged so as to reveal the harmony that is the result of man's toil. It has a simplicity that is not the least intellectual, but invites the intuition of the viewer. And yet, somehow . . . is it a swirl of purple in the sky, or the liquid shadows on the tree trunks? One is no longer in the bondage of the earthly. The possibility of the supernatural exists. Four decades ago, this was, for me, just a village scene. Now, if asked to describe my soul, I would describe that painting.

For more on the Matulka, see the first of two letters dated 12.10.89.

42. Based on the fact that I was publishing his conversations with me, Richard and I teased each other about my being a kind of Boswell to his Johnson—without, of course, identifying ourselves with either of those great talents. "Too bad you didn't get a better subject," he'd say. "Too bad you don't have a better Boswell," I'd say.

43. This is one of Richard's many protestations of love for Anton Chekhov, the man and the work. See especially the paragraphs from Driving the Quill, 1992, dated Who Knows What Date, and February 12.

44. "Seeing Red: A Clinical Look at Rothko's #3" appears in *The Whistlers' Room*. The hardcover edition reproduces the Yale Rothko on the back of the dust jacket.

45. Richard had told me the story of his encounter with Frederick March, placing it in the context of his life then at Yale.

SELZER: There was a party two doors up the street at Bob Brustein's. John Gielgud and Irene Worth were here giving readings in Shakespeare and they were absolutely wonderful. After the theatre we went to Brustein's for a party where everyone could meet the actors. Gielgud was there with this very handsome man who was his lover, and Irene Worth was there by herself shoveling shrimp down her throat, cold, and hardly chewing them once but wolfing them down. She was quite a full-blown woman, a bit puffy but still quite beautiful, swallowing down these shrimp and trying to make polite conversation with the adorers. I could not take my eyes off these people who had just before enacted Macbeth and Lady Macbeth, Othello and Desdemona and all the others, and I thought: "What a peek behind the curtains to find that Desdemona likes shrimp!"

There was a new production at Yale Rep, so Bob called and said: "Would you come to dinner at Maury's?" Maury's is the local Yale restaurant where he was having a private dinner before the performance. The other people were Joseph E. Levine, the great entrepreneur. I remember Mike Nichols being enormously witty, and this beautiful Claire Bloom, who was then his inamorata. Frederick March was a man in his eighties with a shock of white hair, still beautiful, gorgeous. I said to him: "I *loved* you in *Mutiny on the Bounty*."

He said: "I wasn't *in Mutiny on the Bounty*."

JOSYPH: You were thinking of Trevor Howard.

SELZER: Yes, I was. I didn't know! I mean, I was so nervous sitting next to this man! And when he said: "I wasn't *in Mutiny on the Bounty*," I was *completely* destroyed. He then began to ask me: "Well who are you—why are you here?" I said: "Well I'm just a doctor—I'm a surgeon," and we talked about Vitamin C, which is a very safe subject and which I *clung* to. I remembered, of course, seeing him in many movies but I couldn't recall exactly what they were.

JOSYPH: There's no way to adjust once you've done a thing like that.

SELZER: No, I thought: "I should die now—there is just *no way* I should go on living—I don't deserve it." But you see Bob Brustein was trying to get Joseph E. Levine to give a million or two to support the Yale Drama School, so we were all to be nice to this little fat frog, revolting man, he was absolutely disgusting and he was lording it over us because we were Yale, pathetic Yale, and he had the money, so he was dangling it in front of us. We wanted him to give it, so everyone was being very charming. The dinner ended and we ran out. It was a block and a half to the theatre and it was humiliating to me because they held up the performance until we got there. Twenty minutes, twenty-five, thirty—why wasn't it starting? Well, it wasn't starting because we—Frederick March and Joseph E. Levine and Mike Nichols—

JOSYPH: You were having your dessert.

SELZER: We were having our dessert and we weren't ready. We had to walk down the aisle in front of all these people and I am the only one who is a citizen of New Haven. These people in the audience, waiting for us to arrive, were my patients!

JOSYPH: You had to take their gall bladders out the next day.

SELZER: Yes, and my colleagues, my fellow surgeons and their wives, are all irked at being held up—then I walk down the aisle in the party—*in the party*. O, I died.

JOSYPH: But how did Joe respond?

SELZER: He gave *a bunch* of money.

INTO THE CAVE OF AEOLUS
1990

1. This passage does not appear in the published story, which contains a scene of almost marital domesticity but nothing as overtly homoerotic.

2. During rehearsals for an evening of Chekhov at Victory Rep, a play had to be scrapped, leaving a hole that I filled by writing a one-act play overnight about a Russian theatre company playing Chekhov—with Chekhov in the audience—under conditions of constant catastrophe. I did not play Chekhov but an actor-director who, like myself, tries to prevent the evening from falling apart. Richard saw my picture in a review that appeared in *Newsday*.

3. Richard's near-participation in an assisted-death incident for someone who was suffering with AIDS is chronicled in chapter 13 of *Down from Troy*, which first appeared as "A Question of Mercy" in the *New York Times Magazine* (9.22.91). It was later adapted into a play by David Rabe (New York: Grove Press, 1998), which premiered at the New York Theatre Workshop on February 7, 1997, directed by Douglas Hughes. It is far from Rabe's best work. When "Mercy" first appeared in the *Times*, Richard went to deliver the Robert Penn Warren Lecture at the Yale University Medical School. The man who was slated to introduce him refused to come to the hall—he apparently felt the piece was a sanction of euthanasia. Meanwhile, a gay activist organization threatened to disrupt the proceedings, presumably in protest that Richard did *not* go through with the plan. Ultimately the talk, which had nothing to do with either AIDS or euthanasia, was given without incident. See also Into the Cave of Aeolus, 1990, n.15; and Lazarus Rising, 1991, n.16.

4. *Raising the Dead* is the book Richard wrote for Whittle Communications' Grand Rounds Press series. It was published in 1993 and reissued in 1994 by Viking Penguin in association with Whittle. It is based on Richard's near-death bout with Legionnaire's Disease. The first twenty pages recount an operation on the English writer Fanny d'Arblay.

5. I tried to prevent, or at least ration, Richard's further use of the phrase "All at once." The attempt was a failure.

6. It is interesting to compare this version of the paragraph with the one on pp. 167–168 of *Imagine a Woman*. Richard's subtle revisions make the published version better. Concerning the well of the lighthouse, there is this from a letter of 3.25.06:

> Last night I awoke from a deep sleep thinking about "Poe's Light-house." Without consciously being aware of it, I had echoed Poe's preoccupation with menace and foreboding. The undersea chamber at the bottom of the lighthouse is none other than the tarn into which the House of Usher sinks at the end of that story, or the maelstrom into which the narrator descends in "Descent into the Maelstrom," or the Pit over which the Pendulum swings back and forth above the doomed man. I never thought about this, but I see quite clearly that it is what I was up to.

7. In my preface to the Michigan State paperback of *Repairs*, I compare Richard's work to that of Tanazaki, one of his favorite Japanese writers. Richard and Janet spent a year in Japan together after he served in Korea. His letters to her from Korea do reveal a different Selzer, for he is not yet a fully formed writer. Also, the content and tone of the letters are formed—and limited—by the fact that the couple are newlyweds who have yet to start their life together. The distance between the harsh, often brutal facts of his Korean odyssey and the overall thrust of his letters to Janet is reflected and intensified in *Knife Song Korea*. In that novel, when the surgeon, Sloane, writes a letter that is too close to the bone, he tears it up and tries another. The illusion becomes increasingly harder to sustain. See Sleepwalking and Daydreaming, 1989, n.28.

8. Richard is referring to the events recounted in one of his best essays, "Diary of an Infidel: Notes from a Monastery," the opening memoir in *Repairs*. When I visited the Abbey of San Giorgio Maggiore, a monk who remembered Richard's visit there told me that one of the chief characters in the piece had "gone to Amer-i-ca. To Chi-*ca*-go!"

9. Richard Seltzer—with a *t*—is a writer who, upon receiving requests for engagements that he knew were meant for Richard, undertook them anyway. Richard's friends were annoyed that he did not take more vigorous action against Seltzer, for Seltzer was not only appropriating his livelihood and disappointing the organizations who booked him: he was menacing Richard's own repu-

tation. But Richard told me something about Seltzer's situation that tempered Richard's approbation of him. Richard's compassion in this instance was staggering to me.

10. In "Poe's Light-house," the main narrator is given pistols for his eighteenth birthday and, as an escape from the torments of his Tourette's, he decides to use one to kill himself at midnight. Describing the moment at which he intended to pull the trigger, "Youth bids farewell to the moon more easily than to the sun," he says. When Richard writes to me, on February 1, "I fully understand that it is harder to bid farewell to the sun than to the moon," he is talking about the suicide of a man he calls Luis who is suffering with AIDS. His assisted death is scheduled for February 10. This is also the narrator's birthday in "Poe's Light-house," and thus the date of his attempted suicide. Richard has assured me that he was unaware of this connection.

11. Richard discusses the assignment that Richard Ellmann gave him in chapter 3 of *Said*, "This Little Street."

12. When Richard was asked to write about his choice of a medical painting for *Art & Antiques*, I had suggested Picasso's *Science and Charity*.

13. This "Editor's Note" is Richard's note as it appears in the letter.

14. In *The New Criterion* of February 1996 (Vol. 14, No. 6), Richard reviewed another book by Gerald Weissmann called *Democracy and DNA: American Dreams and Medical Progress* (New York: Hill & Wang, 1996). This review, which is titled "The Body Politic," is both flattering and critical of Weissmann's book. It is especially interesting in that, perhaps because of the venue, it presents a slightly different—less personal, less playful—Selzer than is found in most of his essays. It takes Weissmann to task for his views on Emily Dickinson and her editor at the *Atlantic*, Thomas Wentworth Higginson. It also challenges some of Weissmann's larger notions about science and the arts. "The Body Politic" can be found at www.newcriterion.com.

15. My exhibition *New York Signatures* was opening at the Cannon Office Building of the House of Representatives in Washington, D.C. When large portraits of Poe, Wharton, James, and Ginsberg were then exhibited at the Apple Bank on Broadway and 73rd Street, they were written up in the *New Yorker*. Richard refers to this in the letters of 1991.

16. "The Occasion Fleeting" is chapter 8 of *Said*.

17. "Whither Thou Goest" was adapted by Kenneth Cavander into a TV drama, called *Harvest*, that was broadcast in 1992 on Trinity Broadcast Network, which is owned by Trinity Church in Lower Manhattan. Details of this production are discussed in subsequent letters. In the story, a widow locates and listens to the transplanted heart of her departed husband.

18. *Vietnam in My Kitchen* was a solo exhibition for the New York State Vietnam Memorial Gallery in the state complex in Albany, close to where my show *The Legacy* was hung.

19. At the conference in Buffalo where I received an award, Allen Ginsberg, who gave the keynote, read several poems about sex. Ginsberg was one of the writers in *New York Signatures* and my portrait of him was based on a photo I had taken of him in Buffalo.

20. When I was in D.C. to hang *New York Signatures*, I stayed in a tiny basement room, the "closet" Richard is having fun with.

21. *Lives of the Saints* was a collaborative project with Kevin Larkin under the name Josyph & Larkin. We showed the work on Long Island and in Manhattan at Church of the Advent, 93rd Street and Broadway, where we filled up the walls and installed a large mural, *St. Jerome in His Study*, above the existing altarpiece. Richard proposed writing about the work for *Art & Antiques* but nothing came of it. His letters about *Saints* (8.20.91 and 8.22.91) are examples of how uniquely he approaches visual art. As the group of original *Saints* that weren't sold had to be dumpstered when I lost my studio space, Josyph & Larkin have always been grateful to have Richard's letters about the work. Seven of his essays on art are published in *The Whistlers' Room*. See Lazarus Rising, 1991, n.12.

LAZARUS RISING
1991

1. This piece opens the book *Raising the Dead*.

2. From Richard's diary, 8.15.92: "Visited with Saad Ahmet, who was born and raised in the Iraqi desert, the son and grandson of sheiks. Living in exile, he earns a living teaching English to foreigners. Presently, to twelve bearded Siberians at the University of New Haven. They point to their villages on the map. Saad's blood runs cold when they troop into the classroom bringing the idea of snow with them. Saad is writing a book of stories set in old Iraq. They are delicate, beautiful and unearthly." From an undated entry in Richard's diary:

> Visited with Saad at the library. He said that great as Shakespeare is, he was only a man, his works not divinely inspired, and so are lesser works of literature than the Koran or the Bible. It is the first evidence I have that Saad is a believing Muslim. I asked him why he did not teach his son Arabic. "Because," he replied, "my wife does not speak it and it would be exclusionary." He is presently tutoring a number of Iraqi engineers in English. They are Jews whose parents fled from Iraq to Israel many years ago when they were small children or before they were even born. But they have all heard stories and reminiscences of the Baghdad that was, how beautiful the city, how proud their parents were to live there. Now Saad tells them about the city they never knew, speaks of the same parks, streets, buildings, markets, which the Israelis have heard tell of. And the Tigris, the food, the smells. He watches their eyes go muzzy with longing for their heritage. It is a passing down of culture from their parents through Saad. He is the conduit. And to think that he and the parents have never met!

From an entry of January 2001:

> Grand visit with Saad in Machine City. The man's purity and sweetness serve as a reproach to one as soiled as I. It seems to me that the disease and pain he suffered as a child in Iraq transported him into a state of innocence from which he would never return. A more elegant, tender, and refined gentleman does not exist. He brought me his newest poem, "Rocks." It is exquisitely wrought. I have encouraged him to create a small number of bound volumes of his works, for gifts if for no other reason. He is devoid of ambition and would not pursue commercial publication. Saad teaches remedial writing to adult students at the University of New Haven. How lucky for these students, mostly foreigners, and many from the various professions, to have this saintly, patient Saad as mentor.

3. The "good people of Halifax" (as he describes them elsewhere) invited Richard back for a month-long residency, but he was unable to make it.

4. This important figure of speech appears on the opening page of *Down from Troy*: "More than once, I have tied dried apricots and paper leaves to the branches of a long-dead tree to give it the appearance of life." Richard is openly sharing a fact that some of his readers prefer to ignore: even when he is writing about himself, he sometimes makes things up. Compare this with his statement on the copyright page of *Repairs*: "Each chapter of this book is a blend of fact and fiction, and all written in accordance with the First Law of the Imagination: The moment an artist picks up his pen, he is no longer himself or entirely of this world." And there is this in the diary of 1993:

> Thinking of *Raising the Dead*. How, at the beginning, it is true to life, but once under way the allegiance to art takes over. One crops here, shapes there, works in a metaphor; there will be elisions, asides, all the dishonesties of art. And, worst, there will be an incident such as never took place—my death and resurrection—until the book has slipped its anchor to fact and is no longer the case history of a man with Legionnaire's Disease. The solemnity and sadness of death have been transformed. Death itself will have been seized by the author and wrenched from the pages.

And this, also about the death in *Repairs*, in the diary of 1997:

> In my defense, I did reveal later in the book that it was pure invention. The reviewers were not amused. "An act of pure mischief," it was termed. Had I been courageous I would not have confessed at all. I did so out of authorial cowardice. The real miracle was not my death and resurrection but the fact that the great majority of those who read *Raising the Dead* believed that it had happened. I admit that the mere writing of it has made it almost as real as anything that has happened to me. What I can say truthfully is that the patient released from the hospital after a close brush with death sees the world in a fresh way. It has been transformed by the possibility of having lost it.

See also n.8.

5. The letters and diaries feature a range of vignettes of the Sterling Library. From Richard's diary of July 1991:

> There is a kind of molestation that takes place in the Main Reading Room of the library. There one sits, racking his brains, when plock! Plock! Plock! comes the sharp punitive tap of high heels on marble, followed by the echo. This, until the miscreant has achieved her destination. Not a word writ nor read, but we must all wait for the racket to abate. Such a felonious assault ought to be punished by having both shoe-heels amputated and the culprit made to walk around with her feet wrapped in felt. O Lord! Here she comes again! Plock! Plock! Plock! Where is my orthopedic saw?

At the Sterling on 10.16.89 with nothing to write to me on, Richard enlisted a flimsy sheet (out of the garbage?) containing a mathematical formula and he simply wrote around it. "Can you make anything of this?" he asked of the equations. "Perhaps it is the formula for achieving human happiness." To the formula's query, "What additional conditions on f will allow $F(x, y)$ to be soluble for y at Po?" he appended a notation that f = f—ing, and gave the solution as follows: "(1) a woman; (2) 6 pillows; (3) a bowl of cold green grapes."

One afternoon when we entered the Sterling together, I said: "It's pretty remarkable that you have this whenever you want it."

"I *never* lose the sense of awe," he said. "Each time I enter this building I feel lucky."

6. In discussing the ardor with which he adapted *The Black Swan* into a play, Richard once said to me: "I *was* Rosalie." He was not, at the time, consciously echoing Flaubert's famous remark: "Madame Bovary is me."

7. For Richard's harrowing encounter with John Cheever at Yaddo, see chapter 9 of *Said*, "The John Cheever Story."

8. After the previous letter, Richard contracted and nearly died of Legionnaire's Disease, the subject of *Raising the Dead*. This accounts for the loss of a month of correspondence. When I visited Richard in the garden at St. Ronan, he looked emaciated, shockingly so, but his spirits were reviving, despite bouts of what, even in July, he called "hollow, bottomless fatigue." There is this about the illness in the diary of 1997:

> It is now more than five years later and I still reflect on it, but the horror has not chased me. I remember only the closeness of Death, that I was reconciled to it; welcomed it, even. That is the way with me: I have left behind all but one or two seemingly insignificant moments, but it is upon these that the whole of my life has been focused. I remain stupidly cheerful by and large. Should an errant gust of melancholy stir the curtain, I think of that early morning when I was carried home from the hospital and put to bed in my own room. The cardinals, mockingbirds, and wrens were in full throat just outside the window. It was as if I were hearing their charivari for the first time. What a relief from the mortuary cooing of the pigeons that roost on the window ledges of the hospital.

See also n.13.

9. I had checked into a sleazy motel on Long Island in order to write my application for a Pollock-Krasner grant, to which Richard added his recommendation. When I received the grant, it enabled me to rent an apartment and to continue painting. The "memoir" is my letter about the motel.

10. A profile of me called "A Life of Austerity for Art," by Fred Bruning, had appeared in *Newsday* (7.17.91). It discussed several projects, including *Vietnam*, *Saints*, and *Said*.

11. "Great guy" is an apt description of Joe Caldwell, author of *The Uncle from Rome* and other novels. At the time that I met him at Yaddo, where I painted two portraits of him, Joe was volunteering to help patients with AIDS. Richard glows whenever he speaks of him.

12. Richard is referring to a Josyph & Larkin assemblage that became the postcard for *Lives of the Saints*. The piece included a headshot of Marlon Brando. In addition to being supportive about this and other projects, Richard was encouraging about my short stories. Around this time he showed one to Janet for her approval and suggested that we celebrate its completion. I have deleted many of these references, but they were important for me to hear and I have left some of them stand as examples of how diligent he was, and continues to be, about encouraging the efforts of younger artists.

13. As *Raising the Dead* was being written, Richard called it *Lazarus Rising*, *Lazarus*, *Laz*, or *Legionnaire*. Two undated notes enclosed with manuscripts that he sent me during the writing of the book provide clues as to how he developed it. Based on these notes, one might imagine that the book was fiction and that the author hadn't suffered through the disease. The first of these notes is signed "Love, Hopeless."

> What I want to do is put the narrative in the third person, but describe the setting in terms of the hero—what he sees, hears, imagines. The reader must witness the action from the hero's standpoint. Narrator and hero are intimately integrated. One must embrace both the hero's subjective response and the observations of the narrator, e.g., "It seemed to him that he was floating in a giant seashell thrown up by the respiration of the sea." Such a technique achieves the important effect of distancing which enables the reader to assess the central character. This would be lost if written in the first person. The dialogue is realistic, but the description is poetic—full of evocative images that illustrate his preoccupations. The hero's feelings are described in terms of his surroundings, e.g., "He had the feeling that he was throwing out ballast, concentrating, slimming down to a purpose; he was growing light and profound at one and the same time." Do you know what I mean?

> The piece as I see it should begin with my having fallen sick after a lecture tour. I am taken to the emergency room and lose consciousness. The reader is not informed that the author is rewriting his lost hospital chart. At some point he dies and is resurrected. The next section deals with his stay in the hospital after transfer from the ICU. Here he is in and out of madness, assailed by dreams, etc. At last he is discharged home. The next section portrays him musing over the experience, trying to make sense of it. I know that I need some transitional material to make it seamless. I also know that I have repeated myself. The trick will be to arrange these pages in a sensible and reasonable order so that a story emerges. A mythical, impressionistic account rather than anything reportorial. Thanks for anything you can do.

I do not recall doing much of anything, for sometimes a writer needs to say that he is hopeless as part of the natural process of taking the next step, which of course Richard did. Even his notes to me were revised before he mailed them. In the second paragraph, "I am taken to the emergency room" is changed to "He is taken to the emergency room," and "The reader is informed" becomes "The reader is not informed." These minor shifts in wording represent major reconceptions of *Raising the Dead*. At the bottom of the second page of these notes, he appended the following postscript: "Just read it over and put the pages loosely in the general order they belong. It is *mightily repetitive*. Needs boiling down? Needs clarification."

14. Richard took my suggestion to reuse the title *Down from Troy*, a section title from *Mortal Lessons*. It was combined with the subtitle *A Doctor Comes of Age*.

15. From Richard's diary, December 1991:

With all my heart I wish I had not published that account of assisted death in the *New York Times Magazine*. The heap of opprobrium is unnerving. For months I have been attacked left and right. The right considers me a would-be murderer or accessory to the fact. The left, an unreliable instrument of mercy, someone who couldn't be counted on, gutless. These were somewhat balanced by the many letters from gay men whose lovers had died slowly, horribly. Yesterday, a letter from a man who had nursed his lover of twenty years, then cremated the body. "Day by day, half-teaspoon by half-teaspoon, I am eating the ashes." My initial revulsion later turned to sympathetic understanding. It seems to me now that this man is striving to incorporate the beloved into his very tissues, to absorb his DNA, and thus to become one with him. In a way, it is a triumph over death. Weren't there primitive tribes in which, upon the death of father or chieftain, a portion of the body was eaten by the sons to take upon themselves his wisdom and courage? In this way the strength and potency of the tribe are passed on. There is something of the sublime omophagy of the Mass in the devouring of the lover's ashes. It is, for him, a celebratory act.

"Not to worry," I wrote to the man. "You are following in the footsteps of the faithful Artemesia, wife of King Mausoleus, the same who in the fourth century B.C. built his tomb at Helicarnassus and gave his name to that generic structure. When he died, his body was cremated and Artemesia drank her husband's ashes mixed with wine."

DRIVING THE QUILL

1992

1. As Richard was on the other side of the Long Island Sound roughly opposite my cliffside apartment in Rocky Point, I would joke about the fact that we could practically see and hear each other across the water. As for picking up the phone, we never conversed that way more than a few times a year, and Richard would always begin by saying: "I just sent off a letter to you." The discussion that ensued was invariably informed by an attempt, on both our parts, to not blunt the thrust of the letters we had sent. Stopping himself mid-sentence, "You'll see," he would say. "It's all in the letter." When we would preface a piece of news by saying: "As I wrote in my last letter," we were, in effect, quoting the correspondence out of respect for its primacy.

2. This verse from Éluard's "Blason Dédoré de Mes Rêves" is the epigraph for *Raising the Dead*. On 11.7.89, Richard wrote to me: "There'll be no Luis again today. I can only sit hour by hour waiting 'to be stung by the splendour of a sudden thought.' I wish I had a sprightly story for you, but my brain has turned into a turnip. So I'll give you a fine thing by the French poet Paul Éluard." He then quotes the verse, adding: "As an expression for the sense of emerging from anesthesia, it can't be matched." Once, when he read me a line of it in French—*En me couchant comme le cendre sous la flamme*—the phonic delight was audible in his voice. "It *is* better that way," he said. But he has not been able to track down the author of his preferred translation. "I know that *I* didn't do it." A different translation by Gilbert Bowen can be found in "Tarnished Emblems of My Dreams" in *Unbroken Poetry II* (Northumberland: Bloodaxe Books Ltd., 1996).

3. See Into the Cave of Aeolus, 1990, n.18.

4. The play *Little Saint Hugh* was conceived as a reader's theatre piece to accompany the *Saints* exhibition at Church of the Advent, where we planned to perform it once for free. As several of the performers, myself included, were Equity actors, the production needed showcase status for us to avoid prohibitive union contracts. Despite our explanation that we were performing in a church, Actors Equity refused on the grounds that the space contained too many seats. When we offered to rope off the rest of the church so that none of the "extra" pews could be used, Equity insisted that

unless we *removed* them, the show could not go on. As explained in n.31 for Sleepwalking and Daydreaming, 1989, the play was done eventually at the Inner Space Theatre, where the actors put down their scripts and a few simple actions were blocked into the show.

5. Carol Bullard was in charge of fundraising at Yaddo. She is an excellent photographer who took one of the best author photographs of Richard, which is on the dust jacket of *Imagine a Woman*. This rendition of his evening with Carol typifies the conversational posture in which he places himself respecting beautiful women, that of the almost-but-not-quite-successful worshipper. The flipside of this is the innocent old writer whose charm over women is beyond his control. Of course both of these postures are a form of comedy.

6. Compare this note of departure with Richard's letter to the Yaddo community, dated 10.10.88, after the pleasant stay in which Richard and I met. Also present were the writer Louisa Ermelino and the composer Tom Whitman.

> My beloved Yaddish,
> I cannot leave this magic kingdom without saying to each of you what is there in the chambers of my heart. I feel myself to have been *gifted* with three of the happiest weeks of my life. To have lived amongst you in a tiny society predicated on affection and courtesy—it is a condition that must be rare in the history of the world. Certainly it has been rare in the history of my life. Perhaps none of us will ever achieve it again, but that doesn't matter. We have had it once and it is something that no one can take away. I have seen your great talents. All that is missing is the luck to achieve success and the renown that each of you deserves. Believe me when I wish it for you with all my heart.

7. Richard arranged for me to talk at Alma College while I was on a summer fellowship at the Alden B. Dow Creativity Center in Midland, Michigan.

8. I had asked Richard for a short paragraph about the Lam Qua Grotesques to include in the exhibition. The paragraph (reproduced at n.39 for Sleepwalking and Daydreaming, 1989) was published in *MD* with a mangled version of my article about Lam Qua and Peter Parker.

9. The *New York Times Book Review*'s front-page review of *Down from Troy*, called "Dickie, the Doctor's Boy," appeared on Sunday, July 26, 1992. This long review, written by Susan Cheever, is highly favorable. The cover features three photographs: Richard's mother and father, Julius and Gertrude Selzer, standing together in long overcoats; a closeup of Richard's father; and Richard's mother sitting with her sons, Dickie and Billy. Inside there is a picture of baby Richard on a Troy sidewalk with his parents, and a current photograph of Richard for a profile, "The Mirages of Home," written by Lynn Karpen. In it Richard claims that the book was inspired by Eudora Welty's *One Writer's Beginnings*.

10. Neither man directed *The Black Swan*. About this situation Richard wrote to me on 8.28.92: "I don't care what happens to any of my little bits. I just don't want to lose Kenneth for a friend. It isn't my way of life."

11. I had suggested collaborating on Moliere's *Imaginary Invalid*. Richard would translate and I would fashion something new and musical out of it. The project never materialized.

12. See "The Ivory Crucifixion" in *The Whistlers' Room* for a picture and a discussion of this anonymous seventeenth-century Goan sculpture. Richard's treatment of the carving, first published in *MD* as "Yale's Ivory Christ" (January 1994), constitutes his best essay on art. Whenever he took me to see it in the Yale Art Gallery, his fascination with this work was far from academic, and he was deeply disappointed when the sculpture would disappear or return in a different, less congenial location (e.g., too close to the elevator). Discussing any crucifixion with Richard is enlightening, for he examines it as a lover of both sculptural poetry and human anatomy, which for him, on some level, are one and the same.

13. The speaker on this occasion was allegedly Richard's friend, about whom he told me: "When I called him to account, he bristled and turned icy cold—until he needed me for some-

thing." I was present at a similarly warped interpretation of "Brute," a story in which a physician confesses lasting remorse over giving in to fatigue and responding to a difficult Emergency Room patient by suturing his ears to a mattress and grinning at him. The patient, a large black man with a lacerated brow, is brought into the hospital by the police. He is portrayed with compassion and admiration. "There is a vast dignity about him. He keeps his own council." The physician speculates that the wound might have been caused by the police. "Or was there any blow? Here is a brow that might have burst on its own, spilling out its excess of rage, bleeding itself toward ease."

In November 1994, when Michigan State University Press invited us to a signing in East Lansing to launch the publication of *Said* and the MSU edition of *Repairs*, Richard was also booked into a dialogue with students about "Brute." When I arrived at the auditorium, Richard was on stage, the session was in progress, and it was clear that it was an intellectual ambush, the students having prepared to criticize the author for racial insensitivity. He was not at all defensive and he was listening intently, but the attack was an example of academic rudeness under the cover of political correctness, for Richard had not been sufficiently forewarned as to the adversarial nature of the event. At one point a student pointed out that in describing the patient's confinement in a police van, Richard wrote: "Through the back window of the wagon—a netted panther." This, she said, was proof of racism, for Richard was thinking of the man as an animal. I reminded her that the Black Panthers used that word proudly. I also reminded her than man *is* an animal, and that "Brute" explores a theme running throughout Richard's work: the powerful and sometimes mysterious effect of a wound on the human organism, as when the narrator refers to the man's "raw, untreated flesh, his very wildness which suggests less a human than a great and beautiful animal. As though by the addition of the wound, his body is more than it was, more of a body." From a letter of 2.20.07: "My poor 'Brute' is a most misunderstood fellow."

14. From an undated entry in the diary:

In fact, I relish the chance to keep company with my notebook. Every entry is caught on the fly. A tiny chip of life flecks off the pen, arcs, strikes, ricochets and lies half-buried among the leaves. Let it lie, I say. It is my workbench no less than was the operating table. (Years ago, the regular whoosh-whoosh of the respirators in the intensive care unit used to pace my pen.) It is where I dissect, peel, pare, whittle, carve, hammer, burnish, and even taste. Swatches, fragments, and snippets are strewn about, leftovers either discarded once and for all, or waiting to catch the eye and be incorporated into an as yet unborn paragraph. I prefer to think of these fragments as *spazzature*, the sweepings of gold or silver left in the tray of the goldsmith—worth a little something, but nowhere near the value of the crafted piece. A diary is not composed: it simply grows.

thing." I was present at a similarly warped interpretation of "Brute," a story in which a physician confesses lasting remorse over giving in to fatigue and responding to a difficult Emergency Room patient by suturing his ears to a mattress and grinning at him. The patient, a large black man with a lacerated brow, is brought into the hospital by the police. He is portrayed with compassion and admiration. "There is a vast dignity about him. He keeps his own council." The physician speculates that the wound might have been caused by the police. "Or was there any blow? Here is a brow that might have burst on its own, spilling out its excess of rage, bleeding itself toward ease."

In November 1994, when Michigan State University Press invited us to a signing in East Lansing to launch the publication of *Said* and the MSU edition of *Repairs*, Richard was also booked into a dialogue with students about "Brute." When I arrived at the auditorium, Richard was on stage, the session was in progress, and it was clear that it was an intellectual ambush, the students having prepared to criticize the author for racial insensitivity. He was not at all defensive and he was listening intently, but the attack was an example of academic rudeness under the cover of political correctness, for Richard had not been sufficiently forewarned as to the adversarial nature of the event. At one point a student pointed out that in describing the patient's confinement in a police van, Richard wrote: "Through the back window of the wagon—a netted panther." This, she said, was proof of racism, for Richard was thinking of the man as an animal. I reminded her that the Black Panthers used that word proudly. I also reminded her than man *is* an animal, and that "Brute" explores a theme running throughout Richard's work: the powerful and sometimes mysterious effect of a wound on the human organism, as when the narrator refers to the man's "raw, untreated flesh, his very wildness which suggests less a human than a great and beautiful animal. As though by the addition of the wound, his body is more than it was, more of a body." From a letter of 2.20.07: "My poor 'Brute' is a most misunderstood fellow."

14. From an undated entry in the diary:

In fact, I relish the chance to keep company with my notebook. Every entry is caught on the fly. A tiny chip of life flecks off the pen, arcs, strikes, ricochets and lies half-buried among the leaves. Let it lie, I say. It is my workbench no less than was the operating table. (Years ago, the regular whoosh-whoosh of the respirators in the intensive care unit used to pace my pen.) It is where I dissect, peel, pare, whittle, carve, hammer, burnish, and even taste. Swatches, fragments, and snippets are strewn about, leftovers either discarded once and for all, or waiting to catch the eye and be incorporated into an as yet unborn paragraph. I prefer to think of these fragments as *spazzature*, the sweepings of gold or silver left in the tray of the goldsmith—worth a little something, but nowhere near the value of the crafted piece. A diary is not composed: it simply grows.

Bibliography

BY RICHARD SELZER

Rituals of Surgery. New York: Harper's Magazine Press, 1974.

Mortal Lessons: Notes on the Art of Surgery. New York: Simon and Schuster, 1976.

Confessions of a Knife. New York: Simon and Schuster, 1979.

Letters to a Young Doctor. New York: Simon and Schuster, 1982.

Taking the World in for Repairs. New York: William Morrow, 1986.

Down from Troy: A Doctor Comes of Age. New York: William Morrow, 1992.

Raising the Dead. Knoxville: Whittle Direct Books, 1993; and New York: Viking Penguin, 1994.

Imagine a Woman and Other Tales. New York: Random House, 1994.

The Doctor Stories. New York: Picador USA, 1998.

The Exact Location of the Soul. New York: Picador USA, 2001.

The Whistlers' Room. Washington, D.C.: Shoemaker & Hoard, 2004.

Knife Song Korea. Albany: State University of New York Press, 2009.

WITH PETER JOSYPH

What One Man Said to Another: Talks with Richard Selzer. East Lansing: Michigan State University Press, 1994. Also, Blackstone Audiobooks, 2002, narrated by Raymond Todd and Peter Josyph.

Editor's Acknowledgments

Thanks to Barbara Mann for her invaluable assistance in transcribing these letters; to Janet Selzer for her warm hospitality; and to Richard Selzer for his friendship and trust.

Thanks, too, to Dr. Richard Soden; to Dr. Arthur Miller; to Henry Purslow; to the Corporation of Yaddo; to the Gardner Earl Memorial Chapel and Crematorium; to the Troy Public Library; to the Yale Elizabethan Club; to Anne Borchardt; and to James Peltz and all the superb staff at SUNY Press.